G.T.   *A Musical Instrument*

'' What was he doing, the great God Pan, down in the
reeds by the river.''

THE GOLDEN TREASURY
WITH ADDITIONAL POEMS

F. T. PALGRAVE

ILLUSTRATED BY MARGARET R. CAIRD

LONDON & GLASGOW
COLLINS' CLEAR-TYPE PRESS

TO

ALFRED TENNYSON,

POET LAUREATE

THIS book in its progress has recalled often to my memory a man with whose friendship we were once honoured, to whom no region of English Literature was unfamiliar, and who, whilst rich in all the noble gifts of Nature, was most eminently distinguished by the noblest and the rarest— just judgment and high-hearted patriotism. It would have been hence a peculiar pleasure and pride to dedicate what I have endeavoured to make a true national Anthology of three centuries to Henry Hallam. But he is beyond the reach of any human tokens of love and reverence; and I desire therefore to place before it a name united with his by associations which, whilst Poetry retains her hold on the minds of Englishmen, are not likely to be forgotten.

Your encouragement, given while traversing the wild scenery of Treryn Dinas, led me to begin the work; and it has been completed under your advice and assistance. For the favour now asked I have thus a second reason: and to this I may add, the homage which is your right as Poet, and the gratitude due to a Friend, whose regard I rate at no common value.

Permit me then to inscribe to yourself a book which, I hope, may be found by many a lifelong fountain of innocent and exalted pleasure; a source of animation to friends when they meet; and able to sweeten solitude itself with best society—with the companionship of the wise and the good, with the beauty which the eye cannot see, and the music only heard in silence. If this Collection proves a storehouse of delight to Labour and to Poverty—if it teaches those indifferent to the Poets to love them, and those who love them to love them more, the aim and the desire entertained in framing it will be fully accomplished.

F. T. P.

May, 1861.

ORIGINAL PREFACE

By F. T. PALGRAVE

THIS little Collection differs, it is believed, from others in the attempt made to include in it all the best original Lyrical pieces and Songs in our language, by writers not living—and none beside the best. Many familiar verses will hence be met with; many also which should be familiar :—the Editor will regard as his fittest readers those who love Poetry so well, that he can offer them nothing not already known and valued. For those who take up the book in a serious and scholarly spirit, the following remarks on the plan and the execution are added.

The Editor is acquainted with no strict and exhaustive definition of Lyrical Poetry; but he has found the task of practical decision increase in clearness and in facility as he advanced with the work, whilst keeping in view a few simple principles. Lyrical has been here held essentially to imply that each Poem shall turn on some single thought, feeling, or situation. In accordance with this, narrative, descriptive, and didactic poems—unless accompanied by rapidity of movement, brevity, and the colouring of human passion—have been excluded. Humorous poetry, except in the very unfrequent instances where a truly poetical tone pervades the whole, with what is strictly personal, occasional, and religious, has been considered foreign to the idea of the book. Blank verse and the ten-syllable couplet, with all pieces markedly dramatic, have been rejected as alien from what is commonly understood by Song, and rarely conforming to Lyrical conditions in treatment. But it is not anticipated, nor is it possible, that all readers shall think the line accurately drawn. Some poems, as Gray's *Elegy*, the *Allegro* and *Penseroso*, Wordsworth's *Ruth* or Campbell's *Lord Ullin*, might be claimed with perhaps equal justice for a narrative or descriptive selection : whilst with reference especially to Ballads and Sonnets, the Editor can only state that he has taken his utmost pains to decide without caprice or partiality.

This also is all he can plead in regard to a point even more liable to question ;—what degree of merit should give rank among the Best. That a Poem shall be worthy of the writer's genius—that it shall reach a perfection commensurate with its aim—that we should require finish in proportion to brevity—that passion, colour, and originality cannot atone for serious imperfections in clearness, unity, or truth—that a few good lines do not make a good poem—that popular estimate is serviceable as a guidepost more than as a compass—above all, that Excellence should be looked for rather in the Whole than in the Parts—such and other such canons have been always steadily regarded. He may however add that the pieces chosen, and a far larger number rejected, have been carefully and repeatedly considered ; and that he has been aided throughout by two friends of independent and exercised judgment, besides the distinguished person addressed in the Dedication. It is hoped that by this procedure the volume has been freed from that one-sidedness which must beset individual decisions :—but for the final choice the Editor is alone responsible.

Chalmers' vast collection, with the whole works of all accessible poets not contained in it, and the best Anthologies of different periods, have been twice systematically read through : and it is hence improbable that any omissions which may be regretted are due to oversight. The poems are printed entire, except in a very few instances (specified in the notes) where a stanza has been omitted. The omissions have been risked only when the piece could be thus brought to a closer lyrical unity : and, as essentially opposed to this unity, extracts, obviously such, are excluded. In regard to the text, the purpose of the book has appeared to justify the choice of the most poetical version, wherever more than one exists : and much labour has been given to present each poem, in disposition, spelling, and punctuation, to the greatest advantage.

In the arrangement, the most poetically effective order has been attempted. The English mind has passed through phases of thought and cultivation so various and so opposed during these three centuries of Poetry, that a rapid passage between Old and New, like rapid alteration of the eye's focus in looking at the landscape, will always be wearisome and hurtful to the sense of Beauty. The poems have been therefore distributed into Books corresponding, I. to the ninety years closing about 1616, II. thence to 1700, III. to 1800, IV. to the half century just ended. Or, looking at

the Poets who more or less give each portion its distinctive
character, they might be called the Books of Shakespeare,
Milton, Gray, and Wordsworth. The volume, in this
respect, so far as the limitations of its range allow, accurately
reflects the natural growth and evolution of our Poetry.
A rigidly chronological sequence, however, rather fits a
collection aiming at instruction than at pleasure, and the
Wisdom which comes through Pleasure :—within each
book the pieces have therefore been arranged in gradations
of feeling or subject. The development of the symphonies
of Mozart and Beethoven has been here thought of as a
model, and nothing placed without careful consideration.
And it is hoped that the contents of this Anthology will
thus be found to present a certain unity, " as episodes," in
the noble language of Shelley, " to that great Poem which
all poets, like the co-operating thoughts of one great mind,
have built up since the beginning of the world."

As he closes his long survey, the Editor trusts he may
add without egotism, that he has found the vague general
verdict of popular Fame more just than those have thought,
who, with too severe a criticism, would confine judgments
on Poetry to " the selected few of many generations."
Not many appear to have gained reputation without some
gift or performance that, in due degree, deserved it : and
if no verses by certain writers who show less strength than
sweetness, or more thought than mastery in expression,
are printed in this volume, it should not be imagined that
they have been excluded without much hesitation and
regret—far less that they have been slighted. Throughout
this vast and pathetic array of Singers now silent, few have
been honoured with the name Poet, and have not possessed
a skill in words, a sympathy with beauty, a tenderness of
feeling, or seriousness in reflection, which render their
works, although never perhaps attaining that loftier and
finer excellence here required—better worth reading than
much of what fills the scanty hours that most men spare
for self-improvement, or for pleasure in any of its more
elevated and permanent forms. And if this be true of even
mediocre poetry, for how much more are we indebted to
the best ! Like the fabled fountain of the Azores, but with
a more various power, the magic of this Art can confer on
each period of life its appropriate blessing : on early years
Experience, on maturity Calm, on age Youthfulness.
Poetry gives treasures " more golden than gold," leading

us in higher and healthier ways than those of the world, and interpreting to us the lessons of Nature. But she speaks best for herself. Her true accents, if the plan has been executed with success, may be heard throughout the following pages :—wherever the Poets of England are honoured, wherever the dominant language of the world is spoken, it is hoped that they will find fit audience.

F. T. PALGRAVE.

ACKNOWLEDGMENTS

The Editor's thanks are due to the authors (or their literary executors) and publishers of the following poems :—

For the Fallen, by Laurence Binyon. Reprinted by permission of the Proprietors of *Punch*.

A Passer-by and *My Delight and Thy Delight*, by Robert Bridges. Published by the Oxford University Press.

The Soldier, by Rupert Brooke. Reprinted by permission of the Literary Executor of Rupert Brooke and Sidgwick and Jackson, Ltd.

Epilogue to *Asolando*, by Robert Browning. Published by John Murray.

The Old Woman, by Joseph Campbell. Reprinted by permission of the author.

The Donkey, by G. K. Chesterton. Published by J. M. Dent & Sons, Ltd.

A Cradle Song and *No Child*, by Padraic Colum. Reprinted by permission of the author.

Heraclitus, by William Cory, from *Ionica*. Published by George Allen & Unwin, Ltd.

". . . But a Short Time to Live," by Leslie Coulson. Published by Erskine Macdonald, Ltd.

The Example, *Leisure*, and *The Moon*, by W. H. Davies. Published by Jonathan Cape, Ltd.

The Scribe, *An Epitaph*, and *Fare Well*, by Walter de la Mare, from *Collected Poems*. Reprinted by permission of the author.

Song, by Edward Dowden. Reprinted by permission of Mrs. Elizabeth D. Dowden.

"*Non Sum Qualis Eram Bonæ Sub Regno Cynaræ*," by Ernest Dowson, from *The Poems of Ernest Dowson*. Published by John Lane, The Bodley Head, Ltd.

Yasmin, and *Epilogue to The Golden Journey to Samarkand*, by James Elroy Flecker. Published by Martin Secker, Ltd.

The Country Faith, by Norman Gale. Reprinted by permission of the author.

Into Battle and *To a Black Greyhound*, by Julian Grenfell. Reprinted by permission of the Lady Desborough.

By the Statue of King Charles at Charing Cross, by Lionel Johnson. Reprinted by permission of Elkin Mathews and Marrot, Ltd.

Trees, by Joyce Kilmer. Published by Doubleday, Doran and Company.

Recessional, by Rudyard Kipling, from *The Five Nations*. Published by Methuen & Co., Ltd.

The Odyssey, by Andrew Lang, from *The Poetical Works of Andrew Lang*. Published by Longmans Green & Co., Ltd.

Sea Fever and *Beauty*, by John Masefield, from *Collected Poems*. Published by William Heinemann, Ltd.

Extract from *Love in the Valley*, by George Meredith. By permission of Messrs. Constable & Co., London, and Messrs. Charles Scribner's Sons, New York.

Renouncement, *The Shepherdess*, and *A Letter from a Girl to her own Old Age*, by Alice Meynell. Reprinted by permission of Wilfrid Meynell, Esq.

Yattendon, by Henry Newbolt, from *Poems New and Old*. Published by John Murray.

The Married Lover, *Unthrift*, and *The Toys*, by Coventry Patmore. Published by G. Bell & Sons, Ltd.

The Blessed Damozel, by D. G. Rossetti. Reprinted by permission of Messrs. Ellis.

"*I have a Rendezvous with Death*," by Alan Seeger. Published by Constable & Co.

To S. R. Crockett, *My Wife*, *Requiem*, *Romance*, "*Bright is the ring of words*," by Robert Louis Stevenson. Reprinted by permission of Mr. Lloyd Osbourne.

Itylus, Stanzas from *The Triumph of Time*, *Chorus from "Atalanta*," and *A Forsaken Garden*, by A. C. Swinburne, from *Poems and Ballads*. Published by William Heinemann, Ltd.

The Crying of Water, by Arthur Symons. Published by William Heinemann, Ltd.

Romance, by W. J. Turner. Reprinted by permission of the author and Sidgwick and Jackson, Ltd.

The Making of Birds, by Katharine Tynan. Reprinted by permission of the author.

"*April, April*," by William Watson. Reprinted by permission of the author.

The Heart of the Woman, by W. B. Yeats, from *Early Poems*, published by Macmillan & Co., Ltd., and *A Cradle Song*, *When You Are Old*, and *Down by the Salley Gardens*, by W. B. Yeats, from *Poems*, published by Ernest Benn, Ltd.

FIRST BOOK

SUMMARY

THE Elizabethan Poetry, as it is rather vaguely termed, forms the substance of this Book, which contains pieces from Wyat under Henry VIII. to Shakespeare midway through the reign of James I., and Drummond who carried on the early manner to a still later period. There is here a wide range of style;—from simplicity expressed in a language hardly yet broken into verse—through the pastoral fancies and Italian conceits of the strictly Elizabethan time—to the passionate reality of Shakespeare : yet a general uniformity of tone prevails. Few readers can fail to observe the natural sweetness of the verse, the single-hearted straightforwardness of the thoughts :—nor less, the limitation of subject to the many phases of one passion, which then characterised our lyrical poetry—unless when, as with Drummond and Shakespeare, the " purple light of Love " is tempered by a spirit of sterner reflection.

It should be observed that this and the following Summaries apply in the main to the Collection here presented, in which (besides its restriction to Lyrical Poetry) a strictly representative or historical Anthology has not been aimed at. Great Excellence, in human art as in human character, has from the beginning of things been even more uniform than Mediocrity, by virtue of the closeness of its approach to Nature :—and so far as the standard of Excellence kept in view has been attained in this volume, a comparative absence of extreme or temporary phases in style, a similarity of tone and manner, will be found throughout :—something neither modern nor ancient, but true in all ages, and like the works of Creation, perfect as on the first day.

1. SPRING

Spring, the sweet Spring, is the year's pleasant king;
Then blooms each thing, then maids dance in a ring,
Cold doth not sting, the pretty birds do sing,
    Cuckoo, jug-jug, pu-we, to-witta-woo!

The palm and may make country houses gay,
Lambs frisk and play, the shepherds pipe all day,
And we hear aye birds tune their merry lay,
    Cuckoo, jug-jug, pu-we, to-witta-woo!

The fields breathe sweet, the daises kiss our feet,
Young lovers meet, old wives a-sunning sit,
In every street these tunes our ears do greet,
    Cuckoo, jug-jug, pu-we, to-witta-woo!
        Spring! the sweet Spring!

T. NASH.

2. SUMMONS TO LOVE

Phœbus, arise!
And paint the sable skies
With azure, white, and red:
Rouse Memnon's mother from her Tithon's bed
That she may thy career with roses spread:
The nightingales thy coming eachwhere sing:
Make an eternal spring!
Give life to this dark world which lieth dead;
Spread forth thy golden hair
In larger locks than thou wast wont before,
And emperor-like decore
With diadem of pearl thy temples fair:
Chase hence the ugly night
Which serves but to make dear thy glorious light.

—This is that happy morn.
That day, long-wishèd day
Of all my life so dark,
(If cruel stars have not my ruin sworn
And fates my hopes betray),
Which, purely white, deserves
An everlasting diamond should it mark.
This is the morn should bring unto this grove
My Love, to hear and recompense my love.

Fair King, who all preserves,
But show thy blushing beams,
And thou two sweeter eyes
Shalt see than those which by Penéus' streams
Did once thy heart surprise.
Now, Flora, deck thyself in fairest guise :
If that ye winds would hear
A voice surpassing far Amphion's lyre,
Your furious chiding stay ;
Let Zephyr only breathe,
And with her tresses play.
—The winds all silent are,
And Phœbus in his chair
Ensaffroning sea and air
Makes vanish every star :
Night like a drunkard reels
Beyond the hills, to shun his flaming wheels :
The fields with flowers are deck'd in every hue,
The clouds with orient gold spangle their blue ;
Here is the pleasant place—
And nothing wanting is, save She, alas !

                    W. DRUMMOND OF HAWTHORNDEN.

3. TIME AND LOVE

When I have seen by Time's fell hand defaced
The rich proud cost of out-worn buried age ;
When sometime lofty towers I see down-razed,
And brass eternal slave to mortal rage ;

When I have seen the hungry ocean gain
Advantage on the kingdom of the shore,
And the firm soil win of the watery main,
Increasing store with loss, and loss with store ;

When I have seen such interchange of state,
Or state itself confounded to decay,
Ruin hath taught me thus to ruminate—
That Time will come and take my Love away :

—This thought is as a death, which cannot choose
But weep to have that which it fears to lose.

                    W. SHAKESPEARE.

4

Since brass, nor stone, nor earth, nor boundless sea,
But sad mortality o'ersways their power,
How with this rage shall beauty hold a plea,
Whose action is no stronger than a flower?

O how shall summer's honey breath hold out
Against the wreckful siege of battering days,
When rocks impregnable are not so stout
Nor gates of steel so strong, but time decays?

O fearful meditation! where, alack!
Shall Time's best jewel from Time's chest lie hid?
Or what strong hand can hold his swift foot back,
Or who his spoil of beauty can forbid?

O! none, unless this miracle have might,
That in black ink my love may still shine bright.

W. SHAKESPEARE.

5. THE PASSIONATE SHEPHERD TO HIS LOVE

Come live with me and be my Love,
And we will all the pleasure prove
That hills and valleys, dale and field,
And all the craggy mountains yield.

There will we sit upon the rocks
And see the shepherds feed their flocks,
By shallow rivers, to whose falls
Melodious birds sing madrigals.

There will I make thee beds of roses
And a thousand fragrant posies,
A cap of flowers, and a kirtle
Embroider'd all with leaves of myrtle.

A gown made of the finest wool,
Which from our pretty lambs we pull,
Fair linéd slippers for the cold,
With buckles of the purest gold.

A belt of straw and ivy buds
With coral clasps and amber studs:
And if these pleasures may thee move,
Come live with me and be my Love.

Thy silver dishes for thyme eat
As precious as the gods do eat,
Shall on an ivory table be
Prepared each day for thee and me.
The shepherd swains shall dance and sing
For thy delight each May-morning :
If these delights thy mind may move,
Then live with me and be my Love.

C. MARLOWE.

6. A MADRIGAL

Crabbed Age and Youth
Cannot live together :
Youth is full of pleasance,
Age is full of care :
Youth is like summer morn,
Age like winter weather,
Youth like summer brave,
Age like winter care :
Youth is full of sport
Age's breath is short,
Youth is nimble, Age is lame :
Youth is hot and bold,
Age is weak and cold,
Youth is wild, and Age is tame :—
Age, I do abhor thee,
Youth, I do adore thee ;
O ! my Love, my Love is young !
Age, I do defy thee—
O sweet shepherd, hie thee,
For methinks thou stay'st too long.

W. SHAKESPEARE.

7.

Under the greenwood tree
    Who loves to lie with me,
    And tune his merry note
    Unto the sweet bird's throat—
Come hither, come hither, come hither !
    Here shall we see
    No enemy
But winter and rough weather.

Who doth ambition shun
And loves to live i' the sun,
Seeking the food he eats
And pleased with what he gets
Come hither, come hither, come hither !
Here shall he see
No enemy
But winter and rough weather.

W. SHAKESPEARE.

8

It was a lover and his lass
With a hey and a ho, and a hey-nonino !
That o'er the green cornfield did pass
In the spring time, the only pretty ring time,
When birds do sing hey ding a ding :
Sweet lovers love the Spring.
Between the acres of the rye
These pretty country folks would lie :
This carol they began that hour,
How that life was but a flower :
And therefore take the present time
With a hey and a ho and a hey-nonino !
For love is crownèd with the prime
In spring time, the only pretty ring time,
When birds do sing hey ding a ding :
Sweet lovers love the Spring.

W. SHAKESPEARE.

9. PRESENT IN ABSENCE

Absence, hear thou my protestation
Against thy strength,
Distance, and length ;
Do what thou canst for alteration :
For hearts of truest mettle
Absence doth join, and Time doth settle.

Who loves a mistress of such quality,
He soon hath found
Affection's ground
Beyond time, place, and all mortality.
To hearts that cannot vary
Absence is Presence, Time doth tarry.

By absence this good means I gain,
    That I can catch her,
    Where none can watch her,
In some close corner of my brain :
    There I embrace and kiss her ;
And so I both enjoy and miss her.

ANON.

10. ABSENCE

Being your slave, what should I do but tend
Upon the hours and times of your desire ?
I have no precious time at all to spend,
Nor services to do, till you require :

Nor dare I chide the world-without-end hour
Whilst I, my sovereign, watch the clock for you,
Nor think the bitterness of absence sour
When you have bid your servant once adieu :

Nor dare I question with my jealous thought
Where you may be, or your affairs suppose,
But like a sad slave, stay and think of nought
Save, where you are, how happy you make those ;—

So true a fool is love, that in your will,
Though you do anything, he thinks no ill

W. SHAKESPEARE.

11

How like a winter hath my absence been
From Thee, the pleasure of the fleeting year !
What freezings have I felt, what dark days seen,
What old December's bareness everywhere !

And yet this time removed was summer's time :
The teeming autumn, big with rich increase,
Bearing the wanton burden of the prime
Like widow'd wombs after their lords' decease :

Yet this abundant issue seem'd to me
But hope of orphans, and unfather'd fruit ;
For summer and his pleasures wait on thee,
And, thou away, the very birds are mute ;

Or, if they sing, 'tis with so dull a cheer,
That leaves look pale, dreading the winter's near.

W. SHAKESPEARE.

12. A CONSOLATION

When in disgrace with fortune and men's eyes
I all alone beweep my outcast state,
And trouble deaf heaven with my bootless cries,
And look upon myself, and curse my fate;

Wishing me like to one more rich in hope,
Featured like him, like him with friends possest,
Desiring this man's art, and that man's scope,
With what I most enjoy contented least;

Yet in these thoughts myself almost despising,
Haply I think on Thee—and then my state,
Like to the lark at break of day arising
From sullen earth, sings hymns at heaven's gate;

For thy sweet love remember'd, such wealth brings
That then I scorn to change my state with kings.

W. SHAKESPEARE.

13. THE UNCHANGEABLE

O never say that I was false of heart,
Though absence seem'd my flame to qualify:
As easy might I from myself depart
As from my soul, which in thy breast doth lie;

That is my home of love; if I have ranged,
Like him that travels, I return again,
Just to the time, not with the time exchanged,
So that myself bring water for my stain.

Never believe, though in my nature reign'd
All frailties that besiege all kinds of blood,
That it could so preposterously be stain'd
To leave for nothing all thy sum of good:

For nothing this wide universe I call,
Save thou, my rose: in it thou art my all.

W. SHAKESPEARE.

To me, fair Friend, you never can be old,
For as you were when first your eye I eyed
Such seems your beauty still. Three winters cold
Have from the forests shook three summers' pride ;

Three beauteous springs to yellow autumn turn'd
In process of the season have I seen,
Three April perfumes in three hot Junes burn'd,
Since first I saw you fresh which yet are green.

Ah ! yet doth beauty, like a dial hand,
Steal from his figure, and no pace perceived ;
So your sweet hue, which methinks still doth stand
Hath motion, and my eye may be deceived.

For fear of which, hear this, thou age unbred.—
Ere you were born, was beauty's summer dead.

W. SHAKESPEARE.

15. DIAPHENIA

Diaphenia like the daffadowndilly,
White as the sun, fair as the lily,
Heigh ho, how I do love thee !
I do love thee as my lambs
Are belovéd of their dams ;
How blest were I if thou woulds't prove me.

Diaphenia like the spreading roses,
That in thy sweets all sweets encloses,
Fair sweet, how I do love thee !
I do love thee as each flower
Loves the sun's life-giving power ;
For dead, thy breath to life might move me.

Diaphenia like to all things blessed
When all thy praises are expressèd,
Dear joy, how I do love thee !
As the birds do love the spring,
Or the bees their careful king :
Then in requite, sweet virgin, love me !

H. CONSTABLE.

16. ROSALINE

Like to the clear in highest sphere
Where all imperial glory shines,
Of selfsame colour is her hair
Whether unfolded, or in twines :
   Heigh ho, fair Rosaline !
Her eyes are sapphires set in snow,
Resembling heaven by every wink ;
The Gods do fear whenas they glow,
And I do tremble when I think
   Heigh ho, would she were mine !

Her cheeks are like the blushing cloud
That beautifies Aurora's face,
Or like the silver crimson shroud
That Phœbus' smiling looks doth grace ;
   Heigh ho, fair Rosaline !
Her lips are like two budded roses
Whom ranks of lilies neighbour nigh
Within which bounds she balm encloses
Apt to entice a deity :
   Heigh ho, would she were mine !

Her neck is like a stately tower
Where Love himself imprison'd lies,
To watch for glances every hour
From her divine and sacred eyes :
   Heigh ho, fair Rosaline !
Her paps are centres of delight,
Her breasts are orbs of heavenly frame,
Where Nature moulds the dew of light
To feed perfection with the same :
   Heigh ho, would she were mine !

With orient pearl, with ruby red,
With marble white, with sapphire blue
Her body every way is fed,
Yet soft in touch and sweet in view :
   Heigh ho, fair Rosaline !
Nature herself her shape admires ;
The Gods are wounded in her sight ;
And Love forsakes his heavenly fires
And at her eyes his brand doth light :
   Heigh ho, would she were mine !

Then muse not, Nymphs, though I bemoan
The absence of fair Rosaline,
Since for a fair there's fairer none,
Nor for her virtues so divine :
    Heigh ho, fair Rosaline ;
Heigh ho, my heart ! would God that she were mine !

                T. LODGE.

17. COLIN

Beauty sat bathing by a spring
    Where fairest shades did hide her ;
The winds blew calm, the birds did sing,
    The cool streams ran beside her.
My wanton thoughts enticed mine eye
    To see what was forbidden :
But better memory said, fie !
    So vain desire was chidden :—
        Hey nonny nonny O !
        Hey nonny nonny !

Into a slumber then I fell,
    When fond imagination
Seeméd to see, but could not tell
    Her feature or her fashion.
But ev'n as babes in dreams do smile,
    And sometimes fall a-weeping,
So I.awaked, as wise this while
    As when I fell a-sleeping :—
        Hey nonny nonny O !
        Hey nonny nonny !

            THE SHEPHERD TONIE.

18. TO HIS LOVE

Shall I compare thee to a summer's day ?
Thou art more lovely and more temperate :
Rough winds do shake the darling buds of May,
And summer's lease hath all too short a date :

Sometime too hot the eye of heaven shines,
And often is his gold complexion dimm'd :
And every fair from fair sometime declines,
By chance, or nature's changing course, untrimm'd.

But thy eternal summer shall not fade
Nor lose possession of that fair thou owest ;
Nor shall death brag thou wanderest in his shade,
When in eternal lines to time thou growest.

So long as men can breathe, or eyes can see,
So long lives this, and this gives life to thee.
                              W. SHAKESPEARE.

19. TO HIS LOVE

When in the chronicle of wasted time
I see descriptions of the fairest wights,
And beauty making beautiful old rhyme
In praise of ladies dead, and lovely knights ;

Then in the blazon of sweet beauty's best
Of hand, of foot, of lip, of eye, of brow,
I see their antique pen would have exprest
Ev'n such a beauty as you master now.

So all their praises are but prophecies
Of this our time, all, you prefiguring ;
And for they look'd but with divining eyes,
They had not skill enough your worth to sing :

For we, which now behold these present days,
Have eyes to wonder, but lack tongues to praise.
                              W. SHAKESPEARE.

20. LOVE'S PERJURIES

On a day, alack the day !
Love, whose month is ever May,
Spied a blossom passing fair
Playing in the wanton air :
Through the velvet leaves the wind
All unseen 'gan passage find ;
That the lover, sick to death,
Wish'd himself the heaven's breath.
Air, quoth he, thy cheeks may blow ;
Air, would I might triumph so !
But, alack, my hand is sworn
Ne'er to pluck thee from thy thorn :

Vow, alack, for youth unmeet;
Youth so apt to pluck a sweet.
Do not call it sin in me
That I am forsworn for thee:
Thou for whom e'en Jove would swear
Juno but an Ethiope were,
And deny himself for Jove,
Turning mortal for thy love.
                                                W. SHAKESPEARE.

21. A SUPPLICATION

Forget not yet the tried intent
Of such a truth as I have meant;
My great travail so gladly spent,
                    Forget not yet!

Forget not yet when first began
The weary life ye know, since whan
The suit, the service none tell can;
                    Forget not yet!

Forget not yet the great assays,
The cruel wrong, the scornful ways
The painful patience in delays,
                    Forget not yet!

Forget not! O, forget not this,
How long ago hath been, and is
The mind that never meant amiss—
                    Forget not yet!

Forget not then thine own approved,
The which so long hath thee so loved,
Whose steadfast faith yet never moved—
                    Forget not this!
                                                SIR T. WYAT.

22. TO AURORA

O if though knew'st how thou thyself dost harm,
And dost prejudge thy bliss, and spoil my rest;
Then thou would'st melt the ice out of thy breast
And thy relenting heart would kindly warm.

O if thy pride did not our joys controul,
What world of loving wonders should'st thou see !
For if I saw thee once transform'd in me,
Then in thy bosom I would pour my soul ;

Then all my thoughts should in thy visage shine,
And if that aught mischanced thou should'st not moan
Nor bear the burthen of thy griefs alone ;
No, I would have my share in what were thine :

And whilst we thus should make our sorrows one,
This happy harmony would make them none.

W. ALEXANDER, EARL OF STERLINE.

23. TRUE LOVE

Let me not to the marriage of true minds
Admit impediments. Love is not love
Which alters when it alteration finds,
Or bends with the remover to remove :——

O no ! it is an ever-fixéd mark
That looks on tempests, and is never shaken ;
It is the star to ever wandering bark
Whose worth's unknown, although his height be taken.

Love's not Time's fool, though rosy lips and cheeks
Within his bending sickle's compass come ;
Love alters not with his brief hours and weeks,
But bears it out ev'n to the edge of doom :——

If this be error, and upon me proved,
I never writ, nor no man ever loved.

W. SHAKESPEARE.

24. A DITTY

My true-love hath my heart, and I have his,
By just exchange one to the other given :
I hold his dear, and mine he cannot miss,
There never was a better bargain driven :
  My true-love hath my heart, and I have his.

His heart in me keeps him and me in one,
My heart in him his thoughts and senses guides :
He loves my heart, for once it was his own,
I cherish his because in me it bides :
  My true-love hath my heart, and I have his.
                                          SIR. P. SIDNEY.

25. LOVE'S OMNIPRESENCE

Were I as base as is the lowly plain,
And you, my Love, as high as heaven above,
Yet should the thoughts of me your humble swain
Ascend to heaven, in honour of my Love.

Were I as high as heaven above the plain,
And you, my Love, as humble and as low
As are the deepest bottoms of the main,
Whereso'er you were, with you my love should go.

Were you the earth, dear Love, and I the skies,
My love should shine on you like to the sun,
And look upon you with ten thousand eyes
Till heaven wax'd blind, and till the world were done.

Whereso'er I am, below, or else above you,
Whereso'er you are, my heart shall truly love you.
                                          J. SYLVESTER.

26. CARPE DIEM

O Mistress mine, where are you roaming ?
O stay and hear ! your true-love's coming
      That can sing both high and low ;
Trip no further, pretty sweeting,
Journeys end in lovers' meeting—
      Every wise man's son doth know.

What is love ? 'tis not hereafter ;
Present mirth hath present laughter ;
      What's to come is still unsure :
In delay there lies no plenty.—
Then come kiss me, Sweet-and-twenty,
      Youth's a stuff will not endure.
                                          W. SHAKESPEARE.

27. WINTER

When icicles hang by the wall
 And Dick the shepherd blows his nail,
And Tom bears logs into the hall,
 And milk comes frozen home in pail ;
When blood is nipt, and ways be foul,
Then nightly sings the staring owl
   Tuwhoo !
Tuwhit ! tuwhoo ! A merry note !
While greasy Joan doth keel the pot.

When all around the wind doth blow,
 And coughing drowns the parson's saw,
And birds sit brooding in the snow,
 And Marian's nose looks red and raw ;
When roasted crabs hiss in the bowl—
Then nightly sings the staring owl
   Tuwhoo !
Tuwhit ! tuwhoo ! A merry note !
While greasy Joan doth keel the pot.

W. SHAKESPEARE.

28

That time of year thou may'st in me behold
When yellow leaves, or none, or few do hang
Upon those boughs which shake against the cold,
Bare ruin'd choirs, where late the sweet birds sang.

In me thou seest the twilight of such day
As after sunset fadeth in the west,
Which by and by black night doth take away,
Death's second self, that seals up all in rest.

In me thou seest the glowing of such fire,
That on the ashes of his youth doth lie
As the deathbed whereon it must expire,
Consumed with that which it was nourish'd by :

—This thou perceiv'st, which makes thy love more strong,
To love that well which thou must leave ere long.

W. SHAKESPEARE.

29. REMEMBRANCE

When to the sessions of sweet silent thought
I summon up remembrance of things past,
I sigh the lack of many a thing I sought,
And with old woes new wail my dear time's waste ;

Then can I drown an eye, unused to flow,
For precious friends hid in death's dateless night,
And weep afresh love's long-since-cancell'd woe,
And moan the expense of many a vanish'd sight.

Then can I grieve at grievances foregone,
And heavily from woe to woe tell o'er
The sad account of fore-bemoanéd moan,
Which I new pay as if not paid before :

—But if the while I think on thee, dear friend,
All losses are restored, and sorrows end.

W. SHAKESPEARE.

30. REVOLUTIONS

Like as the waves make towards the pebbled shore
So do our minutes hasten to their end ;
Each changing place with that which goes before,
In sequent toil all forwards do contend.

Nativity once in the main of light
Crawls to maturity, wherewith being crown'd,
Crooked eclipses 'gainst his glory fight,
And Time that gave, doth now his gift confound.

Time doth transfix the flourish set on youth,
And delves the parallels in beauty's brow ;
Feeds on the rarities of nature's truth,
And nothing stands but for his scythe to mow.

And yet, to times in hope, my verse shall stand
Praising Thy worth, despite his cruel hand.

W. SHAKESPEARE.

31

Farewell! thou art too dear for my possessing,
And like enough thou know'st thy estimate:
Thy charter of thy worth gives thee releasing,
My bonds in thee are all determinate.

For how do I hold thee but by thy granting?
And for that riches where is my deserving?
The cause of this fair gift in me is wanting,
And so my patent back again is swerving.

Thyself thou gav'st, thy own worth then not knowing.
Or me, to whom thou gav'st it, else mistaking;
So thy great gift, upon misprision growing,
Comes home again, on better judgment making.

Thus have I had thee as a dream doth flatter;
In sleep, a king; but waking, no such matter.

W. SHAKESPEARE.

32. THE LIFE WITHOUT PASSION

They that have power to hurt, and will do none,
That do not do the thing they most do show,
Who, moving others, are themselves as stone,
Unmovéd, cold, and to temptation slow,—

They rightly do inherit Heaven's graces,
And husband nature's riches from expense;
They are the lords and owners of their faces,
Others, but stewards of their excellence.

The summer's flower is to the summer sweet,
Though to itself it only live and die;
But if that flower with base infection meet,
The basest weed outbraves his dignity:

For sweetest things turn sourest by their deeds;
Lilies that fester smell far worse than weeds.

W. SHAKESPEARE.

33. THE LOVER'S APPEAL

And wilt thou leave me thus?
Say nay! say nay! for shame,
To save thee from the blame
Of all my grief and grame.
And wilt thou leave me thus?
Say nay! say nay!

And wilt thou leave me thus,
That hath loved thee so long
In wealth and woe among:
And is thy heart so strong
As for to leave me thus?
Say nay! say nay!

And wilt thou leave me thus,
That hath given thee my heart
Never for to depart
Neither for pain nor smart:
And wilt thou leave me thus?
Say nay! say nay!

And wilt thou leave me thus,
And have no more pity
Of him that loveth thee?
Alas! thy cruelty!
And wilt thou leave me thus?
Say nay! say nay!

SIR T. WYAT.

34. THE NIGHTINGALE

As it fell upon a day
In the merry month of May,
Sitting in a pleasant shade
Which a grove of myrtles made,
Beasts did leap and birds did sing,
Trees did grow and plants did spring,
Everything did banish moan
Save the nightingale alone.
She, poor, bird, as all forlorn,
Lean'd her breast against a thorn,
And there sung the dolefullest ditty
That to hear it was great pity.

Fie, fie, fie, now would she cry ;
Tereu, tereu, by and by :
That to hear her so complain
Scarce I could from tears refrain ;
For her griefs so lively shown
Made me think upon mine own.
—Ah, thought I, thou mourn'st in vain,
None takes pity on thy pain :
Senseless trees, they cannot hear thee,
Ruthless beasts, they will not cheer thee ;
King Pandion, he is dead,
All thy friends are lapp'd in lead :
All thy fellow birds do sing
Careless of thy sorrowing :
Even so, poor bird, like thee
None alive will pity me.

R. BARNEFIELD.

35

Care-charmer Sleep, son of the sable Night,
Brother to Death, in silent darkness born,
Relieve my languish, and restore the light ;
With dark forgetting of my care return.

And let the day be time enough to mourn
The shipwreck of my ill adventured youth :
Let waking eyes suffice to wail their scorn,
Without the torment of the night's untruth.

Cease, dreams, the images of day-desires,
To model forth the passions of the morrow ;
Never let rising Sun approve you liars
To add more grief to aggravate my sorrow :

Still let me sleep, embracing clouds in vain,
And never wake to feel the day's disdain.

S. DANIEL.

36. MADRIGAL

Take O take those lips away
That so sweetly were forsworn,
And those eyes, the break of day,
Lights that do mislead the morn :
But my kisses bring again,
           Bring again—
Seals of love, but seal'd in vain,
           Seal'd in vain !

W. SHAKESPEARE.

37. LOVE'S FAREWELL

Since there's no help, come let us kiss and part,—
Nay, I have done, you get no more of me ;
And I am glad, yea glad with all my heart,
That thus so cleanly I myself can free ;

Shake hands for ever, cancel all our vows,
And when we meet at any time again,
Be it not seen in either of our brows
That we one jot of former love retain.

Now at the last gasp of love's latest breath,
When his pulse failing, passion speechless lies,
When faith is kneeling by his bed of death,
And innocence is closing up his eyes,

—Now if thou would'st, when all have given him over,
From death to life thou might'st him yet recover !

M. DRAYTON.

38. TO HIS LUTE

My lute, be as thou wert when thou didst grow
With thy green mother in some shady grove,
When immelodious winds but made thee move,
And birds their ramage did on thee bestow.

Since that dear Voice which did thy sounds approve,
Which wont in such harmonious strains to flow,
Is reft from Earth to tune those spheres above,
What art thou but a harbinger of woe ?

Thy pleasing notes be pleasing notes no more,
But orphans' wailings to the fainting ear ;

Each stroke a sigh, each sound draws forth a tear ;
For which be silent as in woods before :

Or if any hand to touch thee deign,
Like widow'd turtle still her loss complain.

W. DRUMMOND.

39. BLIND LOVE

O me ! what eyes hath love put in my head
Which have no correspondence with true sight ;
Or if they have, where is my judgment fled
That censures falsely what they see aright ?

If that be fair whereon my false eyes dote,
What means the world to say it is not so ?
If it be not, then love doth well denote
Love's eye is not so true as all men's : No,

How can it ? O how can love's eye be true,
That is so vex'd with watching and with tears ?
No marvel then though I mistake my view :
The sun itself sees not till heaven clears.

O cunning Love ! with tears thou keep'st me blind,
Lest eyes well-seeing thy foul faults should find !

W. SHAKESPEARE.

40. THE UNFAITHFUL SHEPHERDESS

While that the sun with his beams hot
Scorchéd the fruits in vale and mountain,
Philon the shepherd, late forgot,
Sitting beside a crystal fountain,
    In shadow of a green oak tree
    Upon his pipe this song play'd he :
Adieu Love, adieu Love, untrue Love,
Untrue Love, untrue Love, adieu Love ;
Your mind is light, soon lost for new love.

So long as I was in your sight
I was your heart, your soul, and treasure ;
And evermore you sobb'd and sigh'd
Burning in flames beyond all measure :
    —Three days endured your love to me,
    And it was lost in other three !
Adieu Love, adieu Love, untrue Love,

Untrue Love, untrue Love, adieu Love ;
Your mind is light, soon lost for new love.

Another Shepherd you did see
To whom your heart was soon enchainéd ;
Full soon your love was leapt from me,
Full soon my place he had obtainéd.
   Soon came a third, your love to win,
   And we were out and he was in.
Adieu Love, adieu Love, untrue Love,
Untrue Love, untrue Love, adieu Love ;
Your mind is light, soon lost for new love.

Sure you have made me passing glad
That you your mind so soon removéd,
Before that I the leisure had
To choose you for my best belovéd.
   For all your love was past and done
   Two days before it was begun :—
Adieu Love, adieu Love, untrue Love,
Untrue Love, untrue Love, adieu Love ;
Your mind is light, soon lost for new love.

ANON.

41. A RENUNCIATION

If women could be fair, and yet not fond,
Or that their love were firm, not fickle still,
I would not marvel that they make men bond
By service long to purchase their good will ;
Bu⁺ when I see how frail those creatures are,
I muse that men forget themselves so far.

To mark the choice they make, and how they change,
How oft from Phœbus they do flee to Pan ;
Unsettled still, like haggards wild they range,
These gentle birds that fly from man to man ;
Who would not scorn and shake them from the fist,
And let them fly, fair fools, which way they list ?

Yet for disport we fawn and flatter both,
To pass the time when nothing else can please,
And train them to our lure with subtle oath,
Till, weary of their wiles, ourselves we ease ;
And then we say when we their fancy try,
To play with fools, O what a fool was I !

E. VERE, EARL OF OXFORD.

42

Blow, blow, thou winter wind
Thou art not so unkind
As man's ingratitude ;
Thy tooth is not so keen
Because thou art not seen,
Although thy breath be rude.
Heigh ho ! sing heigh ho ! unto the green holly :
Most friendship is feigning, most loving mere folly :
Then, heigh ho ! the holly !
This life is most jolly.

Freeze, freeze, thou bitter sky,
Thou dost not bite so nigh
As benefits forgot :
Though thou the waters warp,
Thy sting is not so sharp
As friend remember'd not.
Heigh ho ! sing heigh ho ! unto the green holly :
Most friendship is feigning, most loving mere folly :
Then, heigh ho ! the holly !
This life is most jolly.

W. SHAKESPEARE.

43. MADRIGAL

My thoughts hold mortal strife ;
I do detest my life,
And with lamenting cries
Peace to my soul to bring
Oft call that prince which here doth monarchise :
—But he, grim grinning King,
Who caitiffs scorns, and doth the blest surprise,
Late having deck'd with beauty's rose his tomb,
Disdains to crop a weed, and will not come.

W. DRUMMOND.

44. DIRGE OF LOVE

Come away, come away, Death,
And in sad cypres let me be laid ;
Fly away, fly away, breath ;
I am slain by a fair cruel maid.

My shroud of white, stuck all with yew,
　　O prepare it !
My part of death no one so true
　　Did share it.

Not a flower, not a flower sweet
On my black coffin let there be strown ;
　　Not a friend, not a friend greet
My poor corpse, where my bones shall be thrown :
A thousand thousand sighs to save,
　　Lay me, O where
Sad true lover never find my grave,
　　To weep there.
　　　　　　　　　W. SHAKESPEARE.

45. FIDELE

Fear no more the heat o' the sun
　　Nor the furious winter's rages :
Thou thy worldly task hast done,
　　Home art gone and ta'en thy wages :
Golden lads and girls all must,
As chimney sweepers, come to dust.

Fear no more the frown o' the great,
　　Thou art past the tyrant's stroke ;
Care no more to clothe and eat ;
　　To thee the reed is as the oak :
The sceptre, learning, physic, must
All follow this, and come to dust.

Fear no more the lightning flash
　　Nor the all-dreaded thunder-stone ;
Fear not slander, censure rash ;
　　Thou hast finish'd joy and moan :
All lovers young, all lovers must
Consign to thee, and come to dust.
　　　　　　　　　W. SHAKESPEARE.

46. A SEA DIRGE

Full fathom five thy father lies :
　　Of his bones are coral made ;
Those are pearls that were his eyes :
　　Nothing of him that doth fade,

But doth suffer a sea-change
Into something rich and strange ;
Sea-nymphs hourly ring his knell :
Hark ! now I hear them,—
    Ding, dong, Bell.

W. SHAKESPEARE.

47. A LAND DIRGE

Call for the robin-redbreast and the wren,
Since o'er shady groves they hover
And with leaves and flowers do cover
The friendless bodies of unburied men.
Call unto his funeral dole
The ant, the field-mouse, and the mole
To rear him hillocks that shall keep him warm
And (when gay tombs are robb'd) sustain no harm ;
But keep the wolf far thence, that's foe to men,
For with his nails he'll dig them up again.

J. WEBSTER.

48. POST MORTEM

If Thou survive my well-contented day
When that churl Death my bones with dust shall cover,
And shalt by fortune once more re-survey
These poor rude lines of thy deceasèd lover ;

Compare them with the bettering of the time,
And though they be outstripp'd by every pen,
Reserve them for my love, not for their rhyme
Exceeded by the height of happier men.

O then vouchsafe me but this loving thought—
" Had my friend's muse grown with this growing age,
A dearer birth than this his love had brought,
To march in ranks of better equipage :

But since he died, and poets better prove,
Theirs for their style I'll read, his for his love."

49. THE TRIUMPH OF DEATH

No longer mourn for me when I am dead
Than you shall hear the surly sullen bell
Give warning to the world, that I am fled
From this vile world, with vilest worms to dwell ;

Nay, if you read this line, remember not
The hand that writ it ; for I love you so,
That I in your sweet thoughts would be forgot
If thinking on me then should make you woe.

O if, I say, you look upon this verse
When I perhaps compounded am with clay,
Do not so much as my poor name rehearse,
But let your love even with my life decay ;

Lest the wise world should look into your moan,
And mock you with me after I am gone.

W. SHAKESPEARE.

50. MADRIGAL

Tell me where is Fancy bred,
Or in the heart, or in the head ?
How begot, how nourishéd ?
    Reply, reply.
It is engender'd in the eyes,
With gazing fed ; and Fancy dies
In the cradle where it lies :
Let us all ring fancy's knell ;
I'll begin it,—Ding, dong, bell.
    —Ding, dong, bell.

W. SHAKESPEARE.

51. CUPID AND CAMPASPE

Cupid and my Campaspe play'd
At cards for kisses ; Cupid paid :
He stakes his quiver, bow, and arrows,
His mother's doves, and team of sparrows ;
Loses them too ; then down he throws
The coral of his lips, the rose
Growing on's cheek (but none knows how) ;
With these, the crystal of his brow,
And then the dimple on his chin ;
All these did my Campaspe win :
At last he set her both his eyes—
She won, and Cupid blind did rise.
    O Love ! has she done this to thee ?
    What shall, alas ! become of me ?

J. LYLE.

52

Pack, clouds, away, and welcome day,
　With night we banish sorrow ;
Sweet air blow soft, mount larks aloft
　To give my Love good-morrow !
Wings from the wind to please her mind,
　Notes from the lark I'll borrow ;
Bird prune thy wing, nightingale sing,
　To give my Love good-morrow ;
　　To give my Love good-morrow
　　Notes from them both I'll borrow.
Wake from thy nest, Robin-redbreast,
　Sing, birds, in every furrow ;
And from each bill, let music shrill
　Give my fair Love good-morrow !
Blackbird and thrush in every bush,
　Stare, linnet, and cock-sparrow !
You pretty elves, amongst yourselves
　Sing my fair Love good-morrow ;
　　To give my Love good-morrow
　　Sing birds in every furrow !

T. Heywood.

53. PROTHALAMION

Calm was the day, and through the trembling air
Sweet-breathing Zephyrus did softly play—
A gentle spirit, that lightly did delay
Hot Titan's beams, which then did glister fair ;
When I, (whom sullen care,
Through discontent of my long fruitless stay
In princes' court, and expectation vain.
Of idle hopes, which still do fly away
Like empty shadows, did afflict my brain)
Walk'd forth to ease my pain
Along the shore of silver-streaming Thames ;
Whose rutty bank, the which his river hems,
Was painted all with variable flowers,
And all the meads adorn'd with dainty gems
Fit to deck maidens' bowers,
And crown their paramours
Against the bridal day, which is not long :
　Sweet Thames ! run softly, till I end my song.

There in a meadow by the river's side
A flock of nymphs I chancéd to espy,
All lovely daughters of the flood thereby,
With goodly greenish locks all loose untied
As each had been a bride ;
And each one had a little wicker basket
Made of fine twigs, entrailéd curiously,
In which they gather'd flowers to fill their flasket,
And with fine fingers cropt full feateously
The tender stalks on high.
Of every sort which in that meadow grew
They gather'd some ; the violet, pallid blue,
The little daisy that at evening closes,
The virgin lily and the primrose true :
With store of vermeil roses,
To deck their bridegrooms' posies
Against the bridal day, which was not long :
　　Sweet Thames ! run softly, till I end my song.

With that I saw two swans of goodly hue
Come softly swimming down along the lee ;
Two fairer birds I yet did never see ;
The snow which doth the top of Pindus strow
Did never whiter show,
Nor Jove himself, when he a swan would be
For love of Leda, whiter did appear ;
Yet Leda was (they say) as white as he,
Yet not so white as these, nor nothing near ;
So purely white they were
That even the gentle stream, the which them bare,
Seem'd foul to them, and bade his billows spare
To wet their silken feathers, lest they might
Soil their fair plumes with water not so fair,
And mar their beauties bright
That shone as Heaven's light
Against their bridal day, which was not long :
　　Sweet Thames ! run softly, till I end my song.

Eftsoons the nymphs, which now had flowers their fill,
Ran all in haste to see that silver brood
As they came floating on the crystal flood ;
Whom when they saw, they stood amazéd still
Their wondering eyes to fill ;

Them seem'd they never saw a sight so fair
Of fowls, so lovely, that they sure did deem
Them heavenly born, or to be that same pair
Which through the sky draw Venus' silver team ;
For sure they did not seem
To be begot of any earthly seed,
But rather angels, or of angels' breed ;
Yet were they bred of summer's heat, they say,
In sweetest season, when each flower and weed
The earth did fresh array ;
So fresh they seem'd as day,
Even as their bridal day, which was not long :
   Sweet Thames ! run softly, till I end my song.

Then forth they all out of their baskets drew
Great store of flowers, the honour of the field,
That to the sense did fragrant odours yield,
All which upon those goodly birds they threw
And all the waves did strew,
That like old Peneus' waters they did seem
When down along by pleasant Tempe's shore
Scatter'd with flowers, through Thessaly they stream,
That they appear, through lilies' plenteous store,
Like a bride's chamber-floor.
Two of those nymphs meanwhile two garlands bound
Of freshest flowers which in that mead they found,
The which presenting all in trim array,
Their snowy foreheads therewithal they crown'd
Whilst one did sing this lay
Prepared against that day,
Against their bridal day, which was not long :
   Sweet Thames ! run softly, till I end my song.

" Ye gentle birds ! the world's fair ornament,
And Heaven's glory, whom this happy hour
Doth lead unto your lovers' blissful bower,
Joy may you have, and gentle hearts content
Of your love's complement ;
And let fair Venus, that is queen of love,
With her heart-quelling son upon you smile,
Whose smile, they say, hath virtue to remove
All love's dislike, and friendship's faulty guile
For ever to assoil.
Let endless peace your stedfast hearts accord,
And blessèd plenty wait upon your board ;

And let your bed with pleasures chaste abound,
That fruitful issue may to you afford
Which may your foes confound,
And make your joys redound
Upon your bridal day, which is not long :
   Sweet Thames ! run softly, till I end my song."

So ended she ; and all the rest around
To her redoubled that her undersong,
Which said their bridal day should not be long :
And gentle Echo from the neighbour ground
Their accents did resound
So forth those joyous birds did pass along
Adown the lee that to them murmur'd low,
As he would speak but that he lack'd a tongue,
Yet did by signs his glad affection show,
Making his stream run slow.
And all the fowl which in his flood did dwell
'Gan flock about these twain, that did excel
The rest, so far as Cynthia doth shend
The lesser stars. So they, enrangéd well,
Did on those two attend,
And their best service lend
Against their wedding day, which was not long :
   Sweet Thames ! run softly, till I end my song.

At length they all to merry London came,
To merry London, my most kindly nurse,
That to me gave this life's first native source,
Though from another place I take my name,
An house of ancient fame :
There when they came whereas those bricky towers
The which on Thames' broad agéd back do ride,
Where now the studious lawyers have their bowers,
There whilome wont the Templar-knights to bide,
Till they decay'd through pride ;
Next whereunto there stands a stately place,
Where oft I gainéd gifts and goodly grace
Of that great lord, which therein wont to dwell,
Whose want too well now feels my friendless case ;
But ah ! here fits not well
Old woes, but joys to tell
Against the bridal day, which is not long :
   Sweet Thames ! run softly, till I end my song.

Yet therein now doth lodge a noble peer,
Great England's glory and the world's wide wonder,
Whose dreadful name late thro' all Spain did thunder,
And Hercules' two pillars standing near
Did make to quake and fear :
Fair branch of honour, flower of chivalry !
That fillest England with thy triumphs' fame
Joy have thou of thy noble victory,
And endless happiness of thine own name
That promiseth the same ;
That through thy prowess and victorious arms
Thy country may be freed from foreign harms,
And great Eliza's glorious name may ring
Through all the world, fill'd with thy wide alarms
Which some brave Muse may sing
To ages following,
Upon the bridal day, which is not long :
   Sweet Thames ! run softly, till I end my song.

From those high towers this noble lord issuing
Like radiant Hesper, when his golden hair
In th' ocean billows he hath bathéd fair,
Descended to the river's open viewing
With a great train ensuing.
Above the rest were goodly to be seen
Two gentle knights of lovely face and feature,
Beseeming well the bower of any queen,
With gifts of wit and ornaments of nature,
Fit for so goodly stature,
That like the twins of Jove they seem'd in sight
Which deck the baldric of the Heavens bright ;
They two, forth pacing to the river's side,
Received those two fair brides, their love's delight ;
Which, at th' appointed tide,
Each one did make his bride
Against their bridal day, which is not long :
   Sweet Thames ! run softly, till I end my song.
E. SPENSER.

54. THE HAPPY HEART

Art thou poor, yet hast thou golden slumbers ?
      O sweet content !
Art thou rich, yet is thy mind perplexéd ?
      O punishment !
Dost thou laugh to see how fools are vexéd
To add to golden numbers, golden numbers ?
O sweet content ! O sweet, O sweet content !
   Work apace, apace, apace, apace ;
   Honest labour bears a lovely face ;
Then hey nonny nonny, hey nonny nonny !

Canst drink the waters of the crispéd spring ?
      O sweet content !
Swimm'st thou in wealth, yet sink'st in thine own tears ?
      O punishment !
Then he that patiently want's burden bears
No burden bears, but is a king, a king !
O sweet content ! O sweet, O sweet content !
   Work apace, apace, apace, apace ;
   Honest labour bears a lovely face ;
Then hey nonny nonny, hey nonny nonny !

T. DEKKER.

55

This Life, which seems so fair,
Is like a bubble blown up in the air
By sporting children's breath,
Who chase it everywhere
And strive who can most motion it bequeath.
And though it sometimes seem of its own might
Like to an eye of gold to be fix'd there,
And firm to hover in that empty height,
That only is because it is so light.
—But in that pomp it doth not long appear ;
For when 'tis most admiréd, in a thought,
Because it erst was nought, it turns to nought.

W. DRUMMOND.

56. SOUL AND BODY

Poor Soul, the centre of my sinful earth,
Fool'd by those rebel powers that thee array,
Why dost thou pine within, and suffer dearth,
Painting thy outward walls so costly gay?

Why so large cost, having so short a lease,
Dost thou upon thy fading mansion spend?
Shall worms, inheritors of this excess,
Eat up thy charge? is this thy body's end?

Then, Soul, live thou upon thy servant's loss,
And let that pine to aggravate thy store;
Buy terms divine in selling hours of dross;
Within be fed, without be rich no more:—

So shalt thou feed on death, that feeds on men,
And death once dead, there's no more dying then.

W. SHAKESPEARE.

57. LIFE

The World's a bubble, and the Life of Man
        Less than a span:
In his conception wretched, from the womb
        So to the tomb;
Curst from his cradle, and brought up to years
        With cares and fears.
Who then to frail mortality shall trust,
But limns on water, or but writes in dust.

Yet whilst with sorrow here we live opprest,
        What life is best?
Courts are but only superficial schools
        To dandle fools:
The rural parts are turn'd into a den
        Of savage men:
And where's city from foul vice so free,
But may be term'd the worst of all the three?

Domestic cares afflict the husband's bed,
        Or pains his head:
Those that live single, take it for a curse,
        Or do things worse:

Some would have children : those that have them,
  moan
          Or wish them gone :
What is it, then, to have, or have no wife,
But single thraldom, or a double strife ?

Our own affections still at home to please
          Is a disease :
To cross the seas to any foreign soil,
          Peril and toil :
Wars with their noise affright us ; when they cease,
          We are worse in peace ;—
What then remains, but that we still should cry
For being born, or, being born, to die ?

                              LORD BACON.

58. THE LESSONS OF NATURE

Of this fair volume which we World do name
If we the sheets and leaves could turn with care,
Of Him who it corrects, and did it frame,
We clear might read the art and wisdom rare :

Find out His power which wildest powers doth tame,
His providence extending everywhere,
His justice which proud rebels doth not spare,
In every page, no period of the same.

But silly we, like foolish children, rest
Well pleased with colour'd vellum, leaves of gold,
Fair dangling ribbands, leaving what is best,
On the great Writer's sense ne'er taking hold ;

Or if by chance we stay our minds on aught,
It is some picture on the margin wrought.

                              W. DRUMMOND.

59

Doth then the world go thus, doth all thus move ?
Is this the justice which on Earth we find ?
Is this that firm decree which all doth bind ?
Are these your influences, Powers above ?

Those souls which vice's moody mists most blind,
Blind Fortune, blindly, most their friend doth prove ;
And they who thee, poor idol Virtue ! love,
Ply like a feather toss'd by storm and wind.

Ah ! if a Providence doth sway this all,
Why should best minds groan under most distress ?
Or why should pride humility make thrall,
And injuries the innocent oppress ?

Heavens ! hinder, stop this fate ; or grant a time
When good may have, as well as bad, their prime !
                              W. DRUMMOND.

60. THE WORLD'S WAY

Tired with all these, for restful death I cry—
As, to behold desert a beggar born,
And needy nothing trimm'd in jollity,
And purest faith unhappily forsworn,

And gilded honour shamefully misplaced,
And maiden virtue rudely strumpeted,
And right perfection wrongfully disgraced,
And strength by limping sway disabléd,

And art made tongue-tied by authority,
And folly, doctor-like, controlling skill,
And simple truth miscall'd simplicity,
And captive Good attending captain Ill :—

—Tired with all these, from these would I be gone,
Save that, to die, I leave my Love alone.
                              W. SHAKESPEARE.

61. SAINT JOHN BAPTIST

The last and greatest Herald of Heaven's King
Girt with rough skins, hies to the deserts wild,
Among that savage brood the woods forth bring,
Which he more harmless found than man, and mild.

His food was locusts, and what there doth spring
With honey that from virgin hives distill'd ;
Parch'd body, hollow eyes, some uncouth thing
Made him appear, long since from earth exiled.

There burst he forth : All he whose hopes rely
On God, with me amidst these deserts mourn,
Repent, repent, and from old errors turn !
—Who listen'd to his voice, obey'd his cry ?

Only the echoes, which he made relent,
Rung from their flinty caves, Repent ! Repent !

W. DRUMMOND.

SECOND BOOK

SUMMARY

THIS division, embracing the latter eighty years of the
seventeenth century, contains the close of our Early
poetical style and the commencement of the Modern. In
Dryden we see the first master of the new : in Milton,
whose genius dominates here as Shakespeare's in the
former book—the crown and consummation of the early
period. Their splendid Odes are far in advance of any
prior attempts, Spenser's excepted : they exhibit the wider
and grander range which years and experience and the
struggles of the time conferred on Poetry. Poetry now
gave expression to political feeling, to religious thought,
to a high philosophic statesmanship in writers such as
Marvell, Herbert, and Wotton : whilst in Marvell and
Milton, again, we find the first noble attempts at pure
description of nature, destined in our own ages to be
continued and equalled. Meanwhile the poetry of simple
passion, although before 1660 often deformed by verbal
fancies and conceits of thought, and afterward by levity
and an artificial tone—produced in Herrick and Waller
some charming pieces of more finished art than the
Elizabethan : until in the courtly compliments of Sedley
it seems to exhaust itself, and lie almost dormant for the
hundred years between the days of Wither and Suckling
and the days of Burns and Cowper. That the change from
our early style to the modern brought with it at first a
loss of nature and simplicity is undeniable : yet the far
bolder and wider scope which Poetry took between 1620
and 1700, and the successful efforts then made to gain
greater clearness in expression, in their results have been
no slight compensation.

62. ODE ON THE MORNING OF CHRIST'S NATIVITY

This is the month, and this the happy morn
Wherein the Son of Heaven's Eternal King
Of wedded maid and virgin mother born,
Our great redemption from above did bring ;
For so the holy sages once did sing
That He our deadly forfeit should release,
And with His Father work us a perpetual peace.

That glorious Form, that Light unsufferable,
And that far-beaming blaze of Majesty
Wherewith He wont at Heaven's high council-table
To sit the midst of Trinal Unity,
He laid aside ; and, here with us to be,
Forsook the courts of everlasting day,
And chose with us a darksome house of mortal clay.

Say, heavenly Muse, shall not thy sacred vein
Afford a present to the Infant God ?
Hast thou no verse, no hymn, or solemn strain
To welcome Him to this His new abode,
Now while the heaven, by the sun's team untrod,
Hath took no print of the approaching light,
And all the spangled host keep watch in squadrons bright ?

See how from far, upon the eastern road,
The star-led wizards haste with odours sweet :
O run, prevent them with thy humble ode
And lay it lowly at his blessed feet ;
Have thou the honour first thy Lord to greet,
And join thy voice unto the angel quire
From out His secret altar touch'd with hallow'd fire.

J. MILTON.

63. THE HYMN

It was the winter wild
While the heaven-born Child
All meanly wrapt in the rude manger lies ;
Nature in awe to Him
Had doff'd her gaudy trim,
With her great Master so to sympathise :
It was no season then for her
To wanton with the sun, her lusty paramour.

Only with speeches fair
She woos the gentle air
To hide her guilty front with innocent snow ;
And on her naked shame,
Pollute with sinful blame,
The saintly veil of maiden white to throw ;
Confounded, that her Maker's eyes
Should look so near upon her foul deformities.

But He, her fears to cease,
Sent down the meek-eyed Peace ;
She, crown'd with olive green, come softly sliding
Down through the turning sphere
His ready harbinger,
With turtle wing the amorous clouds dividing ;
And waving wide her myrtle wand,
She strikes a universal peace through sea and land.

No war, or battle's sound
Was heard the world around :
The idle spear and shield were high up hung ;
The hookéd chariot stood
Unstain'd with hostile blood ;
The trumpet spake not to the arméd throng ;
And kings sat still with awful eye,
As if they surely knew their sovran Lord was by.

But peace was the night
Wherein the Prince of Light
His reign of peace upon the earth began :
The winds, with wonder whist,
Smoothly the waters kist
Whispering new joys to the mild ocean—
Who now hath quite forgot to rave,
While birds of calm sit brooding on the charméd wave.

The stars, with deep amaze,
Stand fix'd in steadfast gaze,
Bending one way their precious influence ;
And will not take their flight
For all the morning light,
Or Lucifer that often warn'd them thence ;
But in their glimmering orbs did glow
Until their Lord Himself bespake, and bid them go.

And though the shady gloom had given day her room,
The sun himself withheld his wonted speed,
And hid his head for shame,
As his inferior flame
The new-enlighten'd world no more should need :
He saw a greater Sun appear
Than his bright throne, or burning axletree, could bear.

The shepherds on the lawn
Or ere the point of dawn
Sate simply chatting in rustic row :
Full little thought they then
That the mighty Pan
Was kindly come to live with them below ;
Perhaps their loves, or else their sheep
Was all that did their silly thoughts so busy keep.

When such music sweet
Their hearts and ears did greet
As never was by mortal finger strook—
Divinely-warbled voice
Answering the stringèd noise,
As all their souls in blissful rapture took :
The air, such pleasure loth to lose,
With thousand echoes still prolongs each heavenly close.

Nature that heard such sound
Beneath the hollow round
Of Cynthia's seat the airy region thrilling,
Now was almost won
To think her part was done,
And that her reign had here its last fulfilling ;
She knew such harmony alone
Could hold all heaven and earth in happier union.

At last surrounds their sight
A globe of circular light
That with long beams the shamefaced night array'd ;
The helmèd Cherubim
And sworded Seraphim
Are seen in glittering ranks with wings display'd,
Harping in loud and solemn quire
With unexpressive notes, to Heaven's new-born Heir.

Such music (as 'tis said)
Before was never made
But when of old the sons of morning sung,

While the Creator great
His constellations set
And the well-balanced world on hinges hung ;
And cast the dark foundations deep,
And bid the weltering waves their oozy channel keep.

Ring out, ye crystal spheres
Once bless our human ears,
If ye have power to touch our senses so ;
And let your silver chime
Move in melodious time ;
And let the bass of heaven's deep organ blow
And with your ninefold harmony
Make up full concert to the angelic symphony.

For if such holy song
Enwrap our fancy long,
Time will run back, and fetch the age of gold ;
And speckled vanity
Will sicken soon and die,
And leprous sin will melt from earthly mould ;
And Hell itself will pass away,
And leave her dolorous mansions to the peering day.

Yea, Truth and Justice then
Will down return to men,
Orb'd in a rainbow ; and, like glories wearing,
Mercy will sit between
Throned in celestial sheen,
With radiant feet the tissued clouds down steering ;
And Heaven, as at some festival,
Will open wide the gates of her high palace hall.

But wisest Fate says No ;
This must not yet be so ;
The Babe yet lies in smiling infancy
That on the bitter cross
Must redeem our loss ;
So both Himself and us to glorify :
Yet first, to those ychain'd in sleep
The wakeful trump of doom must thunder through the
       deep,

With such a horrid clang
As on mount Sinai rang

While the red fire and smouldering clouds outbrake :
The aged Earth aghast
With terror of that blast
Shall from the surface to the centre shake,
When, at the world's last session,
The dreadful Judge in middle air shall spread His throne.

And then at last our bliss
Full and perfect is,
But now begins ; for from this happy day
The old Dragon, under ground
In straiter limits bound,
Not half so far casts his usurpéd sway ;
And, wroth to see his kingdom fail,
Swinges the scaly horrour of his folded tail.

The oracles are dumb ;
No voice or hideous hum
Runs through the archéd roof in words deceiving :
Apollo from his shrine
Can no more divine,
With hollow shriek the steep of Delphos leaving :
No nightly trance or breathéd spell
Inspires the pale-eyed priest from the prophetic cell.

The lonely mountains o'er
And the resounding shore
A voice of weeping heard, and loud lament ;
From haunted spring and dale
Edged with poplar pale
The parting Genius is with sighing sent ;
With flower-inwoven tresses torn
The nymphs in twilight shade of tangled thickets mourn.

In consecrated earth
And on the holy hearth
The Lars and Lemurés moan with midnight plaint ;
In urns, and altars round
A drear and dying sound
Affrights the Flamens at their service quaint :
And the chill marble seems to sweat,
While each peculiar Power foregoes his wonted seat.

Peor and Baalim
Forsake their temples dim,
With that twice-batter'd god of Palestine ;
And moonéd Ashtaroth

Heaven'd queen and mother both,
Now sits not girt with tapers' holy shine,
The Lybic Hammon shrinks his horn
In vain the Tyrian maids their wounded Thammuz mourn.

And sullen Moloch, fled,
Hath left in shadows dread
His burning idol all of blackest hue ;
In vain with cymbals' ring
They call the grisly king,
In dismal dance about the furnace blue ;
The brutish gods of Nile as fast
Isis, and Orus, and the dog Anubis, haste.

Nor is Osiris seen
In Memphian grove, or green,
Trampling the unshower'd grass with lowings loud :
Nor can he be at rest
Within his sacred chest ;
Nought but profoundest hell can be his shroud ;
In vain with timbrell'd anthems dark
The sable stoléd sorcerers bear his worshipt ark.

He feels from Juda's land
The dreaded infant's hand ;
The rays of Bethlehem blind his dusky eyn ;
Nor all the gods beside
Longer dare abide,
Nor Typhon huge ending in snaky twine :
Our Babe, to show his Godhead true,
Can in his swaddling bands control the damnéd crew.

So, when the sun in bed
Curtain'd with cloudy red
Pillows his chin upon an orient wave,
The flocking shadows pale
Troop to the infernal jail,
Each fetter'd ghost slips to his several grave ;
And the yellow-skirted fays
Fly after the night-steeds, leaving their moon-loved maze.

But see, the Virgin blest
Hath laid her Babe to rest ;
Time is, our tedious song should here have ending :
Heaven's youngest-teeméd star
Hath fixed her polish'd car,
Her sleeping Lord with hand-maid lamp attending :

And all about the courtly stable
Bright-harness'd angels sit in order serviceable.

J. MILTON.

63. SONG FOR SAINT CECILIA'S DAY, 1687

From Harmony, from heavenly Harmony
   This universal frame began :
  When Nature underneath a heap
   Of jarring atoms lay
 And could not heave her head,
The tuneful voice was heard from high
   Arise, ye more than dead !
Then cold, and hot, and moist, and dry
In order to their stations leap,
   And Music's power obey.
From harmony, from heavenly harmony
   This universal frame began :
   From harmony to harmony
Through all the compass of the notes it ran,
The diapason closing full in Man.

What passion cannot Music raise and quell ?
   When Jubal struck the chorded shell
  His listening brethren stood around,
  And, wondering, on their faces fell
  To worship that celestial sound.
Less than a God they thought there could not dwell
   Within the hollow of that shell
   That spoke so sweetly and so well.
What passion cannot Music raise and quell ?

  The trumpet's loud clangor
   Excites us to arms,
 With shrill notes of anger
   And mortal alarms.
 The double double double beat
   Of the thundering drum
   Cries " Hark ! the foes come ;
Charge, charge, 'tis too late to retreat ! "

  The soft complaining flute
  In dying notes discovers

The woes of hopeless lovers,
Whose dirge is whisper'd by the warbling lute.

Sharp violins proclaim
Their jealous pangs and desperation,
Fury, frantic indignation,
Depth of pains, and height of passion
    For the fair disdainful dame.

But oh ! what art can teach,
What human voice can reach
    The sacred organ's praise ?
Notes inspiring holy love,
Notes that wing their heavenly ways
    To mend the choirs above.
Orpheus could lead the savage race,
And trees uprooted left their place
    Sequacious of the lyre :
But bright Cecilia raised the wonder higher :
When to her Organ vocal breath was given
An Angel heard, and straight appear'd—
    Mistaking Earth for Heaven !

Grand Chorus :

As from the power of sacred lays
    The spheres began to move,
And sung the great Creator's praise
    To all the blest above ;
So when the last and dreadful hour
This crumbling pageant shall devour,
The trumpet shall be heard on high,
The dead shall live, the living die,
    And Music shall untune the sky.

                                    J. DRYDEN.

64. ON THE LATE MASSACRE IN PIEMONT

Avenge, O Lord ! thy slaughter'd Saints, whose bones
Lie scatter'd on the Alpine mountains cold ;
Even them who kept Thy truth so pure of old
When all our fathers worshipt stocks and stones.

Forget not : In Thy book record their groans
Who were Thy sheep, and in their ancient fold
Slain by the bloody Piemontese, that roll'd
Mother with infant down the rocks. Their moans

The vales redoubled to the hills, and they
To Heaven. Their martyr'd blood and ashes sow
O'er all the Italian field, where still doth sway
The triple tyrant, that from these may grow
A hundred-fold, who, having learnt Thy way,
Early may fly the Babylonian woe.
                                    J. MILTON.

65. HORATIAN ODE UPON CROMWELL'S RETURN FROM IRELAND

The forward youth that would appear,
Must now forsake his Muses dear,
    Nor in the shadows sing
    His numbers languishing.

'Tis time to leave the books in dust,
And oil the unused armour's rust,
    Removing from the wall
    The corslet of the hall.

So restless Cromwell could not cease
In the inglorious arts of peace,
    But through adventurous war
    Urgéd his active star :

And like the three-fork'd lightning first,
Breaking the clouds where it was nurst,
    Did thorough his own side
    His fiery way divide :

For 'tis all one to courage high
The emulous, or enemy ;
    And with such, to enclose
Is more than to oppose ;

Then burning through the air he went
And palaces and temples rent ;
    And Cæsar's head at last
    Did through his laurels blast.

'Tis madness to resist or blame
The face of angry heaven's flame ;
    And if we would speak true,
    Much to the Man is due

Who, from his private gardens, where
He lived reservéd and austere
    (As if he his highest plot
    To plant the bergamot)

Could by industrious valour climb
To ruin the great work of time,
    And cast the Kingdoms old
    Into another mould.

Though Justice against Fate complain,
And plead the ancient Rights in vain—
    But those do hold or break
    As men are strong or weak ;

Nature, that hateth emptiness,
Allows of penetration less,
    And therefore must make room
    Where greater spirits come.

Where field of all the civil war
Where his were not the deepest scar ?
    And Hampton shows what part
    He had of wiser art,

Where, twining subtle fears with hope,
He wore a net of such a scope
    That Charles himself might chase
    To Carisbrook's narrow case ;

That thence the Royal actor borne
The tragic scaffold might adorn :
    While round the arméd bands
    Did clap their bloody hands ;

He nothing common did or mean
Upon that memorable scene,
    But with his keener eye
    The axe's edge did try ;

Nor call'd the Gods, with vulgar spite,
To vindicate his helpless right ;
    But bow'd his comely head
    Down, as upon a bed.

—This was that memorable hour
Which first assured the forcéd power :

So when they did design
The Capitol's first line,

A Bleeding Head, where they begun,
Did fright the architects to run ;
    And yet in that the State
    Foresaw its happy fate !

And now the Irish are ashamed
To see themselves in one year tamed :
    So much one man can do
    That does both act and know.

They can affirm his praises best,
And have, though overcome, confest
    How good he is, how just
    And fit for highest trust ;

Nor yet grown stiffer with command,
But still in the Republic's hand—
    How fit he is to sway
    That can so well obey !

He to the Commons' feet presents
A Kingdom for his first year's rents,
    And (what he may) forbears
    His fame, to make it theirs :

And has his sword and spoils ungirt
To lay them at the Public's skirt.
    So when the falcon high
    Falls heavy from the sky,

She, having kill'd, no more does search
But on the next green bough to perch,
    Where, when he first does lure,
    The falconer has her sure.

—What may not then our Isle presume
While victory his crest does plume ?
    What may not others fear
    If thus he crowns each year !

As Cæsar he, ere long, to Gaul,
To Italy an Hannibal,
    And to all states not free
    Shall climacteric be.

The Pict no shelter now shall find
Within his parti-colour'd mind,
But from this valour, sad
Shrink underneath the plaid—

Happy, if in the tufted brake
The English hunter him mistake,
Nor lay his hounds in near
The Caledonian deer.

But Thou, the War's and Fortune's son,
March indefatigably on ;
And for the last effect
Still keep the sword erect

Besides the force it has to fright
The spirits of the shady night,
The same arts that did gain
A power, must it maintain.

A. MARVELL.

66. LYCIDAS

Elegy on a Friend drowned in the Irish Channel

Yet once more, O ye laurels, and once more
Ye myrtles brown, with ivy never sere,
I come to pluck your berries harsh and crude,
And with forced fingers rude
Shatter your leaves before the mellowing year.
Bitter constraint, and sad occasion dear
Compels me to disturb your season due :
For Lycidas is dead, dead ere his prime,
Young Lycidas, and hath not left his peer :
Who would not sing for Lycidas ? he knew
Himself to sing, and build the lofty rhyme.
He must not float upon his watery bier
Unwept, and welter to the parching wind,
Without the meed of some melodious tear.

Begin then, Sisters of the sacred well
That from beneath the seat of Jove doth spring ;
Begin, and somewhat loudly sweep the string ;
Hence with denial vain and coy excuse :
So may some gentle Muse
With lucky words favour my destined urn ;
And as he passes, turn
And bid fair peace be to my sable shroud.

For we were nursed upon the self-same hill,
Fed the same flock by fountain, shade, and rill:
Together both, ere the high lawns appear'd
Under the opening eye-lids of the morn,
We drove a-field, and both together heard
What time the gray-fly winds her sultry horn,
Battening our flocks with the fresh dews of night,
Oft till the star that rose at evening bright
Toward heaven's descent had sloped his westering wheel.
Meanwhile the rural ditties were not mute,
Temper'd to the oaten flute;
Rough Satyrs danced, and Fauns with cloven heel
From the glad sound would not be absent long;
And old Damœtas loved to hear our song.

But, O the heavy change, now thou art gone,
Now thou art gone, and never must return!
Thee, Shepherd, thee the woods, and desert caves
With wild thyme and the gadding vine o'ergrown,
And all their echoes, mourn:
The willows and the hazel copses green
Shall now no more be seen
Fanning their joyous leaves to thy soft lays:—
As killing as the canker to the rose,
Or taint-worm to the weanling herds that graze,
Or frost to flowers, that their gay wardrobe wear
When first the white-thorn blows;
Such, Lycidas, thy loss to shepherds' ear.

Where were ye, Nymphs, when the remorseless deep
Closed o'er the head of your loved Lycidas?
For neither were ye playing on the steep
Where your old bards, the famous Druids, lie,
Nor on the shaggy top of Mona high,
Nor yet where Deva spreads her wizard stream:
Ay me! I fondly dream—
Had ye been there—for what could that have done?
What could the Muse herself that Orpheus bore
The Muse herself, for her enchanting son,
Whom universal nature did lament,
When by the rout that made the hideous roar
His gory visage down the stream was sent,
Down the swift Hebrus to the Lesbian shore?

Alas ! what boots it with incessant care
To tend the homely, slighted, shepherd's trade
And strictly meditate the thankless Muse ?
Were it not better done, as others use,
To sport with Amaryllis in the shade,
Or with the tangles of Neæra's hair ?
Fame is the spur that the clear spirit doth raise
(That last infirmity of noble mind)
To scorn delights, and live laborious days ;
But the fair guerdon when we hope to find,
And think to burst out into sudden blaze,
Comes the blind Fury with the abhorréd shears
And slits the thin-spun life. " But not the praise,"
Phœbus replied, and touch'd my trembling ears ;
" Fame is no plant that grows on mortal soil,
  Nor in the glistering foil
Set off to the world, nor in broad rumour lies :
But lives and spreads aloft by those pure eyes
And perfect witness of all-judging Jove ;
As he pronounces lastly on each deed,
Of so much fame in heaven expect thy meed."

O fountain Arethuse, and thou honour'd flood
Smooth-sliding Mincius, crown'd with vocal reeds !
That strain I heard was of a higher mood :
  But now my oat proceeds,
And listens to the herald of the sea
That came in Neptune's plea ;
He ask'd the waves, and ask'd the felon winds,
What hard mishap hath doom'd this gentle swain ?
And question'd every gust of rugged wings
That blows from off each beakéd promontory :
They knew not of his story ;
And sage Hippotadés their answer brings,
That not a blast was from his dungeon stray'd ;
The air was calm, and on the level brine
Sleek Panopé with all her sisters play'd.
It was that fatal and perfidious bark
Built in the eclipse, and rigg'd with curses dark,
That sunk so low that sacred head of thine.

Next Camus, reverend sire, went footing slow,
His mantle hairy, and his bonnet sedge
Inwrought with figures dim, and on the edge
Like to that sanguine flower described with woe :

" Ah ! who hath reft," quoth he, " my dearest pledge ! "
Last came, and last did go
The pilot of the Galilean lake ;
Two massy keys he bore of metals twain
(The golden opes, the iron shuts amain) ;
He shook his mitred locks, and stern bespake :
" How well could I have spared for thee, young swain,
Enow of such, as for their bellies' sake
Creep and intrude and climb into the fold !
Of other care they little reckoning make
Than how to scramble at the shearers' feast,
And shove away the worthy bidden guest ;
Blind mouths ! that scarce themselves know how to hold
A sheep-hook, or have learn'd aught else the least
That to the faithful herdman's art belongs !
What recks it them ? What need they ? They are sped ;
And when they list, their lean and flashy songs
Grate on their scrannel pipes of wretched straw ;
The hungry sheep look up, and are not fed,
But swoln with wind and the rank mist they draw
Rot inwardly, and foul contagion spread :
Besides what the grim wolf with privy paw
Daily devours apace, and nothing said :
—But that two-handed engine at the door
Stands ready to smite once, and smite no more."

Return, Alphéus, the dread voice is past
That shrunk thy streams ; return, Sicilian Muse,
And call the vales, and bid them hither cast
Their bells and flowerets of a thousand hues.
Ye valleys low, where the mild whispers use
Of shades, and wanton winds, and gushing brooks
On whose fresh lap the swart star sparely looks ;
Throw hither all your quaint enamell'd eyes
That on the green turf suck the honey'd showers
And purple all the ground with vernal flowers.
Bring the rathe primrose that forsaken dies,
The tufted crow-toe, and pale jessamine,
The white pink, and the pansy freak'd with jet,
The glowing violet,
The musk-rose, and the well-attired woodbine,
With cowslips wan that hang the pensive head,
And every flower that sad embroidery wears :
Bid amarantus all his beauty shed,

And daffodillies fill their cups with tears
To strew the laureat hearse where Lycid lies.
For so to interpose a little ease,
Let our frail thoughts dally with false surmise ;
Ay me ! whilst thee the shores and sounding seas
Wash far away,—where'er thy bones are hurl'd,
Whether beyond the stormy Hebrides
Where thou perhaps, under the whelming tide,
Visitest the bottom of the monstrous world ;
Or whether thou, to our moist vows denied,
Sleep'st by the fable of Bellerus old,
Where the great Vision of the guarded mount
Looks towards Namancos and Bayona's hold,
—Look homeward, Angel, now, and melt with ruth :
—And, O ye dolphins, waft the hapless youth !

Weep no more, woeful shepherds, weep no more,
For Lycidas, your sorrow, is not dead,
Sunk though he be beneath the watery floor ;
So sinks the day-star in the ocean-bed,
And yet anon repairs his drooping head
And tricks his beams, and with new-spangled ore
Flames in the forehead of the morning sky :
So Lycidas sunk low, but mounted high
Through the dear might of Him that walk'd the waves ;
Where, other groves and other streams along,
With nectar pure his oozy locks he laves,
And hears the unexpressive nuptial song
In the blest kingdoms meek of joy and love.
There entertain him all the saints above
In solemn troops, and sweet societies,
That sing, and singing, in their glory move,
And wipe the tears for ever from his eyes.
Now, Lycidas, the shepherds weep no more ;
Henceforth thou art the Genius of the shore
In thy large recompense, and shalt be good
To all that wander in that perilous flood.

Thus sang the uncouth swain to the oaks and rills,
While the still morn went out with sandals gray ;
He touch'd the tender stops of various quills,
With eager thought warbling his Doric lay ;
And now the sun had stretch'd out all the hills,
And now was dropt into the western bay ;

At last he rose, and twitch'd his mantle blue :
To-morrow to fresh woods, and pastures new.
J. MILTON.

67. THE TOMBS IN WESTMINSTER ABBEY

Mortality, behold and fear
What a change of flesh is here !
Think how many royal bones
Sleep within these heaps of stones ;
Here they lie, had realms and lands,
Who now want strength to stir their hands,
Where from their pulpits seal'd with dust
They preach, " In greatness is no trust."
Here's an acre sown indeed
With the richest royallest seed
That the earth did e'er suck in
Since the first man died for sin :
Here the bones of birth have cried
" Though gods they were, as men they died ! "
Here are sands, ignoble things,
Dropt from the ruin'd sides of kings
Here's a world of pomp and state
Buried in dust, once dead by fate.
F. BEAUMONT.

68. THE LAST CONQUEROR

Victorious men of earth, no more
  Proclaim how wide your empires are ;
Though you bind-in every shore
  And your triumphs reach as far
    As night or day,
  Yet you, proud monarchs, must obey
And mingle with forgotten ashes, when
Death calls ye to the crowd of common men.

Devouring Famine, Plague, and War,
  Each able to undo mankind,
Death's servile emissaries are ;
  Nor to these alone confined,
    He hath at will
  More quaint and subtle ways to kill ;
A smile or kiss, as he will use the art,
Shall have the cunning skill to break a heart.
J. SHIRLEY.

69. DEATH THE LEVELLER

The glories of our blood and state
   Are shadows, not substantial things
There is no armour against fate ;
   Death lays his icy hand on kings ;
     Sceptre and Crown
     Must tumble down,
And in the dust be equal made
With the poor crooked scythe and spade.

Some men with swords may reap the field,
   And plant fresh laurels where they kill :
But their strong nerves at last must yield ;
   They tame but one another still :
     Early or late
     They stoop to fate,
And must give up their murmuring breath
When they, pale captives, creep to death.

The garlands wither on your brow ;
   Then boast no more your mighty deeds ;
Upon Death's purple altar now
   See where the victor-victim bleeds :
     Your heads must come
     To the cold tomb ;
Only the actions of the just
Smell sweet, and blossom in their dust.

                 J. SHIRLEY.

70. WHEN THE ASSAULT WAS INTENDED TO THE CITY

Captain, or Colonel, or Knight in arms,
Whose chance on these defenceless doors may seize,
If deed of honour did thee ever please,
Guard them, and him within protect from harms.

He can requite thee ; for he knows the charms
That call fame on such gentle acts as these,
And he can spread thy name o'er lands and seas,
Whatever clime the sun's bright circle warms.

Lift not thy spear against the Muses' bower :
The great Emathian conqueror bid spare
The house of Pindarus, when temple and tower
Went to the ground : and the repeated air
Of sad Electra's poet had the power
To save the Athenian walls from ruin bare.

J. MILTON.

71. ON HIS BLINDNESS

When I consider how my light is spent
Ere half my days, in this dark world and wide,
And that one talent which is death to hide
Lodged with me useless, though my soul more bent

To serve therewith my Maker, and present
My true account, lest He returning chide,—
Doth God exact day-labour, light denied ?
I fondly ask :—But Patience, to prevent

That murmur, soon replies ; God doth not need
Either man's work, or His own gifts : who best
Bear His mild yoke, they serve Him best : His state

Is kingly ; thousands at His bidding speed
And post o'er land and ocean without rest :—
They also serve who only stand and wait.

J. MILTON.

72. CHARACTER OF A HAPPY LIFE

How happy is he born and taught
    That serveth not another's will ;
Whose armour is his honest thought
    And simple truth his utmost skill !

Whose passions not his masters are,
    Whose soul is still prepared for death,
Not tied unto the world with care
    Of public fame, or private breath ;

Who envies none that chance doth raise
    Or vice ; Who never understood
How deepest wounds are given by praise ;
    Nor rules of state, but rules of good :

Who hath his life from rumours freed,
Whose conscience is his strong retreat ;
Whose state can neither flatterers feed,
Nor ruin make accusers great ;

Who God doth late and early pray
More of His grace than gifts to lend ;
And entertains the harmless day
With a well-chosen book or friend ;

—This man is freed from servile bands
Of hope to rise, or fear to fall ;
Lord of himself, though not of lands ;
And having nothing, yet hath all.

SIR. H. WOTTON.

73. THE NOBLE NATURE

It is not growing like a tree
In bulk, doth make Man better be ,
Or standing long an oak, three hundred year,
To fall a log at last, dry, bald, and sere :
A lily of a day
Is fairer far in May,
Although it fall and die that night—
It was the plant and flower of Light.
In small proportions we just beauties see ;
And in short measures life may perfect be.

B. JONSON.

74. THE GIFTS OF GOD

When God at first made Man,
Having a glass of blessing standing by ;
Let us (said he) pour on him all we can :
Let the world's riches, which disperséd lie,
Contract into a span.

So strength first made a way ;
Then beauty flow'd, then wisdom, honour, pleasure :
When almost all was out, God made a stay,
Perceiving that alone, of all his treasure,
Rest in the bottom lay.

For if I should (said he)
Bestow this jewel also on my creature,
He would adore My gifts instead of Me,
And rest in Nature, not the God of Nature :
      So both should losers be.

      Yet let him keep the rest,
But keep them with repining restlessness :
Let him be rich and weary, that at least,
If goodness lead him not, yet weariness
      May toss him to my breast.

                                        G. HERBERT.

75. THE RETREAT

Happy those early days, when I
Shined in my Angel-infancy !
Before I understood this place
Appointed for my second race,
Or taught my soul to fancy aught
But a white, celestial thought ;
When yet I had not walk'd above
A mile or two from my first Love,

And looking back, at that short space
Could see a glimpse of his bright face ;
When on some gilded cloud or flower
My gazing soul would dwell an hour,
And in those weaker glories spy
Some shadows of eternity ;
Before I taught my tongue to wound
My conscience with a sinful sound,
Or had the black art to dispense
A several sin to every sense,
But felt through all this fleshly dress
Bright shoots of everlastingness.

O how I long to travel back,
And tread again that ancient track !
That I might once more reach that plain,
Where first I left my glorious train ;
From whence th' enlighten'd spirit sees
That shady City of Palm trees !
But ah ! my soul with too much stay
Is drunk, and staggers in the way :—

Some men a forward motion love,
But I by backward steps would move ;
And when this dust falls to the urn,
In that state I came, return.

H. VAUGHAN.

76. TO MR. LAWRENCE

Lawrence, of virtuous father virtuous son,
Now that the fields are dank and ways are mire,
Where shall we sometimes meet, and by the fire
Help waste a sullen day, what may be won

From the hard season gaining ? Time will run
On smoother, till Favonius re-inspire
The frozen earth, and clothe in fresh attire
The lily and rose, that neither sow'd nor spun.

What neat repast shall feast us, light and choice
Of Attic taste, with wine, whence we may rise
To hear the lute well touch'd, or artful voice

Warble immortal notes and Tuscan air ?
He who of those delights can judge, and spare
To interpose them oft, is not unwise.

J. MILTON.

77. TO CYRIACK SKINNER

Cyriack, whose grandsire, on the royal bench
Of British Themis, with no mean applause
Pronounced, and in his volumes taught, our laws,
Which others at their bar so often wrench ;

To-day deep thoughts resolve with me to drench
In mirth, that after no repenting draws ;
Let Euclid rest, and Archimedes pause,
And what the Swede intends, and what the French.

To measure life learn thou betimes, and know
Toward solid good what leads the nearest way ;
For other things mild Heaven a time ordains,

And disapproves that care, though wise in show,
That with superfluous burden loads the day,
And, when God sends a cheerful hour, refrains.

J. MILTON.

78. HYMN TO DIANA

Queen and Huntress, chaste and fair,
   Now the sun is laid to sleep,
Seated in thy silver chair
   State in wonted manner keep :
     Hesperus entreats thy light,
     Goddess excellently bright.

Earth, let not thy envious shade
   Dare itself to interpose ;
Cynthia's shining orb was made
   Heaven to clear when day did close ;
     Bless us then with wishéd sight,
     Goddess excellently bright.

Lay thy bow of pearl apart
   And thy crystal-shining quiver ;
Give unto the flying hart
   Space to breathe, how short soever ;
     Thou that mak'st a day of night,
     Goddess excellently bright !
                B. JONSON.

79. WISHES FOR THE SUPPOSED MISTRESS

Who'er she be,
That not impossible She
That shall command my heart and me ;

Where'er she lie,
Lock'd up from mortal eye
In shady leaves of destiny :

Till that ripe birth
Of studied Fate stand forth,
And teach her fair steps to our earth ;

Till that divine
Idea take a shrine
Of crystal flesh, through which to shine :

—Meet you her, my Wishes,
Bespeak her to my blisses,
And be ye call'd, my absent kisses.

I wish her beauty
That owes not all its duty
To gaudy tire, or glist'ring shoe-tie :

Something more than
Taffata or tissue can,
Or rampant feather, or rich fan.

A face that's best
By its own beauty drest,
And can alone command the rest :

A face made up
Out of no other shop
Than what Nature's white hand sets ope.

Sydneian showers
Of sweet discourse, whose powers
Can crown old Winter's head with flowers.

Whate'er delight
Can make day's forehead bright
Or give down to the wings of night.

Soft silken hours,
Open suns, shady bowers ;
'Bove all, nothing within that lowers.

Days, that need borrow
No part of their good morrow
From a forespent night of sorrow :

Days, that in spite
Of darkness, by the light
Of a clear mind are day all night.

Life, that dares send
A challenge to his end,
And when it comes, say, " Welcome friend."

I wish her store
Of worth may leave her poor
Of wishes ; and I wish——no more.

—Now, if Time knows
That Her, whose radiant brows
Weave them a garland of my vows ;

Her that dares be
What these lines wish to see;
I seek no further, it is She.

'Tis She, and here
Lo! I unclothe and clear
My wishes' cloudy character.

Such worth as this is
Shall fix my flying wishes,
And determine them to kisses.

Let her full glory,
My fancies, fly before ye;
Be ye my fictions :—but her story.

R. CRASHAW.

80. THE GREAT ADVENTURER

Over the mountains
And over the waves,
Under the fountains
And under the graves;
Under floods that are deepest,
Which Neptune obey;
Over rocks that are steepest
Love will find out the way.

Where there is no place
For the glow-worm to lie;
Where there is no space
For receipt of a fly;
Where the midge dares not venture
Lest herself fast she lay;
If love come, he will enter
And soon find out his way.

You may esteem him
A child for his might;
Or you may deem him
A coward from his flight;
But if she whom love doth honour
Be conceal'd from the day,
Set a thousand guards upon her
Love will find out the way.

Some think to lose him
By having him confined ;
And some do suppose him,
Poor thing, to be blind ;
But if ne'er so close ye wall him,
Do the best that you may,
Blind love, if so ye call him,
Will find out his way.

You may train the eagle
To stoop to your fist ;
Or you may inveigle
The phœnix of the east ;
The lioness, ye may move her
To give o'er her prey ;
But you'll ne'er stop a lover :
He will find out his way.

ANON.

81. CHILD AND MAIDEN

Ah, Chloris ! could I now but sit
  As unconcern'd as when
Your infant beauty could beget
  No happiness or pain !
When I the dawn used to admire,
  And praised the coming day,
I little thought the rising fire
  Would take my rest away.

Your charms in harmless childhood lay
  Like metals in a mine ;
Age from no face takes more away
  Than youth conceal'd in thine.
But as your charms insensibly
  To their perfection prest,
So love as unperceived did fly,
  And center'd in my breast.

My passion with your beauty grew,
  While Cupid at my heart
Still as his mother favour'd you
  Threw a new flaming dart :

Each gloried in their wanton part ;
   To make a lover, he
Employ'd the utmost of his art—
   To make a beauty, she.

Sir C. Sedley.

82. COUNSEL TO GIRLS

Gather ye rose-buds while ye may,
   Old Time is still a-flying :
And this same flower that smiles to-day,
   To-morrow will be dying.

The glorious Lamp of Heaven, the Sun,
   The higher he's a-getting
The sooner will his race be run,
   And nearer he's to setting.

That age is best which is the first,
   When youth and blood are warmer,
But being spent, the worse, and worst
   Times, still succeed the former.

Then be not coy, but use your time ;
   And while ye may, go marry :
For having lost but once your prime,
   You may for ever tarry.

R. Herrick.

83. TO LUCASTA, ON GOING TO THE WARS

Tell me not, Sweet, I am unkind
   That from the nunnery
Of thy chaste breast and quiet mind,
   To war and arms I fly.

True, a new mistress now I chase,
   The first foe in the field ;
And with a stronger faith embrace
   A sword, a horse, a shield.

Yet this inconstancy is such
   As you too shall adore ;
I could not love thee, Dear, so much,
   Loved I not Honour more.

Colonel Lovelace.

84. ELIZABETH OF BOHEMIA

You meaner beauties of the night,
  Which poorly satisfy our eyes
More by your number than your light,
  You common people of the skies,
What are you, when the Moon shall rise?

Ye violets that first appear,
  By your pure purple mantles known
Like the proud virgins of the year
  As if the spring were all your own,—
What are you, when the Rose is blown?

Ye curious chanters of the wood
  That warble forth dame Nature's lays,
Thinking your passions understood
  By your weak accents; what's your praise
When Philomel her voice doth raise?

So when my Mistress shall be seen
  In sweetness of her looks and mind,
By virtue first, then choice, a Queen,
  Tell me, if she were not design'd
Th' eclipse and glory of her kind?

Sir H. Wotton.

85. TO THE LADY MARGARET LEY

Daughter to that good earl, once President
Of England's council and her treasury,
Who lived in both, unstain'd with gold or fee,
And left them both, more in himself content,

Till the sad breaking of that parliament
Broke him, as that dishonest victory
At Chæronea, fatal to liberty,
Kill'd with report that old man eloquent :—

Though later born than to have known the days
Wherein your father flourish'd, yet by you,
Madam, methinks I see him living yet ;

So well your words his noble virtues praise,
That all both judge you to relate them true,
And to possess them, honour'd Margaret.

J. Milton.

86. THE LOVELINESS OF LOVE

It is not Beauty I demand
A crystal brow, the moon's despair,
Nor the snow's daughter, a white hand,
Nor mermaid's yellow pride of hair :

Tell me not of your starry eyes,
Your lips that seem on roses fed,
Your breasts, where Cupid tumbling lies
Nor sleeps for kissing of his bed :—

A bloomy pair of vermeil cheeks
Like Hebe's in her ruddiest hours,
A breath that softer music speaks
Than summer winds a-wooing flowers,

These are but gauds : nay what are lips ?
Coral beneath the ocean-stream,
Whose brink when your adventurer slips
Full oft he perisheth on them.

And what are cheeks, but ensigns oft
That wave hot youth to fields of blood ?
Did Helen's breast, though ne'er so soft,
Do Greece or Ilium any good ?

Eyes can with baleful ardour burn ;
Poison can breath, that erst perfumed ;
There's many a white hand holds an urn
With lovers' hearts to dust consumed.

For crystal brows there's nought within ;
They are but empty cells for pride ;
He who the Syren's hair would win
Is mostly strangled in the tide.

Give me, instead of Beauty's bust,
A tender heart, a loyal mind
Which with temptation I would trust,
Yet never link'd with error find,—

One in whose gentle bosom I
Could pour my secret heart of woes,
Like the care-burthen'd honey-fly
That hides his murmurs in the rose.

My earthly Comforter ! whose love
So indefeasible might be
That, when my spirit wonn'd above,
Hers could not stay, for sympathy.

ANON.

87. THE TRUE BEAUTY

He that loves a rosy cheek
  Or a coral lip admires,
Or from star-like eyes doth seek
  Fuel to maintain his fires ;
As old Time makes these decay,
So his flames must waste away.

But a smooth and steadfast mind,
  Gentle thoughts, and calm desires,
Hearts with equal love combined,
  Kindle never-dying fires :—
Where these are not, I despise
Lovely cheeks or lips or eyes.

T. CAREW.

88. TO DIANEME

Sweet, be not proud of those two eyes
Which starlike sparkle in their skies ;
Nor be you proud, that you can see
All hearts your captives ; yours yet free :
Be you not proud of that rich hair
Which wantons with the lovesick air ;
Whenas that ruby which you wear,
Sunk from the tip of your soft ear,
Will last to be a precious stone
When all your world of beauty's gone.

R. HERRICK

89

Go, lovely Rose !
Tell her, that wastes her time and me,
  That now she knows,
When I resemble her to thee,
How sweet and fair she seems to be.

Tell her that's young
And shuns to have her graces spied,
    That hadst thou sprung
In deserts, where no men abide,
Thou must have uncommended died.

    Small is the worth
Of beauty from the light retired :
    Bid her come forth,
Suffer herself to be desired,
And not blush so to be admired.

    Then die ! that she
The common fate of all things rare
    May read in thee :
How small a part of time they share
That are so wondrous sweet and fair !

E. WALLER.

90. TO CELIA

Drink to me only with thine eyes,
    And I will pledge with mine ;
Or leave a kiss but in the cup
    And I'll not look for wine.
The thirst that from the soul doth rise
    Doth ask a drink divine ;
But might I of Jove's nectar sup,
    I would not change for thine.

I sent thee late a rosy wreath,
    Not so much honouring thee
As giving it a hope that there
    It could not wither'd be ;
But thou thereon didst only breathe
    And sent'st it back to me ;
Since when it grows, and smells, I swear,
    Not of itself but thee !

B. JONSON.

91. CHERRY-RIPE

There is a garden in her face
   Where roses and white lilies blow ;
A heavenly paradise is that place,
   Wherein all pleasant fruits do grow ;
There cherries grow that none may buy,
Till Cherry-Ripe themselves do cry.

Those cherries fairly do enclose
   Of orient pearl a double row,
Which when her lovely laughter shows,
   They look like rose-buds fill'd with snow :
Yet them no peer nor prince may buy,
Till Cherry-Ripe themselves do cry.

Her eyes like angels watch them still ;
   Her brows like bended bows do stand,
Threat'ning with piercing frowns to kill
   All that approach with eye or hand
These sacred cherries to come nigh,
—Till Cherry-Ripe themselves do cry !

ANON.

92. THE POETRY OF DRESS

I

A sweet disorder in the dress
Kindles in clothes a wantonness :—
A lawn about the shoulders thrown
Into a fine distractión,—
An erring lace, which here and there
Enthrals the crimson stomacher,—
A cuff neglectful, and thereby
Ribbands to flow confusedly,—
A winning wave, deserving note,
In the tempestuous petticoat,—
A careless shoe-string, in whose tie
I see a wild civility,—
Do more bewitch me, than when art
Is too precise in every part.

R. HERRICK.

93.—II

Whenas in silks my Julia goes
Then, then (methinks) how sweetly flows
That liquefaction of her clothes.

Next, when I cast mine eyes and see
That brave vibration each way free ;
O how that glittering taketh me !

R. HERRICK.

94.—III

My Love in her attire doth shew her wit,
It doth so well become her ;
For every season she has dressings fit,
For Winter, Spring, and Summer.
No beauty she doth miss
When all her robes are on :
But Beauty's self she is
When all her robes are gone.

ANON.

95. ON A GIRDLE

That which her slender waist confined
Shall now my joyful temples bind :
No monarch but would give his crown
His arms might do what this has done.

It was my Heaven's extremest sphere,
The pale which held that lovely deer :
My joy, my grief, my hope, my love
Did all within this circle move.

A narrow compass ! and yet there
Dwelt all that's good, and all that's fair :
Give me but what this ribband bound,
Take all the rest the Sun goes round.

E. WALLER.

96. TO ANTHEA WHO MAY COMMAND HIM ANY THING

Bid me to live, and I will live
Thy Protestant to be :
Or bid me love, and I will give
A loving heart to thee.

A heart as soft, a heart as kind,
 A heart as sound and free
As in the whole world thou canst find,
 That heart I'll give to thee.

Bid that heart stay, and it will stay,
 To honour thy decree :
Or bid it languish quite away,
 And 't shall do so for thee.

Bid me to weep, and I will weep
 While I have eyes to see :
And having none, yet I will keep
 A heart to weep for thee.

Bid me despair, and I'll despair,
 Under that cypress tree :
Or bid me die, and I will dare
 E'en Death, to die for thee.

Thou art my life, my love, my heart,
 The very eyes of me,
And hast command of every part,
 To live and die for thee.

R. HERRICK.

97

Love not me for comely grace,
For my pleasing eye or face,
Nor for any outward part,
No, nor for my constant heart,—
 For those may fail, or turn to ill,
  So thou and I shall sever :
Keep therefore a true woman's eye,
And love me still, but know not why—
 So hast thou the same reason still
  To doat upon me ever !

ANON.

98

Not, Celia, that I juster am
 Or better than the rest ;
For I would change each hour, like them.
 Were not my heart at rest.

But I am tied to very thee
   By every thought I have ;
Thy face I only care to see,
   Thy heart I only crave.

All that in woman is adored
   In thy dear self I find—
For the whole sex can but afford
   The handsome and the kind.

Why then should I seek further store,
   And still make love anew ?
When change itself can give no more,
   'Tis easy to be true.

Sir C. Sedley.

99. TO ALTHEA FROM PRISON

When Love with unconfinéd wings
   Hovers within my gates,
And my divine Althea brings
   To whisper at the grates ;
When I lie tangled in her hair
   And fetter'd to her eye,
The birds that wanton in the air
   Know no such liberty.

When flowing cups run swiftly round
   With no allaying Thames,
Our careless heads with roses crown'd,
   Our hearts with loyal flames ;
When thirsty grief in wine we steep,
   When healths and draughts go free—
Fishes that tipple in the deep
   Know no such liberty.

When, linnet-like confinéd, I
   With shriller throat shall sing
The sweetness, mercy, majesty
   And glories of my King ;
When I shall voice aloud how good
   He is, how great should be,
Enlargéd winds, that curl the flood,
   Know no such liberty.

Stone walls do not a prison make,
    Nor iron bars a cage ;
Minds innocent and quiet take
    That for an hermitage :
If I have freedom in my love
    And in my soul am free,
Angels alone, that soar above,
    Enjoy such liberty.

COLONEL LOVELACE.

100. TO LUCASTA, ON GOING BEYOND THE SEAS

If to be absent were to be
    Away from thee ;
Or that when I am gone
    You or I were alone ;
Then, my Lucasta, might I crave
Pity from blustering wind, or swallowing wave.

Though seas and land betwixt us both,
    Our faith and troth,
Like separated souls,
    All time and space controls :
Above the highest sphere we meet
Unseen, unknown, and greet as Angels greet.

So then we do anticipate
    Our after-fate,
And are alive i' the skies,
    If thus our lips and eyes
Can speak like spirits unconfined
In Heaven, their earthly bodies left behind.

COLONEL LOVELACE.

101. ENCOURAGEMENTS TO A LOVER

Why so pale and wan, fond lover ?
    Prythee, why so pale ?
Will, if looking well can't move her,
    Looking ill prevail ?
    Prythee, why so pale ?

Why so dull and mute, young sinner ?
  Prythee, why so mute ?
Will, when speaking well can't win her,
  Saying nothing do't ?
  Prythee, why so mute ?

Quit, quit, for shame ! this will not move,
  This cannot take her ;
If of herself she will not love,
  Nothing can make her :
  The D——l take her !

Sir J. Suckling.

102. A SUPPLICATION

Awake, awake, my Lyre !
And tell thy silent master's humble tale
 In sounds that may prevail ;
 Sounds that gentle thoughts inspire :
  Though so exalted she
  And I so lowly be
Tell her, such different notes make all thy harmony.

Hark ! how the strings awake :
And, though the moving hand approach not near,
 Themselves with awful fear
 A kind of numerous trembling make.
  Now all thy forces try ;
  Now all thy charms apply ;
Revenge upon her ear the conquests of her eye.

Weak Lyre ! thy virtue sure
Is useless here, since thou art only found
 To cure, but not to wound,
 And she to wound, but not to cure.
  Too weak too wilt thou prove
  My passion to remove ;
Physic to other ills, thou'rt nourishment to love.

Sleep, sleep again, my Lyre !
For thou canst never tell my humble tale
 In sounds that will prevail,
 Nor gentle thoughts in her inspire :

All thy vain mirth lay by,
Bid thy strings silent lie,
Sleep, sleep, again, my Lyre, and let thy master die.
                                        A. COWLEY.

103. THE MANLY HEART

Shall I, wasting in despair,
Die because a woman's fair ?
Or my cheeks make pale with care
'Cause another's rosy are ?
Be she fairer than the day
Or the flowery meads in May—
    If she be not so to me,
    What care I how fair she be ?

Shall my foolish heart be pined
'Cause I see a woman kind ;
Or a well disposéd nature
Joinéd with a lovely feature ?
Be she meeker, kinder, than
Turtle-dove or pelican,
    If she be not so to me,
    What care I how kind she be ?

Shall a woman's virtues move
Me to perish for her love ?
Or her merit's value known
Make me quite forget mine own ?
Be she with that goodness blest
Which may gain her name of Best ;
    If she seem not such to me,
    What care I how good she be ?

'Cause her fortune seems too high,
Shall I play the fool and die ?
Those that bear a noble mind
Where they want of riches find,
Think what with them they would do
Who without them dare to woo ;
    And unless that mind I see,
    What care I though great she be ?

Great or good, or kind or fair,
I will ne'er the more despair
If she love me, this believe,
I will die ere she shall grieve;
If she slight me when I woo,
I can scorn and let her go;
    For if she be not for me,
    What care I for whom she be?

G. WITHER.

104. MELANCHOLY

Hence, all you vain delights,
As short as are the nights
Wherein you spend your folly
There's nought in this life sweet
If man were wise to see't,
But only melancholy,
O sweetest Melancholy!
Welcome, folded arms, and fixéd eyes,
A sigh that piercing mortifies,
A look that's fasten'd to the ground,
A tongue chain'd up without a sound!
Fountain heads and pathless groves,
Places which pale passion loves!
Moonlight walks, when all the fowls
Are warmly housed save bats and owls!
    A midnight bell, a parting groan!
    These are the sounds we feed upon;
Then stretch our bones in a still gloomy valley;
Nothing's so dainty sweet as lovely melancholy.

J. FLETCHER.

105. TO A LOCK OF HAIR

Thy hue, dear pledge, is pure and bright
As in that well-remember'd night
When first thy mystic braid was wove,
And first my Agnes whisper'd love.

Since then how often hast thou prest
The torrid zone of this wild breast,

Whose wrath and hate have sworn to dwell
With the first sin that peopled hell ;
A breast whose blood's a troubled ocean,
Each throb the earthquake's wild commotion !
O if such clime thou canst endure
Yet keep thy hue unstain'd and pure,
What conquest o'er each erring thought
Of that fierce realm had Agnes wrought !
I had not wander'd far and wide
With such an angel for my guide ;
Nor heaven nor earth could then reprove me
If she had lived, and lived to love me.

Not then this world's wild joys had been
To me one savage hunting scene,
My sole delight the headlong race,
And frantic hurry of the chase ;
To start, pursue, and bring to bay,
Rush in, drag down, and rend my prey,
Then—from the carcass turn away !
Mine ireful mood had sweetness tamed,
And soothed each wound which pride inflamed :—
Yes, God and man might now approve me
If thou hadst lived, and lived to love me !

SIR W. SCOTT.

106. THE FORSAKEN BRIDE

O waly waly up the bank,
　And waly waly down the brae,
And waly waly yon burn-side
　Where I and my Love wont to gae !
I leant my back unto an aik,
　I thought it was a trusty tree ;
But first it bow'd, and syne it brak,
　Sae my true Love did lichtly me.

O waly waly, but love be bonny
　A little time while it is new ;
But when 'tis auld, it waxeth cauld
　And fades awa' like morning dew.
O wherefore should I busk my head ?
　Or wherefore should I kame my hair ?
For my true Love has me forsook,
　And says he'll never loe me mair.

Now Arthur-seat sall be my bed ;
    The sheets sall ne'er be prest by me :
Saint Anton's well sall be my drink,
    Since my true Love has forsaken me.
Marti'mas wind, when wilt thou blaw
    And shake the green leaves aff the tree ?
O gentle Death, when wilt thou come ?
    For of my life I am wearie.

'Tis not the frost, that freezes fell,
    Nor blawing snaw's inclemencie ;
'Tis not sic cauld that makes me cry,
    But my Love's heart grown cauld to me.
When we came in by Glasgow town
    We were a comely sight to see ;
My Love was clad in the black velvét,
    And I mysell in cramasie.

But had I wist, before I kist,
    That love had been sae ill to win ;
I had lockt my heart in a case of gowd
    And pinn'd it with a siller pin.
And, O ! if my young babe were born,
    And set upon the nurse's knee,
And I mysell were dead and gane,
    And the green grass growing over me !

                       ANON.

107. FAIR HELEN

I wish I were where Helen lies ;
Night and day on me she cries ;
O that I were where Helen lies
    On fair Kirconnell lea.

Curst be the heart that thought the thought,
And curst the hand that fired the shot,
When in my arms burd Helen dropt,
    And died to succour me !

O think na but my heart was sair
When my Love dropt down and spak nae mair !
I laid her down wi' meikle care
    On fair Kirconnell lea.

As I went down the water-side,
None but my foe to be my guide,
None but my foe to be my guide,
    On fair Kirconnell lea ;

I lighted down my sword to draw,
I hackéd him in pieces sma',
I hackéd him in pieces sma',
    For her sake that died for me.

O Helen fair, beyond compare !
I'll make a garland of thy hair
Shall bind my heart for evermair
    Until the day I die.

O that I were where Helen lies !
Night and day on me she cries ;
Out of my bed she bids me rise,
    Says, " Haste and come to me ! "

O Helen fair ! O Helen chaste !
If I were with thee, I were blest,
Where thou lies low and takes thy rest
    On fair Kirconnell lea.

I wish my grave were growing green,
A winding-sheet drawn ower my een,
And I in Helen's arms lying,
    On fair Kirconnell lea.

I wish I were where Helen lies :
Night and day on me she cries ;
And I am weary of the skies,
    Since my Love died for me.
                 ANON.

108. THE TWA CORBIES

As I was walking all alane
I heard twa corbies making a mane
The tane unto the t'other say,
" 'Where sall we gang and dine to-day ? "

"—In behint yon auld fail dyke,
I wot there lies a new-slain Knight;
And naebody kens that he lies there,
But his hawk, his hound, and lady fair

" His hound is to the hunting gane,
His hawk to fetch the wild-fowl hame,
His lady's ta'en another mate,
So we may mak our dinner sweet.

" Ye'll sit on his white hause-bane,
And I'll pick out his bonny blue een;
Wi' ae lock o' his gowden hair
We'll theek our nest when it grows bare.

" Mony a one for him makes mane,
But nane sall ken where he is gane;
O'er his white banes, when they are bare,
The wind sall blaw for evermair."

ANON.

109. TO BLOSSOMS

Fair pledges of a fruitful tree,
  Why do ye fall so fast?
  Your date is not so past,
But you may stay yet here awhile
  To blush and gently smile,
    And go at last.

What, were ye born to be
  An hour or half's delight,
  And so to bid good-night?
'Twas pity Nature brought ye forth
  Merely to show your worth,
    And lose you quite.

But you are lovely leaves, where we
  May read how soon things have
  Their end, though ne'er so brave
And after they have shown their pride
  Like you, awhile, they glide
    Into the grave.

R. HERRICK.

110. TO DAFFODILS

Fair Daffodils, we weep to see
    You haste away so soon
As yet the early-rising Sun
    Has not attain'd his noon.
      Stay, stay,
    Until the hasting day
      Has run
    But to the even-song;
And, having pray'd together, we
    Will go with you along.

We have short time to stay, as you
    We have as short a Spring;
As quick a growth to meet decay
    As you, or any thing.
      We die,
    As your hours do, and dry
      Away
    Like to the Summer's rain;
Or as the pearls of morning's dew
    Ne'er to be found again.

R. HERRICK.

111. THOUGHTS IN A GARDEN

How vainly men themselves amaze
To win the palm, the oak, or bays,
And their incessant labours see
Crown'd from some single herb or tree,
Whose short and narrow-vergéd shade
Does prudently their toils upbraid;
While all the flowers and trees do close
To weave the garlands of Repose.

Fair Quiet, have I found thee here,
And Innocence thy sister dear?
Mistaken long, I sought you then
In busy companies of men:
Your sacred plants, if here below,
Only among the plants will grow:
Society is all but rude
To this delicious solitude.

No white nor red was ever seen
So amorous as this lovely green.
Fond lovers, cruel as their flame,
Cut in these trees their mistress' name :
Little, alas, they know or heed
How far these beauties her exceed !
Fair trees ! where'er your barks I wound,
No name shall but your own be found.

When we have run our passions' heat
Love hither makes his best retreat :
The gods, who mortal beauty chase,
Still in a tree did end their race :
Apollo hunted Daphne so
Only that she might laurel grow ;
And Pan did after Syrinx speed
Not as a nymph, but for a reed.

What wondrous life is this I lead !
Ripe apples drop about my head ;
The luscious clusters of the vine
Upon my mouth do crush their wine ;
The nectarine and curious peach
Into my hands themselves do reach ;
Stumbling on melons, as I pass,
Ensnared with flowers, I fall on grass.

Meanwhile the mind from pleasure less
Withdraws into its happiness ;
The mind, that ocean where each kind
Does straight its own resemblance find ;
Yet it creates, transcending these,
Far other worlds, and other seas ;
Annihilating all that's made
To a green thought in a green shade.

Here at the fountain's sliding foot
Or at some fruit-tree's mossy root,
Casting the body's vest aside
My soul into the boughs does glide ;
There, like a bird, it sits and sings,
Then whets and claps its silver wings,
And, till prepared for longer flight,
Waves in its plumes the various light.

Such was that happy Garden-state
While man there walk'd without a mate :
After a place so pure and sweet,
What other help could yet be meet !
But 'twas beyond a mortal's share
To wander solitary there :
Two paradises are in one,
To live in Paradise alone.

How well the skilful gardener drew
Of flowers and herbs this dial new !
Where, from above, the milder sun
Does through a fragrant zodiac run :
And, as it works, th' industrious bee
Computes its time as well as we.
How could such sweet and wholesome hours
Be reckon'd, but with herbs and flowers !

A. MARVELL.

112. L'ALLEGRO

Hence, loathéd Melancholy
    Of Cerberus and blackest Midnight born
In Stygian cave forlorn
    'Mongst horrid shapes, and shrieks, and sights unholy !
Find out some uncouth cell
    Where brooding Darkness spreads his jealous wings
And the night-raven sings ;
    There under ebon shades, and low-brow'd rocks
As ragged as thy locks,
    In dark Cimmerian desert ever dwell.

        But come, thou Goddess fair and free,
    In heaven yclept Euphrosyne,
    And by men, heart-easing Mirth,
    Whom lovely Venus at a birth
    With two sister Graces more
    To ivy-crownéd Bacchus bore :
    Or whether (as some sages sing)
    The frolic wind that breathes the spring
    Zephyr, with Aurora playing,
    As he met her once a-Maying—
    There on beds of violets blue
    And fresh-blown roses wash'd in dew

Fill'd her with thee, a daughter fair,
So buxom, blithe, and debonair.
    Haste thee, Nymph, and bring with thee
Jest, and youthful jollity,
Quips, and cranks, and wanton wiles,
Nods, and becks, and wreathéd smiles
Such as hang on Hebe's cheek,
And love to live in dimple sleek ;
Sport that wrinkled Care derides,
And Laughter holding both his sides :—
Come, and trip it as you go
On the light fantastic toe ;
And in thy right hand lead with thee
The mountain nymph, sweet Liberty ;
And if I give thee honour due,
Mirth, admit me of thy crew,
To live with her, and live with thee
In unreprovéd pleasures free ;
To hear the lark begin his flight
And singing startle the dull night
From his watch-tower in the skies,
Till the dappled dawn doth rise ;
Then to come, in spite of sorrow,
And at my window bid good-morrow
Through the sweetbriar, or the vine,
Or the twisted eglantine :
While the cook with lively din
Scatters the rear of darkness thin,
And to the stack, or the barn-door,
Stoutly struts his dames before :
Oft listening how the hounds and horn
Cheerly rouse the slumbering morn,
From the side of some hoar hill,
Through the high wood echoing shrill :
Sometime walking, not unseen,
By hedge-row elms, on hillocks green,
Right against the eastern gate
Where the great Sun begins his state
Robed in flames and amber light,
The clouds in thousand liveries dight ,
While the ploughman, near at hand,
Whistles o'er the furrow'd land,
And the milkmaid singeth blithe,
And the mower whets his scythe,

And every shepherd tells his tale
Under the hawthorn in the dale.
   Straight mine eye hath caught new pleasures
Whilst the landscape round it measures ;
Russet lawns, and fallows gray,
Where the nibbling flocks do stray ;
Mountains, on whose barren breast
The labouring clouds do often rest ;
Meadows trim with daisies pied,
Shallow brooks, and rivers wide ;
Towers and battlements it sees
Bosom'd high in tufted trees,
Where perhaps some Beauty lies,
The Cynosure of neighbouring eyes.
   Hard by, a cottage chimney smokes
From betwixt two aged oaks,
Where Corydon and Thyrsis, met,
Are at their savoury dinner set
Of herbs, and other country messes
Which the neat-handed Phillis dresses ;
And then in haste her bower she leaves
With Thestylis to bind the sheaves ;
Or, if the earlier season lead,
To the tann'd haycock in the mead.
   Sometimes with secure delight
The upland hamlets will invite,
When the merry bells ring round,
And the jocund rebecks sound
To many a youth and many a maid,
Dancing in the chequer'd shade ;
And young and old come forth to play
On a sun-shine holy-day,
Till the live-long day-light fail :
Then to the spicy nut-brown ale,
With stories told of many a feat,
How faery Mab the junkets eat ;
She was pinch'd, and pull'd, she said ;
And he, by friar's lantern led ;
Tells how the drudging Goblin sweat
To earn his cream-bowl duly set,
When in one night, ere glimpse of morn,
His shadowy flail hath thresh'd the corn
That ten day-labourers could not end ;
Then lies him down the lubber fiend,

G.T.   *L'Allegro*

" Every Shepherd tells his tale
Under the hawthorn in the dale."

And, stretch'd out all the chimney's length,
Basks at the fire his hairy strength ;
And crop-full out of doors he flings,
Ere the first cock his matin rings.
    Thus done the tales, to bed they creep
By whispering winds soon lull'd asleep.
    Tower'd cities please us then
And the busy hum of men,
Where throngs of knights and barons bold,
In weeds of peace high triumphs hold,
With store of ladies, whose bright eyes
Rain influence, and judge the prize
Of wit or arms, while both contend
To win her grace, whom all commend.
There let Hymen oft appear
In saffron robe, with taper clear,
And pomp, and feast, and revelry,
With mask, and antique pageantry ;
Such sights as youthful poets dream
On summer eves by haunted stream.
Then to the well-trod stage anon,
If Jonson's learned sock be on,
Or sweetest Shakespeare, Fancy's child,
Warble his native wood-notes wild.
    And ever against eating cares
Lap me in soft Lydian airs
Married to immortal verse,
Such as the meeting soul may pierce
In notes, with many a winding bout
Of linkéd sweetness long drawn out,
With wanton heed and giddy cunning,
The melting voice through mazes running,
Untwisting all the chains that tie
The hidden soul of harmony ;
That Orpheus' self may heave his head
From golden slumber, on a bed
Of heap'd Elysian flowers, and hear
Such strains as would have won the ear
Of Pluto, to have quite set free
His half-regain'd Eurydice.
    These delights if thou canst give,
Mirth, with thee I mean to live.

                    J. MILTON.

113. IL PENSEROSO

Hence, vain deluding Joys,
The brood of Folly without father bred !
How little you bestead
Or fill the fixéd mind with all your toys !
Dwell in some idle brain,
And fancies fond with gaudy shapes possess
As thick and numberless
As the gay motes that people the sunbeams,
Or likest hovering dreams
The fickle pensioners of Morpheus' train.
   But hail, thou goddess sage and holy,
Hail, divinest Melancholy !
Whose saintly visage is too bright
To hit the sense of human sight,
And therefore to our weaker view
O'erlaid with black, staid Wisdom's hue ;
Black, but such as in esteem
Prince Memnon's sister might beseem.
Or that starr'd Ethiop queen that strove
To set her beauty's praise above
The sea-nymphs, and their powers offended :
Yet thou art higher far descended :
Thee bright-hair'd Vesta, long of yore,
To solitary Saturn bore ;
His daughter she ; in Saturn's reign
Such mixture was not held a stain :
Oft in glimmering bowers and glades
He met her, and in secret shades
Of woody Ida's inmost grove,
While yet there was no fear of Jove.
   Come, pensive nun, devout and pure,
Sober, steadfast, and demure,
All in a robe of darkest grain
Flowing with majestic train,
And sable stole of cypres lawn
Over thy decent shoulders drawn :
Come, but keep thy wonted state,
With even step, and musing gait,
And looks commercing with the skies,
Thy rapt soul sitting in thine eyes :
There, held in holy passion still,
Forget thyself to marble, till

With a sad leaden downward cast
Thou fix them on the earth as fast :
And join with thee calm Peace, and Quiet,
Spare Fast, that oft with gods doth diet,
And hears the Muses in a ring
Aye round about Jove's altar sing :
And add to these retired Leisure
That in trim gardens takes his pleasure :—
But first, and chiefest, with thee bring
Him that yon soars on golden wing
Guiding the fiery-wheeléd throne,
The cherub Contemplatión ;
And the mute Silence hist along,
'Less Philomel will deign a song
In her sweetest saddest plight,
Smoothing the rugged brow of Night,
While Cynthia checks her dragon yoke
Gently o'er the accustom'd oak.
—Sweet bird, that shunn'st the noise of folly,
Most musical, most melancholy !
Thee, chauntress, oft the woods among
I woo, to hear thy even-song ;
And missing thee, I walk unseen
On the dry smooth-shaven green,
To behold the wandering Moon
Riding near her highest noon,
Like one that had been led astray
Through the heaven's wide pathless way,
And oft, as if her head she bow'd,
Stooping through a fleecy cloud.
  Oft, on a plat of rising ground
I hear the far-off curfeu sound
Over some wide-water'd shore,
Swinging slow with sullen roar :
Or, if the air will not permit,
Some still removéd place will fit,
Where glowing embers through the room
Teach light to counterfeit a gloom ;
Far from all resort of mirth,
Save the cricket on the hearth,
Or the bellman's drowsy charm
To bless the doors from nightly harm.
  Or let my lamp at midnight hour
Be seen in some high lonely tower,

Where I may oft out-watch the Bear
With thrice-great Hermes, or unsphere
The spirit of Plato, to unfold
What worlds or what vast regions hold
The immortal mind, that hath forsook
Her mansion in this fleshy nook :
And of those demons that are found
In fire, air, flood, or under ground,
Whose power hath a true consent
With planet, or with element.
Sometimes let gorgeous Tragedy
In scepter'd pall come sweeping by
Presenting Thebes, or Pelops' line,
Or the tale of Troy divine ;
Or what (though rare) or later age
Ennobled hath the buskin'd stage.
    But, O sad Virgin, that thy power
Might raise Musæus from his bower,
Or bid the soul of Orpheus sing
Such notes as, warbled to the string,
Drew iron tears down Pluto's cheek
And made Hell grant what Love did seek !
Or call up him that left half-told
The story of Cambuscan bold,
Of Camball, and of Algarsife,
And who had Canacé to wife
That own'd the virtuous ring and glass ;
And of the wondrous horse of brass
On which the Tartar king did ride :
And if aught else great bards beside
In sage and solemn tunes have sung
Of tourneys, and of trophies hung,
Of forests, and enchantments drear,
Where more is meant than meets the ear.
    Thus, Night, oft see me in thy pale career,
Till civil-suited Morn appear,
Not trick'd and frounced as she was wont
With the Attic Boy to hunt,
But kercheft in a comely cloud
While rocking winds are piping loud,
Or usher'd with a shower still,
When the gust hath blown his fill,
Ending on the rustling leaves
With minute drops from off the eaves.

And when the sun begins to fling
His flaring beams, me, goddess, bring
To archéd walks of twilight groves,
And shadows brown, that Sylvan loves,
Of pine, or monumental oak,
Where the rude axe, with heavéd stroke,
Was never heard the nymphs to daunt
Or fright them from their hallow'd haunt.
There in close covert by some brook
Where no profaner eye may look,
Hide me from day's garish eye,
While the bee with honey'd thigh
That at her flowery work doth sing,
And the waters murmuring,
With such consort as they keep
Entice the dewy-feather'd Sleep ;
And let some strange mysterious dream
Wave at his wings in aery stream
Of lively portraiture display'd,
Softly on my eyelids laid :
And, as I wake, sweet music breathe
Above, about, or underneath,
Sent by some spirit to mortals good,
Or the unseen Genius of the wood.
    But let my due feet never fail
To walk the studious cloister's pale,
And love the high-embowéd roof,
With antique pillars massy proof,
And storied windows richly dight
Casting a dim religious Light :
There let the pealing organ blow
To the full-voiced quire below
In service high and anthems clear,
As may with sweetness, through mine ear,
Dissolve me into ecstasies,
And bring all Heaven before mine eyes.
    And may at last my weary age
Find out the peaceful hermitage,
The hairy gown and mossy cell
Where I may sit and rightly spell
Of every star that heaven doth show,
And every herb that sips the dew ;
Till old experience do attain
To something like prophetic strain.

These pleasures, Melancholy, give,
And I with thee will choose to live.

J. MILTON.

114. SONG OF THE EMIGRANTS IN BERMUDA

Where the remote Bermudas ride
In the ocean's bosom unespied,
From a small boat that row'd along
The listening winds received this song.
  " What should we do but sing His praise
That led us through the watery maze
Where He the huge sea-monsters wracks,
That lift the deep upon their backs,
Unto an isle so long unknown,
And yet far kinder than our own ?
He lands us on a grassy stage,
Safe from the storms, and prelate's rage :
He gave us this eternal spring
Which here enamels everything,
And sends the fowls to us in care
On daily visits through the air.
He hangs in shades the orange bright
Like golden lamps in a green night,
And does in the pomegranates close
Jewels more rich than Ormus shows :
He makes the figs our mouths to meet,
And throws the melons at our feet ;
But apples plants of such a price,
No tree could ever bear them twice.
With cedars chosen by His hand
From Lebanon He stores the land ;
And makes the hollow seas that roar
Proclaim the ambergris on shore.
He cast (of which we rather boast)
The Gospel's pearl upon our coast ;
And in these rocks for us did frame
A temple where to sound His name.
O let our voice His praise exalt
Till it arrive at Heaven's vault,
Which then perhaps rebounding may
Echo beyond the Mexique bay ! "

—Thus sung they in the English boat
A holy and a cheerful note :
And all the way, to guide their chime,
With falling oars they kept the time.

A. MARVELL.

115. AT A SOLEMN MUSIC

Blest pair of Sirens, pledges of Heaven's joy,
Sphere-born harmonious Sisters, Voice and Verse !
Wed your divine sounds, and mixt power employ
Dead things with inbreathed sense able to pierce :
And to our high-raised phantasy present
That undisturbéd Song of pure concent
Aye sung before the sapphire-colour'd throne
    To Him that sits thereon,
With saintly shout and solemn jubilee ;
Where the bright Seraphim in burning row
Their loud uplifted angel-trumpets blow ;
And the Cherubic host in thousand quires
Touch their immortal harps of golden wires,
With those just Spirits that wear victorious palms
    Hymns devout and holy psalms
    Singing everlastingly :
That we on earth, with undiscording voice
May rightly answer that melodious noise ;
As once we did, till disproportion'd sin
Jarr'd against nature's chime, and with harsh din
Broke the fair music that all creatures made
To their great Lord, whose love their motion sway'd
In perfect diapason, whilst they stood
In first obedience, and their state of good.
O may we soon again renew that Song,
And keep in tune with Heaven, till God ere long
  To His celestial concert us unite,
To live with Him, and sing in endless morn of light !

J. MILTON.

116. ALEXANDER'S FEAST, OR, THE POWER OF MUSIC

'Twas at the royal feast for Persia won
By Philip's warlike son—
Aloft in awful state
The godlike hero sate
On his imperial throne ;
His valiant peers were placed around,
Their brows with roses and with myrtles bound
(So should desert in arms be crown'd) ;
The lovely Thais by his side
Sate like a blooming eastern bride
In flower of youth and beauty's pride :—
Happy, happy, happy pair !
None but the brave
None but the brave
None but the brave deserves the fair !

Timotheus placed on high
Amid the tuneful quire
With flying fingers touch'd the lyre :
The trembling notes ascend the sky
And heavenly joys inspire.
The song began from Jove
Who left his blissful seats above—
Such is the power of mighty love !
A dragon's fiery form belied the god ;
Sublime on radiant spires he rode
When he to fair Olympia prest,
And while he sought her snowy breast ;
Then round her slender waist he curl'd,
And stamp'd an image of himself, a sovereign of the world.
—The listening crowd admire the lofty sound !
A present deity ! they shout around :
A present deity ! the vaulted roofs rebound !
With ravish'd ears
The monarch hears,
Assumes the god ;
Affects to nod
And seems to shake the spheres.

The praise of Bacchus then the sweet musician sung :
Of Bacchus ever fair and ever young :

The jolly god in triumph comes !
Sound the trumpets, beat the drums !
Flush'd with a purple grace
He shows his honest face :
Now give the hautboys breath ; he comes, he comes !
Bacchus, ever fair and young,
Drinking joys did first ordain ;
Bacchus' blessings are a treasure,
Drinking is the soldier's pleasure :
Rich the treasure,
Sweet the pleasure,
Sweet is pleasure after pain.

Soothed with the sound, the king grew vain ;
Fought all his battles o'er again,
And thrice he routed all his foes, and thrice he slew the
    slain !
The master saw the madness rise,
His glowing cheeks, his ardent eyes ;
And while he Heaven and Earth defied
Changed his hand and check'd his pride.
He chose a mournful Muse
Soft pity to infuse :
He sung Darius great and good,
By too severe a fate
Fallen, fallen, fallen, fallen,
Fallen from his high estate,
And weltering in his blood ;
Deserted, at his utmost need,
By those his former bounty fed ;
On the bare earth exposed he lies
With not a friend to close his eyes.
—With downcast looks the joyless victor sate,
Revolving in his alter'd soul
The various turns of Chance below
And now and then a sigh he stole,
And tears began to flow.

The mighty master smiled to see
That love was in the next degree ;
'Twas but a kindred-sound to move,
For pity melts the mind to love.
Softly sweet, in Lydian measures
Soon he soothed his soul to pleasures.

War, he sung, is toil and trouble,
Honour but an empty bubble,
Never ending, still beginning ;
Fighting still, and still destroying ;
If the world be worth thy winning,
Think, O think, it worth enjoying :
Lovely Thais sits beside thee,
Take the good the gods provide thee !
—The many rend the skies with loud applause ;
So Love was crown'd, but Music won the cause.
The prince, unable to conceal his pain,
Gazed on the fair
Who caused his care,
And sigh'd and look'd, sigh'd and look'd,
Sigh'd and look'd, and sigh'd again :
At length with love and wine at once opprest
The vanquish'd victor sunk upon her breast.

Now strike the golden lyre again :
A louder yet, and yet a louder strain !
Breaks his bands of sleep asunder
And rouse him like a rattling peal of thunder.
Hark, hark ! the horrid sound
Has raised up his head :
As awaked from the dead
And amazed he stares around.
Revenge, revenge, Timotheus cries,
See the Furies arise !
See the snakes that they rear
How they hiss in their hair,
And the sparkles that flash from their eyes !
Behold a ghastly band
Each a torch in his hand !
Those are Grecian ghosts, that in battle were slain
And unburied remain
Inglorious on the plain :
Give the vengeance due
To the valiant crew !
Behold how they toss their torches on high,
How they point to the Persian abodes
And glittering temples of their hostile gods.
—The princes applaud with a furious joy :
And the King seized a flambeau with zeal to destroy ;

Thais led the way
To light him to his prey,
And like another Helen, fired another Troy !

—Thus, long ago,
Ere heaving bellows learn'd to blow,
While organs yet were mute,
Timotheus, to his breathing flute
And sounding lyre
Could swell the soul to rage, or kindle soft desire.
At last divine Cecilia came,
Inventress of the vocal frame ;
The sweet enthusiast from her sacred store
Enlarged the former narrow bounds,
And added length to solemn sounds,
With Nature's mother-wit, and arts unknown before.
—Let old Timotheus yield the prize
Or both divide the crown ;
He raised a mortal to the skies ;
She drew an angel down !

J. DRYDEN.

THIRD BOOK

SUMMARY

It is more difficult to characterise the English Poetry of the eighteenth century than that of any other. For it was an age not only of spontaneous transition, but of bold experiment: it includes not only such divergences of thought as distinguished the "Rape of the Lock" from the "Parish Register," but such vast contemporaneous differences as lie between Pope and Collins, Burns and Cowper. Yet we may clearly trace three leading moods or tendencies :—the aspects of courtly or educated life represented by Pope and carried to exhaustion by his followers ; the poetry of Nature and of Man, viewed through a cultivated, and at the same time an impassioned frame of mind by Collins and Gray :—lastly, the study of vivid and simple narrative, including natural description, begun by Gay and Thomson, pursued by Burns and others in the north, and established in England by Goldsmith, Percy, Crabbe, and Cowper. Great varieties in style accompanied these diversities in aim : poets could not always distinguish the manner suitable for subjects so far apart ; and the union of the language of courtly and of common life, exhibited most conspicuously by Burns, has given a tone to the poetry of that century which is better explained by reference to its historical origin than by naming it, in the common criticism of our day, artificial. There is again, a nobleness of thought, a courageous aim at high and, in a strict sense manly, excellence in many of the writers :—nor can that period be justly termed tame and wanting in originality, which produced poems such as Pope's Satires, Gray's Odes and Elegy, the ballads of Gay and Carey, the songs of Burns and Cowper. In truth Poetry at this as at all times was a more or less unconscious mirror of the genius of the age ; and the brave and admirable spirit of Enquiry which made the eighteenth century the turning-time in European civilisation is reflected faithfully in its verse. An intelligent reader will find the influence of Newton as markedly in the poems of Pope, as of Elizabeth in the plays of Shakespeare. On this great subject, however, these indications must here be sufficient.

117. ODE ON THE PLEASURE ARISING FROM VICISSITUDE

Now the golden Morn aloft
  Waves her dew-bespangled wing,
With vermeil cheek and whisper soft
  She woos the tardy Spring :
Till April starts, and calls around
The sleeping fragrance from the ground,
And lightly o'er the living scene
Scatters his freshest, tenderest green.

New-born flocks, in rustic dance,
  Frisking ply their feeble feet ;
Forgetful of their wintry trance
  The birds his presence greet :
But chief, the sky-lark warbles high
His trembling thrilling ecstasy ;
And lessening from the dazzled sight,
Melts into air and liquid light.

Yesterday the sullen year
  Saw the snowy whirlwind fly ;
Mute was the music of the air,
  The herd stood drooping by :
Their raptures now that wildly flow
No yesterday nor morrow know ;
'Tis Man alone that joy descries
With forward and reverted eyes.

Smiles on past Misfortune's brow
  Soft Reflection's hand can trace,
And o'er the cheek of Sorrow throw
  A melancholy grace ;
While Hope prolongs our happier hour,
Or deepest shades, that dimly lour
And blacken round our weary way,
Gilds with a gleam of distant day.

Still, where rosy Pleasure leads,
  See a kindred Grief pursue ;
Behind the steps that Misery treads
  Approaching Comfort view :

The hues of bliss more brightly glow
Chastised by sabler tints of woe,
And blended form, with artful strife,
The strength and harmony of life.

See the wretch that long has tost
    On the thorny bed of pain,
At length repair his vigour lost
    And breathe and walk again ;
The meanest floweret of the vale,
The simplest note that swells the gale,
The common sun, the air, the skies,
To him are opening Paradise.

                                        T. GRAY.

118. SOLITUDE

Happy the man, whose wish and care
A few paternal acres bound,
Content to breathe his native air
            In his own ground.

Whose herds with milk, whose fields with bread,
Whose flocks supply him with attire ;
Whose trees in summer yield him shade,
            In winter, fire.

Blest, who can unconcern'dly find
Hours, days, and years, slide soft away
In health of body, peace of mind,
            Quiet by day,

Sound sleep by night ; study and ease
Together mix'd ; sweet recreation,
And innocence, which most does please
            With meditation.

Thus let me live, unseen, unknown ;
Thus unlamented let me die ;
Steal from the world, and not a stone
            Tell where I lie.

                                        A. POPE.

119. THE BLIND BOY

O say what is that thing call'd Light,
  Which I must ne'er enjoy;
What are the blessings of the sight,
  O tell your poor blind boy!

You talk of wondrous things you see,
  You say the sun shines bright;
I feel him warm, but how can he
  Or make it day or night?

My day or night myself I make
  Whene'er I sleep or play;
And could I ever keep awake
  With me 'twere always day.

With heavy sighs I often hear
  You mourn my hapless woe;
But sure with patience I can bear
  A loss I ne'er can know.

Then let not what I cannot have
  My cheer of mind destroy:
Whilst thus I sing, I am a king,
  Although a poor blind boy.

                                    C. CIBBER.

120. ON A FAVOURITE CAT, DROWNED IN A TUB OF GOLD FISHES

'Twas on a lofty vase's side
Where China's gayest art had dyed
  The azure flowers that blow,
Demurest of the tabby kind
The pensive Selima, reclined,
  Gazed on the lake below.

Her conscious tail her joy declared:
The fair round face, the snowy beard,
  The velvet of her paws,
Her coat that with the tortoise vies,
Her ears of jet, and emerald eyes—
  She saw, and purr'd applause.

Still had she gazed, but 'midst the tide
Two angel forms were seen to glide,
The Genii of the stream :
Their scaly armour's Tyrian hue
Through richest purple, to the view
Betray'd a golden gleam.

The hapless Nymph with wonder saw :
A whisker first, and then a claw
With many an ardent wish
She stretch'd, in vain, to reach the prize—
What female heart can gold despise ?
What Cat's averse to fish ?

Presumptuous maid ! with looks intent
Again she stretch'd, again she bent,
Nor knew the gulf between—
Malignant Fate sat by and smiled—
The slippery verge her feet beguiled ;
She tumbled headlong in !

Eight times emerging from the flood
She mew'd to every watery God
Some speedy aid to send :—
No Dolphin came, no Nereid stirr'd,
Nor cruel Tom nor Susan heard—
A favourite has no friend !

From hence, ye Beauties ! undeceived
Know one false step is ne'er retrieved,
And be with caution bold :
Not all that tempts your wandering eyes
And heedless hearts, is lawful prize,
Nor all that glisters, gold !

                                        T. Gray.

121. TO CHARLOTTE PULTENEY

Timely blossom, Infant fair,
Fondling of a happy pair,
Every morn and every night
Their solicitous delight,
Sleeping, waking, still at ease
Pleasing, without skill to please

Little gossip, blithe and hale,
Tattling many a broken tale,
Singing many a tuneless song,
Lavish of a heedless tongue ;
Simple maiden, void of art,
Babbling out the very heart,
Yet abandon'd to thy will,
Yet imagining no ill,
Yet too innocent to blush,
Like the linnet in the bush
To the mother-linnet's note
Moduling her slender throat ;
Chirping forth thy petty joys,
Wanton in the change of toys,
Like the linnet green, in May
Flitting to each bloomy spray ;
Wearied then and glad of rest,
Like the linnet in the nest :—
This thy present happy lot
This, in time will be forgot :
Other pleasures, other cares,
Ever-busy Time prepares ;
And thou shalt in thy daughter see,
This picture, once, resembled thee.

A. PHILIPS.

122. RULE BRITANNIA

When Britain first at Heaven's command
  Arose from out the azure main,
This was the charter of her land,
  And guardian angels sung the strain :
Rule Britannia ! Britannia rules the waves !
  Britons never shall be slaves.

The nations not so blest as thee
  Must in their turn to tyrants fall,
Whilst thou shalt flourish great and free
  The dread and envy of them all.

Still more majestic shalt thou rise,
  More dreadful from each foreign stroke ;
As the loud blast that tears the skies
  Serves but to root thy native oak.

Thee haughty tyrants ne'er shall tame ;
　All their attempts to bend thee down
Will but arouse thy generous flame,
　And work their woe and thy renown.

To thee belongs the rural reign ;
　Thy cities shall with commerce shine ;
All thine shall be the subject main,
　And every shore it circles thine !

The Muses, still with Freedom found,
　Shall to thy happy coast repair ;
Blest Isle, with matchless beauty crown'd,
　And manly hearts to guard the fair :—
Rule Britannia ! Britannia rules the waves !
　Britons never shall be slaves !

J. THOMSON.

123. THE BARD
Pindaric Ode

" Ruin seize thee, ruthless King !
　Confusion on thy banners wait !
Tho' fann'd by Conquest's crimson wing
　They mock the air with idle state.
Helm, nor hauberk's twisted mail
Nor e'en thy virtues, tyrant, shall avail
To save thy secret soul from nightly fears,
From Cambria's curse, from Cambria's tears ! "
—Such were the sounds that o'er the crested pride
　Of the first Edward scatter'd wild dismay,
As down the steep of Snowdon's shaggy side
　He wound with toilsome march his long array :—
Stout Glo'ster stood aghast in speechless trance ;
" To arms ! " cried Mortimer, and couch'd his quiver-
　ing lance.

On a rock, whose haughty brow
Frowns o'er old Conway's foaming flood,
　Robed in the sable garb of woe
With haggard eyes the Poet stood ;
(Loose his beard and hoary hair
Stream'd like a meteor to the troubled air)
And with a master's hand and prophet's fire
Struck the deep sorrows of his lyre :

" Hark, how each giant oak and desert-cave
   Sighs to the torrent's awful voice beneath !
O'er thee, O King ! their hundred arms they wave,
   Revenge on thee in hoarser murmurs breathe ;
Vocal no more, since Cambria's fatal day,
To high-born Hoel's harp, or soft Llewellyn's lay.

" Cold is Cadwallo's tongue,
   That hush'd the stormy main :
Brave Urien sleeps upon his craggy bed :
   Mountains, ye mourn in vain
   Modred, whose magic song
Made huge Plinlimmon bow his cloud-topt head.
   On dreary Arvon's shore they lie
Smear'd with gore and ghastly pale :
Far, far aloof the affrighted ravens sail ;
   The famish'd eagle screams, and passes by.
Dear lost companions of my tuneful art,
   Dear as the light that visits these sad eyes,
Dear as the ruddy drops that warm my heart,
   Ye died amidst your dying country's cries—
No more I weep ; They do not sleep ;
   On yonder cliffs, a griesly band,
I see them sit ; They linger yet,
   Avengers of their native land :
With me in dreadful harmony they join,
And weave with bloody hands the tissue of thy line.

" Weave the warp and weave the woof
   The winding-sheet of Edward's race :
Give ample room and verge enough
   The characters of hell to trace.
Mark the year and mark the night
When Severn shall re-echo with affright
The shrieks of death thro' Berkley's roof that ring,
Shrieks of an agonising king !
   She-wolf of France, with unrelenting fangs
That tear'st the bowels of thy mangled mate,
   From thee be born, who o'er thy country hangs
The scourge of Heaven ! What terrors round him wait !
Amazement in his van, with Flight combined,
And Sorrow's faded form, and Solitude behind.

" Mighty victor, mighty lord,
 Low on his funeral couch he lies !
No pitying heart, no eye, afford
 A tear to grace his obsequies.
Is the sable warrior fled ?
Thy son is gone. He rests among the dead.
The swarm that in thy noon-tide beam were born ?
—Gone to salute the rising morn.
Fair laughs the Morn, and soft the zephyr blows,
 While proudly riding o'er the azure realm
In gallant trim the gilded Vessel goes :
 Youth on the prow, and Pleasure at the helm :
Regardless of the sweeping Whirlwind's sway,
That hush'd in grim repose expects his evening prey.

 " Fill high the sparkling bowl,
The rich repast prepare ;
 Reft of a crown, he yet may share the feast :
Close by the regal chair
 Fell Thirst and Famine scowl
A baleful smile upon their baffled guest.
Heard ye the din of battle bray,
 Lance to lance, and horse to horse ?
 Long years of havock urge their destined course,
And thro' the kindred squadrons mow their way.
 Ye towers of Julius, London's lasting shame,
With many a foul and midnight murder fed,
 Revere his Consort's faith, his Father's fame,
And spare the meek usurper's holy head !
Above, below, the rose of snow,
 Twined with her blushing foe, we spread :
The bristled boar in infant-gore
 Wallows beneath the thorny shade.
Now, brothers, bending o'er the accurséd loom,
Stamp we our vengeance deep, and ratify his doom.

" Edward, lo ! to sudden fate
 (Weave we the woof ; The thread is spun)
Half of thy heart we consecrate.
 (The web is wove ; The work is done ;)
Stay, O stay ! nor thus forlorn
Leave me unbless'd, unpitied, here to mourn :
In yon bright track that fires the western skies
They melt, they vanish from my eyes.

But O ! what solemn scenes on Snowdon's height
  Descending slow their glittering skirts unroll ?
Visions of glory, spare my aching sight,
  Ye unborn ages, crowd not on my soul !
No more our long-lost Arthur we bewail :—
All hail, ye genuine kings ! Britannia's issue, hail !

" Girt with many a baron bold
Sublime their starry fronts they rear ;
  And gorgeous dames, and statesmen old
In bearded majesty, appear.
In the midst a form divine !
Her eye proclaims her of the Briton-Line :
Her lion-port, her awe-commanding face
Attemper'd sweet to virgin-grace.
What strings symphonious tremble in the air,
  What strains of vocal transport round her play ?
Hear from the grave, great Taliessin, hear ;
  They breathe a soul to animate thy clay.
Bright Rapture calls, and soaring as she sings,
Waves in the eye of Heaven her many-colour'd wings.

" The verse adorn again
  Fierce War and faithful Love
And Truth severe by fairy Fiction drest.
  In buskin'd measures move
Pale Grief, and pleasing Pain,
With Horror, tyrant of the throbbing breast.
A voice as of the cherub-choir
  Gales from blooming Eden bear,
  And distant warblings lessen on my ear
That lost in long futurity expire.
Fond impious man, think'st thou yon sanguine cloud
  Raised by thy breath, has quench'd the orb of day ?
To-morrow he repairs the golden flood
  And warms the nations with redoubled ray.
Enough for me : with joy I see
  The different doom our fates assign :
Be thine Despair and sceptred Care ;
  To triumph and to die are mine."
—He spoke, and headlong from the mountain's height
Deep in the roaring tide he plunged to endless night.

                        T. GRAY.

124. ODE WRITTEN IN MDCCXLVI

How sleep the Brave, who sink to rest
By all their Country's wishes blest !
When Spring, with dewy fingers cold,
Returns to deck their hallow'd mould,
She there shall dress a sweeter sod
Than Fancy's feet have ever trod.

By fairy hands their knell is rung,
By forms unseen their dirge is sung :
There honour comes, a pilgrim gray
To bless the turf that wraps their clay,
And Freedom shall awhile repair
To dwell a weeping hermit there !

W. COLLINS.

125. LAMENT FOR CULLODEN

The lovely lass o' Inverness,
Nae joy nor pleasure can she see,
For e'en and morn she cries, Alas !
And aye the saut tear blins her ee :
Drumossie moor—Drumossie day—
A waefu' day it was to me !
For there I lost my father dear,
My father dear, and brethren three.

Their winding-sheet the bluidy clay,
Their graves are growing green to see :
And by them lies the dearest lad
That ever blest a woman's ee !
Now wae to me, thou cruel lord,
A bluidy man I trow thou be ;
For mony a heart thou hast made sair
That ne'er did wrang to thine or thee.

R. BURNS.

126. LAMENT FOR FLODDEN

I've heard them lilting at our ewe-milking,
  Lasses a' lilting before dawn o' day ;
But now they are moaning on ilka green loaning—
  The Flowers of the Forest are a' wede away.

At bughts, in the morning, nae blythe lads are scorning.
   Lasses are lonely and dowie and wae ;
Nae daffin', na gabbin', but sighing and sabbing,
   Ilk ane lifts her leglin and hies her away.

In har'st, at the shearing, nae youths now are jeering,
   Bandsters are lyart, and runkled, and gray ;
At fair or at preaching, nae wooing, nae fleeching—
   The Flowers of the Forest are a' wede away.

At e'en, in the gloaming, nae younkers are roaming
   'Bout stacks wi' the lasses at bogle to play ;
But ilk ane sits drearie, lamenting her dearie—
   The Flowers of the Forest are weded away.

Dool and wae for the order, sent our lads to the Border !
   The English, for ance, by guile wan the day ;
The Flowers of the Forest, that fought aye the foremost,
   The prime of our land, are cauld in the clay.

We'll hear nae mair lilting at the ewe-milking ;
   Women and bairns are heartless and wae ;
Sighing and moaning on ilka green loaning—
   The Flowers of the Forest are a' wede away.
                      J. ELLIOT.

127. THE BRAES OF YARROW

Thy braes were bonny, Yarrow stream,
When first on them I met my lover ;
Thy braes how dreary, Yarrow stream,
When now thy waves his body cover !
For ever now, O Yarrow stream !
Thou art to me a stream of sorrow ;
For never on thy banks shall I
Behold my Love, the flower of Yarrow !

He promised me a milk-white steed
To bear me to his father's bowers ;
He promised me a little page
To squire me to his father's towers ;
He promised me a wedding-ring,—
The wedding-day was fix'd to-morrow ;—
Now he is wedded to his grave,
Alas, his watery grave, in Yarrow !

Sweet were his words when last we met ;
My passion I as freely told him ;
Clasp'd in his arms, I little thought
That I should never more behold him !
Scarce was he gone, I saw his ghost ;
It vanish'd with a shriek of sorrow ;
Thrice did the water-wraith ascend,
And gave a doleful groan thro' Yarrow.

His mother from the window look'd
With all the longing of a mother ;
His little sister weeping walk'd
The green-wood path to meet her brother ;
They sought him east, they sought him west,
They sought him all the forest thorough ;
They only saw the cloud of night,
They only heard the roar of Yarrow.

No longer from thy window look—
Thou hast no son, thou tender mother !
No longer walk, thou lovely maid ;
Alas, thou hast no more a brother !
No longer seek him east or west
And search no more the forest thorough ;
For, wandering in the night so dark,
He fell a lifeless corpse in Yarrow.

The tear shall never leave my cheek,
No other youth shall be my marrow—
I'll seek thy body in the stream,
And then with thee I'll sleep in Yarrow.
—The tear did never leave her cheek,
No other youth became her marrow ;
She found his body in the stream,
And now with him she sleeps in Yarrow.

J. LOGAN.

128. WILLIE DROWNED IN YARROW

Down in yon garden sweet and gay
  Where bonnie grows the lily,
I heard a fair maid sighing say
  " My wish be wi' sweet Willie !

" Willie's rare, and Willie's fair,
    And Willie's wondrous bonny ;
And Willie hecht to marry me
    Gin e'er he married ony.

" O gentle wind, that bloweth south,
    From where my Love repaireth,
Convey a kiss frae his dear mouth
    And tell me how he fareth !

" O tell sweet Willie to come doun
And hear the mavis singing,
And see the birds on ilka bush
    And leaves around them hinging.

" The lav'rock there, wi' her white breast
    And gentle throat sae narrow ;
There's sport eneuch for gentlemen
    On Leader haughs and Yarrow.

" O Leader haughs are wide and braid
    And Yarrow haughs are bonny ;
There Willie hecht to marry me
    If e'er he married ony.

" But Willie's gone, whom I thought on,
    And does not hear me weeping ;
Draws many a tear frae true love's e'e
    When other maids are sleeping.

" Yestreen I made my bed fu' braid,
    The night I'll mak' it narrow,
For a' the live-lang winter night
    I lie twined o' my marrow.

" O came ye by yon water-side ?
    Pou'd you the rose or lily ?
Or came you by yon meadow green,
    Or saw you my sweet Willie ? "

She sought him up, she sought him down,
    She sought him braid and narrow ;
Syne, in the cleaving of a craig,
    She found him drown'd in Yarrow !

                                    ANON.

129. LOSS OF THE *ROYAL GEORGE*

Toll for the Brave !
The brave that are no more !
All sunk beneath the wave
Fast by their native shore !

Eight hundred of the brave
Whose courage well was tried,
Had made the vessel heel
And laid her on her side.

A land-breeze shook the shrouds
And she was overset ;
Down went the *Royal George*,
With all her crew complete.

Toll for the brave !
Brave Kempenfelt is gone :
His last sea-fight is fought,
His work of glory done.

It was not in the battle ;
No tempest gave the shock ;
She sprang no fatal leak,
She ran upon no rock.

His sword was in its sheath,
His fingers held the pen,
When Kempenfelt went down
With twice four hundred men.

Weigh the vessel up
Once dreaded by our foes !
And mingle with our cup
The tear that England owes.

Her timbers yet are sound,
And she may float again
Full charged with England's thunder,
And plough the distant main :

But Kempenfelt is gone,
His victories are o'er ;
And he and his eight hundred
Shall plough the wave no more.

W. COWPER.

130. BLACK-EYED SUSAN

All in the Downs the fleet was moor'd,
  The streamers waving in the wind,
When black-eyed Susan came aboard ;
  " O ! where shall I my true-love find ?
Tell me, ye jovial sailors, tell me true
If my sweet William sails among the crew."

William, who high upon the yard
  Rock'd with the billow to and fro,
Soon as her well-known voice he heard
  He sigh'd, and cast his eyes below ;
The cord slides swiftly through his glowing hands,
And quick as lightning on the deck he stands.

So the sweet lark, high poised in air,
  Shuts close his pinions to his breast
If chance his mate's shrill call he hear,
  And drops at once into her nest :—
The noblest captain in the British fleet
Might envy William's lip those kisses sweet.

" O Susan, Susan, lovely dear,
  My vows shall ever true remain ;
Let me kiss off that falling tear ;
  We only part to meet again.
Change as ye list, ye winds ; my heart shall be
The faithful compass that still points to thee.

" Believe not what the landmen say
  Who tempt with doubts thy constant mind :
They'll tell thee, sailors, when away,
  In every port a mistress find :
Yes, yes, believe them when they tell thee so,
For Thou art present wheresoe'er I go.

" If to fair India's coast we sail,
  Thy eyes are seen in diamonds bright,
Thy breath is Afric's spicy gale,
  Thy skin is ivory so white.
Thus every beauteous object that I view
Wakes in my soul some charm of lovely Sue.

" Though battle call me from thy arms
  Let not my pretty Susan mourn ;

Though cannons roar, yet safe from harms
    William shall to his Dear return.
Love turns aside the balls that round me fly,
Lest precious tears should drop from Susan's eye.

The boatswain gave the dreadful word,
    The sails their swelling bosom spread;
No longer must she stay aboard;
    They kiss'd, she sigh'd, he hung his head.
Her lessening boat unwilling rows to land;
"Adieu!" she cries; and waved her lily hand.

J. GAY.

131. SALLY IN OUR ALLEY

Of all the girls that are so smart
    There's none like pretty Sally;
She is the darling of my heart,
    And she lives in our alley.
There is no lady in the land
    Is half so sweet as Sally;
She is the darling of my heart,
    And she lives in our alley.

Her father he makes cabbage-nets
    And through the streets does cry 'em;
Her mother she sells laces long
    To such as please to buy 'em:
But sure such folks could ne'er beget
    So sweet a girl as Sally!
She is the darling of my heart,
    And she lives in our alley.

When she is by, I leave my work,
    I love her so sincerely;
My master comes like any Turk,
    And bangs me most severely—
But let him bang his bellyful,
    I'll bear it all for Sally;
She is the darling of my heart,
    And she lives in our alley.

Of all the days that's in the week
    I dearly love but one day—
And that's the day that comes betwix
    A Saturday and Monday;

For then I'm drest all in my best
  To walk abroad with Sally :
She is the darling of my heart,
  And she lives in our alley.

My master carries me to church,
  And often am I blamed
Because I leave him in the lurch
  As soon as text is named ;
I leave the church in sermon-time
  And slink away to Sally ;
She is the darling of my heart,
  And she lives in our alley.

When Christmas comes about again
  O then I shall have money ;
I'll board it up, and box it all,
  I'll give it to my honey :
I would it were ten thousand pound,
  I'd give it all to Sally ;
She is the darling of my heart,
  And she lives in our alley.

My master and the neighbours all
  Make game of me and Sally,
And, but for her, I'd better be
  A slave and row a galley ;
But when my seven long years are out
  O then I'll marry Sally,—
O then we'll wed, and then we'll bed,
  But not in our alley !

H. CAREY.

132. A FAREWELL

Go fetch to me a pint o' wine,
  And fill it in a silver tassie ;
That I may drink before I go
  A service to my bonnie lassie :
The boat rocks at the pier of Leith,
  Fu' loud the wind blaws frae the Ferry,
The ship rides by the Berwick-law,
  And I maun leave my bonnie Mary.

The trumpets sound, the banners fly,
  The glittering spears are rankéd ready ;
The shouts o' war are heard afar,
  The battle closes thick and bloody ;
But it's not the roar o' sea or shore
  Wad make me langer wish to tarry ;
Nor shouts o' war that's heard afar—
It's leaving thee, my bonnie Mary.

                                        R. BURNS.

133

If doughty deeds my lady please
  Right soon I'll mount my steed ;
And strong his arm, and fast his seat
  That bears frae me the meed.
I'll wear thy colours in my cap
  Thy picture at my heart ;
And he that bends not to thine eye
  Shall rue it to his smart !
      Then tell me how to woo thee, Love ;
        O tell me how to woo thee !
      For thy dear sake, nae care I'll take
        Tho' ne'er another trow me.

If gay attire delight thine eye
  I'll dight me in array ;
I'll tend thy chamber door all night,
  And squire thee all the day.
If sweetest sounds can win thine ear,
  These sounds I'll strive to catch ;
Thy voice I'll steal to woo thysell,
  That voice that name can match.

But if fond love thy heart can gain,
  I never broke a vow ;
Nae maiden lays her skaith to me,
  I never loved but you.
For you alone I ride the ring,
  For you I wear the blue ;
For you alone I strive to sing,
  O tell me how to woo !
      Then tell me how to woo thee, Love ;
        O tell me how to woo thee !
      For thy dear sake, nae care I'll take,
        Tho' ne'er another trow me.
                        GRAHAM OF GARTMORE.

134. TO A YOUNG LADY

Sweet stream, that winds through yonder glade,
Apt emblem of a virtuous maid—
Silent and chaste she steals along,
Far from the world's gay busy throng:
With gentle yet prevailing force,
Intent upon her destined course;
Graceful and useful all she does,
Blessing and blest where'er she goes;
Pure-bosom'd as that watery glass,
And Heaven reflected in her face.

W. COWPER.

135. THE SLEEPING BEAUTY

Sleep on, and dream of Heaven awhile—
Tho' shut so close thy laughing eyes,
Thy rosy lips still wear a smile
And move, and breathe delicious sighs!

Ah, now soft blushes tinge her cheeks
And mantle o'er her neck of snow:
Ah, now she murmurs, now she speaks
What most I wish—and fear to know!

She starts, she tembles, and she weeps!
Her fair hands folded on her breast:
—And now, how like a saint she sleeps!
A seraph in the realms of rest!

Sleep on secure! Above controul
Thy thoughts belong to Heaven and thee:
And may the secret of thy soul
Remain within its sanctuary!

S. ROGERS

136

For ever, Fortune, wilt thou prove
An unrelenting foe to Love,
And when we meet a mutual heart
Come in between, and bid us part?

Bid us sigh on from day to day,
And wish and wish the soul away
Till youth and genial years are flown,
And all the life of life is gone?

But busy, busy, still art thou,
To bind the loveless joyless vow,
The heart from pleasure to delude,
To join the gentle to the rude.

For once, O Fortune, hear my prayer,
And I absolve thy future care;
All other blessings I resign,
Make but the dear Amanda mine.

J. THOMSON.

137

The merchant, to secure his treasure,
Conveys it in a borrow'd name:
Euphelia serves to grace my measure,
But Cloe is my real flame.

My softest verse, my darling lyre
Upon Euphelia's toilet lay—
When Cloe noted her desire
That I should sing, that I should play.

My lyre I tune, my voice I raise,
But with my numbers mix my sighs
And whilst I sing Euphelia's praise,
I fix my soul on Cloe's eyes.

Fair Cloe blush'd: Euphelia frown'd:
I sung, and gazed; I play'd, and trembled:
And Venus to the Loves around
Remark'd how ill we all dissembled.

M. PRIOR.

138

When lovely woman stoops to folly
And finds too late that men betray,—
What charm can soothe her melancholy,
What art can wash her guilt away?

G.T.   *Cupid and Campaspe*

"Cupid and my Campaspé played at cards for kisses."

The only art her guilt to cover,
    To hide her shame from every eye,
To give repentance to her lover
And wring his bosom, is—to die.
O. GOLDSMITH.

139

Ye banks and braes o' bonnie Doon
    How can ye blume sae fair !
How can ye chant, ye little birds,
    And I sae fu' o' care !

Thou'll break my heart, thou bonnie bird
    That sings upon the bough ;
Thou minds me o' the happy days
    When my fause Luve was true.

Thou'll break my heart, thou bonnie bird
    That sings beside thy mate ;
For sae I sat, and sae I sang,
    And wist na o' my fate.

Aft hae I roved by bonnie Doon
    To see the woodbine twine,
And ilka bird sang o' its love ;
    And sae did I o' mine.

Wi' lightsome heart I pu'd a rose,
    Frae aff its thorny tree ;
And my fause luver staw the rose,
    But left the thorn wi' me.
R. BURNS.

140. THE PROGRESS OF POESY

A Pindaric Ode

Awake, Aeolian lyre, awake,
And give to rapture all thy trembling strings.
From Helicon's harmonious springs
    A thousand rills their mazy progress take :
The laughing flowers that round them blow
Drink life and fragrance as they flow.
Now the rich stream of Music winds along
Deep, majestic, smooth, and strong,

Through verdant vales, and Ceres' golden reign ;
Now rolling down the steep amain
Headlong, impetuous, see it pour :
The rocks and nodding groves re-bellow to the roar.

O Sovereign of the willing soul,
Parent of sweet and solemn-breathing airs,
Enchanting shell ! the sullen Cares
   And frantic Passions hear thy soft control.
On Thracia's hills the Lord of War
Has curb'd the fury of his car
And dropt his thirsty lance at thy command.
Perching on the sceptred hand
Of Jove, thy magic lulls the feather'd king
With ruffled plumes, and flagging wing :
Quench'd in dark clouds of slumber lie
The terror of his beak, and lightnings of his eye.

Thee the voice, the dance, obey,
Temper'd to thy warbled lay.
O'er Idalia's velvet-green
The rosy-crownéd Loves are seen
On Cytherea's day,
With antic Sport, and blue-eyed Pleasures,
Frisking light in frolic measures ;
Now pursuing, now retreating,
   Now in circling troops they meet :
To brisk notes in cadence beating
   Glance their many-twinkling feet.
Slow melting strains their Queen's approach declare :
   Where'er she turns the Graces homage pay :
With arms sublime that float upon the air
   In gliding state she wins her easy way :
O'er her warm cheek and rising bosom move
The bloom of young Desire and purple light of Love.

Man's feeble race what ills await !
Labour, and Penury, the racks of Pain,
Disease, and Sorrow's weeping train,
   And Death, sad refuge from the storms of Fate !
The fond complaint, my song, disprove,
And justify the laws of Jove.
Say, has he given in vain the heavenly Muse ?
Night, and all her sickly dews,

Her spectres wan, and birds of boding cry
He gives to range the dreary sky :
Till down the eastern cliffs afar
Hyperion's march they spy, and glittering shafts of war.

In climes beyond the solar road
Where shaggy forms o'er ice-built mountains roam,
The Muse has broke the twilight gloom
    To cheer the shivering native's dull abode.
And oft, beneath the odorous shade
Of Chili's boundless forests laid,
She deigns to hear the savage youth repeat
In loose numbers wildly sweet
Their feather-cinctured chiefs, and dusky loves.
Her track, where'er the Goddess roves,
Glory pursue, and generous Shame,
Th' unconquerable Mind, and Freedom's holy flame.

Woods, that wave o'er Delphi's steep,
Isles, that crown th' Aegean deep,
Fields that cool Ilissus laves
Or where Mæander's amber waves
In lingering lab'rinths creep,
How do your tuneful echoes languish,
Mute, but to the voice of anguish !
Where each old poetic mountain
    Inspiration breathed around ;
Every shade and hallow'd fountain
    Murmur'd deep a solemn sound :
Till the sad Nine, in Greece's evil hour
    Left their Parnassus for the Latian plains.
Alike they scorn the pomp of tyrant Power,
    And coward Vice, that revels in her chains.
When Latium had her lofty spirit lost,
They sought, O Albion ! next, thy sea-encircled coast.

Far from the sun and summer-gale
In thy green lap was Nature's Darling laid,
What time, where lucid Avon stray'd,
    To him the mighty Mother did unveil
Her awful face : the dauntless Child
Stretch'd forth his little arms, and smiled.
This pencil take (she said), whose colours clear
Richly paint the vernal year :

Thine, too, these golden keys, immortal Boy !
This can unlock the gates of joy ;
Of Horror that, and thrilling Fears,
Or ope the sacred source of sympathetic Tears.

Nor second He, that rode sublime
Upon the seraph-wings of Ecstasy
The secrets of the Abyss to spy :
    He pass'd the flaming bounds of Place and Time :
The living Throne, the sapphire-blaze
Where Angels tremble while they gaze,
He saw ; but blasted with excess of light,
Closed his eyes in endless night.

Behold where Dryden's less presumptuous car
Wide o'er the fields of Glory bear
Two coursers of ethereal race
With necks in thunder clothed, and long-resounding
    pace.

Hark, his hands the lyre explore !
Bright-eyed Fancy, hovering o'er,
Scatters from her pictured urn
Thoughts that breathe, and words that burn.
But ah ! 'tis heard no more——
O ! Lyre divine, what daring Spirit
Wakes thee now ! Tho' he inherit
Nor the pride, nor ample pinion,
    That the Theban Eagle bear,
Sailing with supreme dominion
    Thro' the azure deep of air :
Yet oft before his infant eyes would run
    Such forms as glitter in the Muse's ray
With orient hues, unborrow'd of the sun :
    Yet shall he mount, and keep his distant way
Beyond the limits of a vulgar fate :
Beneath the Good how far—but far above the Great.

                                            T. GRAY.

141. THE PASSIONS

An Ode for Music

When Music, heavenly maid, was young,
While yet in early Greece she sung,
The Passions oft, to hear her shell,
Throng'd around her magic cell

Exulting, trembling, raging, fainting,
Possest beyond the Muse's painting;
By turns they felt the glowing mind
Disturb'd, delighted, raised, refined:
'Till once, 'tis said, when all were fired,
Fill'd with fury, rapt, inspired,
From the supporting myrtles round
They snatch'd her instruments of sound,
And, as they oft had heard apart
Sweet lessons of her forceful art,
Each, for Madness ruled the hour,
Would prove his own expressive power.

First Fear his hand, its skill to try,
  Amid the chords bewilder'd laid,
And back recoil'd, he knew not why,
  E'en at the sound himself had made.

Next Anger rush'd, his eyes on fire,
  In lightnings own'd his secret stings;
In one rude clash he struck the lyre
  And swept with hurried hand the strings.

With woeful measures wan Despair—
  Low sullen sounds his grief beguiled,
A solemn, strange, and mingled air,
  'Twas sad by fits, by starts 'twas wild.

But thou, O Hope, with eyes so fair,
  What was thy delighted measure?
Still it whisper'd promised pleasure
  And bade the lovely scenes at distance hail!
Still would her touch the strain prolong;
  And from the rocks, the woods, the vale
She call'd on Echo still through all the song;
  And, where her sweetest theme she chose,
  A soft responsive voice was heard at every close;
And Hope enchanted smiled, and waved her golden hair:

And longer had she sung:—but with a frown Revenge
    impatient rose:
He threw his blood-stain'd sword in thunder down:
    And with a withering look
  The war-denouncing trumpet took

And blew a blast so loud and dread,
Were ne'er prophetic sounds so full of woe !
    And ever and anon he beat
    The doubling drum with furious heat ;
And, though sometimes, each dreary pause between,
    Dejected Pity at his side
    Her soul-subduing voice applied,
  Yet still he kept his wild unalter'd mien,
While each strain'd ball of sight seem'd bursting from
    his head.

Thy numbers, Jealousy, to nought were fix'd :
    Sad proof of thy distressful state !
Of differing themes the veering song was mix'd ;
    And now it courted Love, now raving call'd on Hate.

With eyes up-raised, as one inspired,
Pale Melancholy sat retired ;
And from her wild sequester'd seat,
In notes by distance made more sweet,
Pour'd through the mellow horn her pensive soul :
    And dashing soft from rocks around
    Bubbling runnels join'd the sound ;
Through glades and glooms the mingled measure stole,
    Or, o'er some haunted stream, with fond delay,
      Round an holy calm diffusing,
      Love of peace, and lonely musing,
  In hollow murmurs died away.

But O ! how alter'd was its sprightlier tone
When Cheerfulness, a nymph of healthiest hue,
    Her bow across her shoulder flung,
    Her buskins gemm'd with morning dew,
Blew an inspiring air, that dale and thicket rung,
    The hunter's call to Faun and Dryad known !
The oak-crown'd Sisters and their chaste-eyed Queen,
    Satyrs and Sylvan Boys, were seen
      Peeping from forth their alleys green
Brown Exercise rejoiced to hear ;
  And Sport leap'd up, and seized his beechen spear.

Last came Joy's ecstatic trial :
He, with viny crown advancing,
    First to the lively pipe his hand addrest :
But soon he saw the brisk awakening viol

Whose sweet entrancing voice he loved the best :
They would have thought who heard the strain
    They saw, in Temple's vale, her native maids
    Amidst the festal-sounding shades
To some unwearied minstrel dancing ;
While, as his flying fingers kiss'd the strings,
  Love framed with Mirth a gay fantastic round :
  Loose were her tresses seen, her zone unbound ;
  And he, amidst his frolic play,
  As if he would the charming air repay,
Shook thousand odours from his dewy wings.
O Music ! sphere-descended maid,
Friend of Pleasure, Wisdom's aid !
Why, goddess, why, to us denied,
Lay'st thou thy ancient lyre aside ?
As in that loved Athenian bower
You learn'd an all-commanding power,
Thy mimic soul, O nymph endear'd !
Can well recall what then it heard.
Where is thy native simple heart
Devote to Virtue, Fancy, Art ?
Arise, as in that elder time,
Warm, energetic, chaste, sublime !
Thy wonders, in that god-like age,
Fill thy recording Sister's page ;—
'Tis said, and I believe the tale,
Thy humblest reed could more prevail
Had more of strength, diviner rage,
Than all which charms this laggard age,
E'en all at once together found
Cecilia's mingled world of sound :—
O bid our vain endeavours cease :
Revive the just designs of Greece :
Return in all thy simple state !
Confirm the tales her sons relate !

W. COLLINS.

142. ODE ON THE SPRING

Lo ! where the rosy-bosom'd Hours
    Fair Venus' train, appear,
Disclose the long-expecting flowers
    And wake the purple year !

The Attic warbler pours her throat
Responsive to the cuckoo's note,
   The untaught harmony of Spring :
While, whispering pleasure as they fly,
Cool Zephyrs through the clear blue sky
   Their gather'd fragrance fling.

Where'er the oak's thick branches stretch
   A broader, browner shade,
Where'er the rude and moss-grown beech
   O'er-canopies the glade,
Beside some water's rushy brink
With me the Muse shall sit, and think
   (At ease reclined in rustic state)
How vain the ardour of the crowd,
How low, how little are the Proud,
   How indigent the Great !

Still is the toiling hand of Care ;
   The panting herds repose :
Yet hark, how thro' the peopled air
   The busy murmur glows !
The insect youth are on the wing,
Eager to taste the honied spring
   And float amid the liquid noon :
Some lightly o'er the current skim,
Some show their gaily-gilded trim
   Quick-glancing to the sun.

To Contemplation's sober eye
   Such is the race of Man :
And they that creep, and they that fly,
   Shall end where they began.
Alike the busy and the gay
But flutter thro' life's little day,
   In Fortune's varying colours drest :
Brush'd by the hand of rough Mischance
Or chill'd by Age, their airy dance
   They leave, in dust to rest.

Methinks I hear in accents low
   The sportive kind reply :
Poor moralist ! and what art thou ?
   A solitary fly !

Thy joys no glittering female meets,
No hive hast thou of hoarded sweets,
No painted plumage to display :
On hasty wings thy youth is flown ;
Thy sun is set, thy spring is gone—
    We frolic while 'tis May.

T. GRAY.

143. THE POPLAR FIELD

The poplars are fell'd, farewell to the shade
And the whispering sound of the cool colonade ;
The winds play no longer and sing in the leaves,
Nor Ouse on his bosom their image receives.

Twelve years have elapsed since I last took a view
Of my favourite field, and the bank where they grew
And now in the grass behold they are laid,
And the tree is my seat that once lent me a shade.

The blackbird has fled to another retreat
Where the hazels afford him a screen from the heat ;
And the scene where his melody charm'd me before
Resounds with his sweet-flowing ditty no more.

My fugitive years are all hasting away,
And I must ere long lie as lowly as they,
With a turf on my breast and a stone at my head,
Ere another such grove shall arise in its stead.

'Tis a sight to engage me, if anything can,
To muse on the perishing pleasures of man ;
Short-lived as we are, our enjoyments, I see,
Have a still shorter date, and die sooner than we.

W. COWPER.

144. TO A FIELD-MOUSE

Wee, sleekit, cow'rin, tim'rous beastie,
O what a panic's in thy breastie !
Thou need na start awa sae hasty,
    Wi' bickering brattle !
I wad be laith to rin and chase thee
    Wi' murd'ring pattle !

I'm truly sorry man's dominion
Has broken nature's social union,
And justifies that ill opinion
Which makes thee startle
At me, thy poor earth-born companion,
And fellow-mortal !

I doubt na, whyles, but thou may thieve ;
What then ? poor beastie, thou maun live !
A daimen icker in a thrave
'S a sma' request :
I'll get a blessin' wi' the lave,
And never miss't !

Thy wee bit housie, too, in ruin !
Its silly wa's the win's are strewin' :
And naething, now, to big a new ane,
O' foggage green !
And bleak December's winds ensuin'
Baith snell and keen !

Thou saw the fields laid bare and waste
And weary winter comin' fast,
And cozie here, beneath the blast,
Thou thought to dwell,
Till, crash ! the cruel coulter past
Out thro' thy cell.

That wee bit heap o' leaves and stibble
Has cost thee mony a weary nibble !
Now thou'd turn'd out for a' thy trouble
But house or hald,
To thole the winter's sleety dribble
And cranreuch cauld ?

But, Mousie, thou art no thy lane
In proving foresight may be vain :
The best laid schemes o' mice and men
Gang aft a-gley,
And lea'e us nought but grief and pain,
For promised joy.

Still thou art blest, compared wi' me !
The present only toucheth thee :

But, och ! I backward cast my e'e
On prospects drear !
And forward, tho' I canna see,
I guess and fear.

R. BURNS.

145. A WISH

Mine be a cot beside the hill ;
A bee-hive's hum shall soothe my ear ;
A willowy brook that turns a mill,
With many a fall shall linger near.

The swallow, oft, beneath my thatch
Shall twitter from her clay-built nest ;
Oft shall the pilgrim lift the latch,
And share my meal, a welcome guest.

Around my ivied porch shall spring
Each fragrant flower that drinks the dew ;
And Lucy, at her wheel, shall sing
In russet-gown and apron blue.

The village-church among the trees,
Where first our marriage-vows were given,
With merry peals shall swell the breeze
And point with taper spire to Heaven.

S. ROGERS.

146. TO EVENING

If aught of oaten stop or pastoral song
May hope, chaste Eve, to soothe thy modest ear
  Like thy own solemn springs,
  Thy springs, and dying gales ;

O Nymph reserved,—while now the bright-hair'd sun
Sits in yon western tent, whose cloudy skirts
  With brede ethereal wove,
  O'erhang his wavvy bed,

Now air is hush'd, save where the weak-eyed bat
With short shrill shriek flits by on leathern wing,
  Or where the beetle winds
  His small but sullen horn,

As oft he rises midst the twilight path,
Against the pilgrim borne in heedless hum,—
    Now teach me, maid composed,
    To breathe some soften'd strain

Whose numbers, stealing through thy dark'ning vale,
May not unseemly with its stillness suit;
    As musing slow I hail
    Thy genial loved return.

For when thy folding-star arising shows
His paly circlet, at his warning lamp
    The fragrant Hours, and Elves
    Who slept in buds the day,

And many a Nymph who wreathes her brows with sedge
And sheds the freshening dew, and lovelier still
    The pensive Pleasures sweet,
    Prepare thy shadowy car.

Then let me rove some wild and heathy scene;
Or find some ruin midst its dreary dells,
    Whose walls more awful nod
    By thy religious gleams.

Or if chill blustering winds or driving rain
Prevent my willing feet, be mine the hut
    That, from the mountain's side,
    Views wilds and swelling floods,

And hamlets brown, and dim-discover'd spires;
And hears their simple bell; and marks o'er all
    Thy dewy fingers draw
    The gradual dusky veil.

While Spring shall pour his showers, as oft he wont,
And bathe thy breathing tresses, meekest Eve!
    While Summer loves to sport
    Beneath thy lingering light;

While sallow Autumn fills thy lap with leaves;
Or Winter, yelling through the troublous air,
    Affrights thy shrinking train
    And rudely rends thy robes;

So long, regardful of thy quiet rule,
Shall Fancy, Friendship, Science, smiling Peace,
   Thy gentlest influence own,
    And love thy favourite name!

                  W. COLLINS.

147. ELEGY WRITTEN IN A COUNTRY CHURCH-YARD

The curfew tolls the knell of parting day,
The lowing herd winds slowly o'er the lea,
The ploughman homeward plods his weary way,
And leaves the world to darkness and to me.

Now fades the glimmering landscape on the sight,
And all the air a solemn stillness holds,
Save where the beetle wheels his droning flight,
And drowsy tinklings lull the distant folds:

Save that from yonder ivy-mantled tower
The moping owl does to the moon complain
Of such as, wandering near her secret bower,
Molest her ancient solitary reign.

Beneath those rugged elms, that yew-tree's shade
Where heaves the turf in many a mouldering heap,
Each in his narrow cell for ever laid,
The rude Forefathers of the hamlet sleep.

The breezy call of incense-breathing morn,
The swallow twittering from the straw-built shed,
The cock's shrill clarion, or the echoing horn,
No more shall rouse them from their lowly bed.

For them no more the blazing hearth shall burn
Or busy housewife ply her evening care:
No children run to lisp their sire's return,
Or climb his knees the envied kiss to share.

Oft did the harvest to their sickle yield,
Their furrow oft the stubborn glebe has broke;
How jocund did they drive their team afield!
How bow'd the woods beneath their sturdy stroke!

Let not Ambition mock their useful toil,
Their homely joys, and destiny obscure;
Nor Grandeur hear with a disdainful smile
The short and simple annals of the Poor.

The boast of heraldry, the pomp of power,
And all that beauty, all that wealth e'er gave
Await alike th' inevitable hour :—
The paths of glory lead but to the grave.

Nor you, ye Proud, impute to these the fault
If Memory o'er their tomb no trophies raise,
Where through the long-drawn aisle and fretted vault
The pealing anthem swells the note of praise.

Can storied urn or animated bust
Back to its mansion call the fleeting breath ?
Can Honour's voice provoke the silent dust,
Or Flattery soothe the dull cold ear of Death ?

Perhaps in this neglected spot is laid
Some heart once pregnant with celestial fire ;
Hands, that the rod of empire might have sway'd,
Or waked to ecstasy the living lyre :

But Knowledge to their eyes her ample page
Rich with the spoils of time, did ne'er unroll ;
Chill Penury repress'd their noble rage,
And froze the genial current of the soul.

Full many a gem of purest ray serene
The dark unfathom'd caves of ocean bear :
Full many a flower is born to blush unseen,
And waste its sweetness on the desert air.

Some village-Hampden, that with dauntless breast
The little tyrant of his fields withstood,
Some mute inglorious Milton here may rest,
Some Cromwell, guiltless of his country's blood.

Th' applause of listening senates to command,
The threats of pain and ruin to despise,
To scatter plenty o'er a smiling land,
And read their history in a nation's eyes

Their lot forbad ; nor circumscribed alone
Their growing virtues, but their crimes confined ;
Forbad to wade through slaughter to a throne,
And shut the gates of mercy on mankind ;

The struggling pangs of conscious truth to hide,
To quench the blushes of ingenuous shame,
Or heap the shrine of Luxury and Pride
With incense kindled at the Muse's flame.

Far from the madding crowd's ignoble strife
Their sober wishes never learn'd to stray ;
Along the cool sequester'd vale of life
They kept the noiseless tenour of their way.

Yet e'en these bones from insult to protect
Some frail memorial still erected nigh,
With uncouth rhymes and shapeless sculpture deck'd,
Implores the passing tribute of a sigh.

Their name, their years, spelt by th' unletter'd Muse,
The place of fame and elegy supply :
And many a holy text around she strews
That teach the rustic moralist to die.

For who, to dumb forgetfulness a prey,
This pleasing anxious being e'er resign'd,
Left the warm precincts of the cheerful day,
Nor cast one longing lingering look behind ?

On some fond breast the parting soul relies,
Some pious drops the closing eye requires ;
E'en from the tomb the voice of Nature cries,
E'en in our ashes live their wonted fires.

For thee, who, mindful of th' unhonour'd dead,
Dost in these lines their artless tale relate ;
If chance, by lonely Contemplation led,
Some kindred spirit shall inquire thy fate,—

Haply some hoary-headed swain may say,
Oft have we seen him at the peep of dawn
Brushing with hasty steps the dews away,
To meet the sun upon the upland lawn ;

There at the foot of yonder nodding beech
That wreathes its old fantastic roots so high,
His listless length at noon-tide would he stretch,
And pore upon the brook that babbles by.

Hard by yon wood, now smiling as in scorn,
Muttering his wayward fancies he would rove ;
Now drooping, woeful-wan, like one forlorn,
Or crazed with care, or cross'd in hopeless love.

One morn I miss'd him on the custom'd hill,
Along the heath, and near his favourite tree ;
Another came ; nor yet beside the rill,
Nor up the lawn, nor at the wood was he ;

The next with dirges due in sad array
Slow through the church-way path we saw him borne,—
Approach and read (for thou canst read) the lay
Graved on the stone beneath yon aged thorn.

THE EPITAPH

Here rests his head upon the lap of Earth
A Youth, to Fortune and to Fame unknown ;
Fair Science frown'd not on his humble birth,
And Melancholy mark'd him for her own.

Large was his bounty, and his soul sincere ;
Heaven did a recompense as largely send :
He gave to Misery all he had, a tear,
He gain'd from Heaven, 'twas all he wish'd, a friend.

No farther seek his merits to disclose,
Or draw his frailties from their dread abode,
(There they alike in trembling hope repose),
The bosom of his Father and his God.

T. GRAY.

148. MARY MORISON

O Mary, at thy window be,
It is the wish'd, the trysted hour !
Those smiles and glances let me see
That make the miser's treasure poor :
How blythely was I bide the stoure,
A weary slave frae sun to sun,
Could I the rich reward secure,
The lovely Mary Morison.

Yestreen when to the trembling string
The dance gaed thro' the lighted ha',
To thee my fancy took its wing,—
I sat, but neither heard nor saw::
Tho' this was fair, and that was braw,
And yon the toast of a' the town,
I sigh'd, and said amang them a',
" Ye are na Mary Morison."

O Mary, canst thou wreck his peace
Wha for thy sake wad gladly dee?
Or canst thou break that heart of his,
Whase only faut is loving thee?
If love for love thou wilt na gie,
At least be pity to me shown;
A thought ungentle canna be
The thought o' Mary Morison.

R. BURNS.

149. BONNIE LESLEY

O saw ye bonnie Lesley
  As she gaed o'er the border?
She's gane, like Alexander,
  To spread her conquests farther.

To see her is to love her,
  And love but her for ever;
For nature made her what she is,
  And ne'er made sic anither!

Thou art a queen, fair Lesley,
  Thy subjects we, before thee;
Thou art divine, fair Lesley,
  The hearts o' men adore thee.

The deil he could na scaith thee,
  Or aught that wad belang thee;
He'd look into thy bonnie face,
  And say "I canna wrang thee!"

The Powers aboon will tent thee;
  Misfortune sha' na steer thee;
Thou'rt like themselves sae lovely
  That ill they'll ne'er let near thee.

Return again, fair Lesley,
  Return to Caledonie!
That we may brag we hae a lass
  There's nane again sae bonnie.

R. BURNS.

150

O my Luve's like a red, red rose
 That's newly sprung in June :
O my Luve's like the melodie
 That's sweetly play'd in tune.

As fair art thou, my bonnie lass,
 So deep in luve am I :
And I will luve thee still, my dear,
 Till a' the seas gang dry :

Till a' the seas gang dry, my Dear,
 And the rocks melt wi' the sun ;
I will luve thee still, my dear,
 While the sands o' life shall run.

And fare thee weel, my only Luve !
 And fare thee weel a while !
And I will come again, my Luve,
 Tho' it were ten thousand mile.

R. BURNS.

151. HIGHLAND MARY

Ye banks and braes and streams around
 The castle o' Montgomery,
Green be your woods, and fair your flowers,
 Your waters never drumlie !
There simmer first unfauld her robes,
 And there the langest tarry ;
For there I took the last fareweel
 O' my sweet Highland Mary.

How sweetly bloom'd the gay green birk,
 How rich the hawthorn's blossom,
As underneath their fragrant shade
 I clasp'd her to my bosom !
The golden hours on angel wings
 Flew o'er me and my dearie ;
For dear to me as light and life
 Was my sweet Highland Mary.

Wi' mony a vow and lock'd embrace
  Our parting was fu' tender ;
And pledging aft to meet again,
  We tore oursels asunder ;
But, O ! fell Death's untimely frost,
  That nipt my flower sae early !
Now green's the sod, and cauld's the clay,
  That wraps my Highland Mary !

O pale, pale now, those rosy lips,
  I aft hae kiss'd sae fondly !
And closed for aye the sparkling glance
  That dwelt on me sae kindly ;
And mouldering now in silent dust
  That heart that lo'ed me dearly !
But still within my bosom's core
  Shall live my Highland Mary.

R. BURNS.

152. AULD ROBIN GRAY

When the sheep are in the fauld, and the kye at hame,
And a' the warld to rest are gane,
The waes o' my heart fa' in showers frae my e'e,
While my gudeman lies sound by me.

Young Jamie lo'ed me weel, and sought me for his bride ;
But saving a croun he had naething else beside :
To make the croun a pund, young Jamie gaed to sea ;
And the croun and the pund were baith for me.

He hadna been awa' a week but only twa,
When my father brak his arm, and the cow was stown awa ;
My mother she fell sick, and my Jamie at the sea—
And auld Robin Gray came a-courtin' me.

My father couldna work, and my mother couldna spin ;
I toil'd day and night, but their bread I couldna win ;
Auld Rob maintain'd them baith, and wi' tears in his e'e
Said, Jennie, for their sakes, O, marry me !

My heart it said nay ; I look'd for Jamie back ;
But the wind it blew high, and the ship it was a wrack ;
His ship it was a wrack—why didna Jamie dee ?
Or why do I live to cry, Wae's me ?

My father urgit sair : my mother didna speak ;
But she look'd in my face till my heart was like to break :
They gi'ed him my hand, but my heart was at the sea ;
Sae auld Robin Gray he was gudeman to me.

I hadna been a wife a week but only four,
When mournfu' as I sat on the stane at the door,
I saw my Jamie's wraith, for I couldna think it he——
Till he said, I'm come hame to marry thee.

O sair, sair did we greet, and muckle did we say ;
We took but ae kiss, and I bad him gang away ;
I wish that I were dead, but I'm no like to dee ;
And why was I born to say, Wae's me !

I gang like a ghaist, and I carena to spin ;
I daurna think on Jamie, for that wad be a sin ;
But I'll do my best a gude wife aye to be,
For auld Robin Gray he is kind unto me.

LADY A. LINDSAY.

153. DUNCAN GRAY

Duncan Gray cam here to woo,
 Ha, ha, the wooing o't
On blythe Yule night when we were fou,
 Ha, ha, the wooing o't :
Maggie coost her head fu' high,
Look'd asklent and unco skeigh,
Gart poor Duncan stand abeigh ;
 Ha, ha, the wooing o't !

Duncan fleech'd, and Duncan pray'd ;
Meg was deaf as Ailsa Craig ;
Duncan sigh'd baith out and in,
Grat his een baith bleert and blin',
Spak o' lowpin' ower a linn !

Time and chance are but a tide,
Slighted love is sair to bide ;
Shall I, like a fool, quoth he,
For a haughty hizzie dee ?
She may gae to——France for me !

How it comes let doctors tell,
Meg grew sick—as he grew heal ;
Something in her bosom wrings,
For relief a sigh she brings ;
And O, her een, they spak sic things !

Duncan was a lad o' grace ;
Maggie's was a piteous case ;
Duncan could na be her death,
Swelling pity smoor'd his wrath ;
Now they're crouse and canty baith :
    Ha, ha, the wooing o't !

                    R. BURNS.

154. THE SAILOR'S WIFE

And are ye sure the news is true ?
    And are ye sure he's weel ?
Is this a time to think o' wrak ?
    Ye jades, lay by your wheel ;
Is this the time to spin a thread,
    When Colin's at the door ?
Reach down my cloak, I'll to the quay,
    And see him come ashore.
For there's nae luck about the house,
    There's nae luck at a' ;
There's little pleasure in the house
    When our gudeman's awa'.

And gie to me my bigonet,
    My bishop's satin gown ;
For I maun tell the baillie's wife
    That Colin's in the town.
My Turkey slippers maun gae on,
    My stockins pearly blue ;
It's a' to pleasure our gudeman,
    For he's baith leal and true.

Rise, lass, and mak a clean fireside,
    Put on the muckle pot ;
Gie little Kate her button gown
    And Jock his Sunday coat ;
And mak their shoon as black as slaes,
    Their hose as white as snaw ;
It's a' to please my ain gudeman,
    For he's been long awa.

There's twa fat hens upo' the coop
   Been fed this month and mair ;
Mak haste and thraw their necks about,
   That Colin weel may fare ;
And spread the table neat and clean,
   Gar ilka thing look braw,
For wha can tell how Colin fared
   When he was far awa ?

Sae true his heart, sae smooth his speech,
   His breath like caller air ;
His very foot has music in't
   As he comes up the stair—
And will I see his face again ?
   And will I hear him speak ?
I'm downright dizzy wi' the thought,
   In troth I'm like to greet !

If Colin's weel, and weel content,
   I hae nae mair to crave :
And gin I live to keep him sae,
   I'm blest aboon the lave :
And will I see his face again,
   And will I hear him speak ?
I'm downright dizzy wi' the thought,
   In troth I'm like to greet.

For there's nae luck about the house,
   There's nae luck at a' ;
There's little pleasure in the house
   When our gudeman's awa.

                W. J. MICKLE.

155. JEAN

Of a' the airts the wind can blaw
   I dearly like the West,
For there the bonnie lassie lives,
   The lassie I lo'e best :
There wild woods grow, and rivers row,
   And mony a hill between ;
But day and night my fancy's flight
   Is ever wi' my Jean.

I see her in the dewy flowers,
I see her sweet and fair :

I hear her in the tunefu' birds,
  I hear her charm the air :
There's not a bonnie flower that springs,
  By fountain, shaw, or green,
There's not a bonnie bird that sings
  But minds me o' my Jean.

O blaw ye westlin winds, blaw saft
  Amang the leafy trees ;
Wi' balmy gale, frae hill and dale
  Bring hame the laden bees ;
And bring the lassie back to me
  That's aye sae neat and clean ;
Ae smile o' her wad banish care,
  Sae charming is my Jean.

What sighs and vows amang the knowes
  Hae pass'd atween us twa !
How fond to meet, how wae to part
  That night she gaed awa !
The Powers aboon can only ken
  To whom the heart is seen,
That nane can be sae dear to me
  As my sweet lovely Jean !

R. BURNS.

156. JOHN ANDERSON

John Anderson my jo, John,
When we were first acquent
Your locks were like the raven,
Your bonnie brow was brent ;
But now your brow is bald, John,
Your locks are like the snow ;
But blessings on your frosty pow,
John Anderson my jo.

John Anderson my jo, John,
We clamb the hill thegither,
And mony a canty day, John,
We've had wi' ane anither :
Now we maun totter down, John,
But hand in hand we'll go,
And sleep thegither at the foot,
John Anderson my jo.

R. BURNS.

157. THE LAND O' THE LEAL

I'm wearing awa', Jean,
Like snaw when it's thaw, Jean,
I'm wearing awa'
    To the land o' the leal.
There's nae sorrow there, Jean,
There's neither cauld nor care, Jean,
The day is aye fair
    In the land o' the leal.

Ye were aye leal and true, Jean,
Your task's ended noo, Jean,
And I'll welcome you
    To the land o' the leal.
Our bonnie bairn's there, Jean,
She was baith guid and fair, Jean ;
O we grudged her right sair
    To the land o' the leal !

Then dry that tearfu' e'e, Jean,
My soul langs to be free, Jean,
And angels wait on me
    To the land o' the leal.
Now fare ye weel, my ain Jean,
This warld's care is vain, Jean ;
We'll meet and aye be fain
    In the land o' the leal.

                                    LADY NAIRN.

158. ODE ON A DISTANT PROSPECT OF ETON COLLEGE

Ye distant spires, ye antique towers
    That crown the wat'ry glade,
Where grateful Science still adores
    Her Henry's holy shade ;
And ye, that from the stately brow
Of Windsor's heights th' expanse below
Of grove, of lawn, of mead survey,
Whose turf, whose shade, whose flowers among
Wanders the hoary Thames along
    His silver-winding way :

Ah happy hills ! ah pleasing shade !
　　Ah fields beloved in vain !
Where once my careless childhood stray'd,
　　A stranger yet to pain !
I feel the gales that from ye blow
A momentary bliss bestow,
As waving fresh their gladsome wing
My weary soul they seem to soothe,
And, redolent of joy and youth,
　　To breathe a second spring.

Say, Father Thames, for thou hast seen
Full many a sprightly race
Disporting on thy margent green
　　The paths of pleasure trace ;
Who foremost now delight to cleave
With pliant arm, thy glassy wave ?
The captive linnet which enthral ?
What idle progeny succeed
To chase the rolling circle's speed
　　Or urge the flying ball ?

While some on earnest business bent
　　Their murmuring labours ply
'Gainst graver hours, that bring constraint
　　To sweeten liberty :
Some bold adventurers disdain
The limits of their little reign
And unknown regions dare descry :
Still as they run they look behind,
They hear a voice in every wind
　　And snatch a fearful joy.

Gay Hope is theirs by fancy fed,
　　Less pleasing when possest ;
The tear forgot as soon as shed,
　　The sunshine of the breast :
Theirs buxom Health, of rosy hue,
Wild Wit, Invention ever new,
And lively Cheer, of Vigour born ;
The thoughtless day, the easy night,
The spirits pure, the slumbers light
　　That fly th' approach of morn.

Alas ! regardless of their doom
The little victims play !
No sense have they of ills to come
Nor care beyond to-day :
Yet see how all around 'em wait
The ministers of human fate
And black Misfortune's baleful train !
Ah shew them where in ambush stand
To seize their prey, the murderous band !
    Ah, tell them they are men !

These shall the fury Passions tear,
    The vultures of the mind,
Disdainful Anger, pallid Fear,
    And Shame that skulks behind ;
Or pining Love shall waste their youth,
Or Jealousy with rankling tooth
That inly gnaws the secret heart,
And Envy wan, and faded Care,
Grim-visaged comfortless Despair,
    And Sorrow's piercing dart.

Ambition this shall tempt to rise,
    Then whirl the wretch from high
To bitter Scorn a sacrifice
    And grinning Infamy.
The stings of Falsehood those shall try,
And hard Unkindness' alter'd eye
That mocks the tear it forced to flow ;
And keen Remorse with blood defiled,
And moody Madness laughing wild
    Amid severest woe.

Lo, in the Vale of Years beneath
    A griesly troop are seen,
The painful family of Death,
    More hideous than their Queen :
This racks the joints, this fires the veins,
That every labouring sinew strains,
Those in the deeper vitals rage :
Lo, Poverty, to fill the band,
That numbs the soul with icy hand,
    And slow-consuming Age.

To each his sufferings : all are men,
 Condemn'd alike to groan ;
The tender for another's pain,
 Th' unfeeling for his own.
Yet, ah ! why should they know their fate,
Since sorrow never comes too late,
And happiness too swiftly flies ?
Thought would destroy their paradise !
No more ;—where ignorance is bliss,
 'Tis folly to be wise.

T. GRAY.

159. HYMN TO ADVERSITY

Daughter of Jove, relentless power,
 Thou tamer of the human breast,
Whose iron scourge and torturing hour
 The bad affright, afflict the best !
Bound in thy adamantine chain
The proud are taught to taste of pain,
And purple tyrants vainly groan
With pangs unfelt before, unpitied and alone.

When first thy Sire to send on earth
 Virtue, his darling child, design'd,
To thee he gave the heavenly birth
 And bade to form her infant mind.
Stern rugged Nurse ! thy rigid lore
With patience many a year she bore :
What sorrow was, thou bad'st her know,
And from her own she learn'd to melt at others' woe.

Scared at thy frown terrific, fly
 Self-pleasing Folly's idle brood,
Wild Laughter, Noise, and thoughtless Joy,
 And leave us leisure to be good.
Light they disperse, and with them go
The summer Friend, the flattering Foe ;
By vain Prosperity received
To her they vow their truth, and are again believed.

Wisdom in sable garb array'd
 Immersed in rapturous thought profound,
And Melancholy, silent maid,
 With leaden eye, that loves the ground

Still on thy solemn steps attend :
Warm Charity, the general friend,
   With Justice, to herself severe,
And Pity dropping soft the sadly-pleasing tear.

Oh, gently on thy suppliant's head,
   Dread Goddess, lay thy chastening hand !
Not in thy Gorgon terrors clad,
   Not circled with the vengeful band
   (As by the impious thou art seen)
With thundering voice, and threatening mien,
With screaming Horror's funeral cry,
Despair, and fell Disease, and ghastly Poverty :

Thy form benign, O Goddess, wear,
   Thy milder influence impart,
Thy philosophic train be there
   To soften, not to wound my heart.
The generous spark extinct revive,
Teach me to love and to forgive,
Exact my own defects to scan,
What others are to feel, and know myself a Man.

T. GRAY.

160. THE SOLITUDE OF ALEXANDER
SELKIRK

I am monarch of all I survey ;
   My right there is none to dispute ;
From the centre all round to the sea
   I am lord of the fowl and the brute.
O Solitude ! where are the charms
That sages have seen in thy face ?
Better dwell in the midst of alarms
   Than reign in this horrible place.

I am out of humanity's reach,
   I must finish my journey alone,
Never hear the sweet music of speech ;
   I start at the sound of my own.
The beasts that roam over the plain
My form with indifference see ;
They are so unacquainted with man,
   Their tameness is shocking to me.

Society, Friendship, and Love
Divinely bestow'd upon man,
O had I the wings of a dove
How soon would I taste you again !
My sorrows I then might assuage
In the ways of religion and truth,
Might learn from the wisdom of age,
And be cheer'd by the sallies of youth.

Ye winds that have made me your sport,
Convey to this desolate shore
Some cordial endearing report
Of a land I shall visit no more :
My friends, do they now and then send
A wish or a thought after me ?
O tell me I yet have a friend,
Though a friend I am never to see.

How fleet is a glance of the mind !
Compared with the speed of its flight,
The tempest itself lags behind,
And the swift-wingéd arrows of light.
When I think of my own native land
In a moment I seem to be there ;
But alas ! recollection at hand
Soon hurries me back to despair.

But the seafowl is gone to her nest,
The beast is laid down in his lair ;
Even here is a season of rest,
And I to my cabin repair.
There's mercy in every place,
And mercy, encouraging thought !
Gives even affliction a grace
And reconciles man to his lot.

W. COWPER.

161. TO MARY UNWIN

Mary ! I want a lyre with other strings,
Such aid from heaven as some have feign'd they drew,
An eloquence scarce given to mortals, new
And undebased by praise of meaner things,

That ere through age or woe I shed my wings
I may record thy worth with honour due,
In verse as musical as thou art true
And that immortalises whom it sings :—

But thou hast little need. There is a Book
By seraphs writ with beams of heavenly light,
On which the eyes of God not rarely look,

A chronicle of actions just and bright—
There all thy deeds, my faithful Mary, shine ;
And since, thou own'st that praise, I spare thee mine.
W. COWPER.

162. TO THE SAME

The twentieth year is well nigh past
Since first our sky was overcast ;
Ah would that this might be the last !
  My Mary !

Thy spirits have a fainter flow,
I see thee daily weaker grow—
'Twas my distress that brought thee low,
  My Mary !

Thy needles, once a shining store,
For my sake restless heretofore,
Now rust disused, and shine no more ;
  My Mary !

For though thou gladly wouldst fulfil
The same kind office for me still,
Thy sight now seconds not thy will,
  My Mary !

But well thou play'dst the housewife's part,
And all thy threads with magic art
Have wound themselves about this heart,
  My Mary !

Thy indistinct expressions seem
Like language utter'd in a dream ;
Yet me they charm, whate'er the theme,
  My Mary !

Thy silver locks, once auburn bright,
Are still more lovely in my sight
Than golden beams of orient light,
    My Mary !

For could I view nor them nor thee,
What sight worth seeing could I see ?
The sun would rise in vain for me,
    My Mary !

Partakers of thy sad decline
Thy hands their little force resign ;
Yet gently press'd, press gently mine,
    My Mary !

Such feebleness of limbs thou prov'st
That now at every step thou mov'st
Upheld by two ; yet still thou lov'st,
    My Mary !

And still to love, though press'd with ill,
In wintry age to feel no chill,
With me is to be lovely still,
    My Mary !

But ah ! by constant heed I know
How oft the sadness that I show
Transforms thy smiles to looks of woe,
    My Mary !

And should my future lot be cast
With much resemblance of the past
Thy worn-out heart will break at last—
    My Mary !

                 W. Cowper.

163. THE DYING MAN IN HIS GARDEN

Why, Damon, with the forward day
Dost thou thy little spot survey,
From tree to tree, with doubtful cheer,
Pursue the progress of the year,
What winds arise, what rains descend,
When thou before that year shalt end ?

What do thy noontide walks avail,
    To clear the leaf, and pick the snail,
Then wantonly to death decree
    An insect usefuller than thee ?
Thou and the worm are brother-kind,
As low, as earthly, and as blind.

Vain wretch ! canst thou expect to see
The downy peach make court to thee ?
    Or that thy sense shall ever meet
The bean-flower's deep-embosom'd sweet
Exhaling with an evening blast ?
Thy evenings then will all be past !

Thy narrow pride, thy fancied green
(For vanity's in little seen),
    All must be left when Death appears,
In spite of wishes, groans, and tears ;
Nor one of all thy plants that grow
But Rosemary will with thee go.

G. SEWELL.

164. TO-MORROW

In the downhill of life, when I find I'm declining,
    May my lot no less fortunate be
Than a snug elbow-chair can afford for reclining,
    And a cot that o'erlooks the wide sea ;
With an ambling pad-pony to pace o'er the lawn,
    While I carol away idle sorrow,
And blithe as the lark that each day hails the dawn
    Look forward with hope for to-morrow.

With a porch at my door, both for shelter and shade too
    As the sunshine or rain may prevail ;
And a small spot of ground for the use of the spade too
    With a barn for the use of the flail :
A cow for my dairy, a dog for my game,
    And a purse when a friend wants to borrow ;
I'll envy no nabob his riches or fame,
    Nor what honours await him to-morrow.

G.T.   *Solitude of Alexander Selkirk*

" I am monarch of all I survey."

From the bleak northern blast may my cot be completely
   Secured by a neighbouring hill ;
And at night may repose steal upon me more sweetly
   By the sound of a murmuring rill :
And while peace and plenty I find at my board,
   With a heart free from sickness and sorrow,
With my friends may I share what to-day may afford,
   And let them spread the table to-morrow.

And when I at last must throw off this frail covering
   Which I've worn for three-score years and ten,
On the brink of the grave I'll not seek to keep hovering,
   Nor my thread wish to spin o'er again :
But my face in the glass I'll serenely survey,
   And with smiles count each wrinkle and furrow ;
As this old worn-out stuff, which is threadbare to-day
   May become everlasting to-morrow.

JOHN COLLINS.

165

Life ! I know not what thou art
  But I know that thou and I must part ;
And when, or how, or where we met
  I own to me's a secret yet.
Life ! we've been long together
Through pleasant and through cloudy weather ;
'Tis hard to part when friends are dear—
  Perhaps 'twill cost a sigh, a tear ;
—Then steal away, give little warning,
  Choose thine own time ;
Say not Good Night,—but in some brighter clime
  Bid me Good Morning.

A. L. BARBAULD.

FOURTH BOOK

SUMMARY

IT proves sufficiently the lavish wealth of our own age in Poetry, that the pieces which, without conscious departure from the standard of Excellence, render this Book by far the longest, were with very few exceptions composed during the first thirty years of the nineteenth century. Exhaustive reasons can hardly be given for the strangely sudden appearance of individual genius : but none, in the Editor's judgment, can be less adequate than that which assigns the splendid national achievements of our recent poetry to an impulse from the frantic follies and criminal war that at the time disgraced the least essentially civilised of our foreign neighbours. The first French Revolution was rather, in his opinion, one result, and in itself by no means the most important, of that far wider and greater spirit which through inquiry and doubt, through pain and triumph, sweeps mankind round the circles of its gradual development : and it is to this that we must trace the literature of modern Europe. But, without more detailed discussion on the motive causes of Scott, Wordsworth, Campbell, Keats, and Shelley, we may observe that these Poets, with others, carried to further perfection the later tendencies of the Century preceding, in simplicity of narrative, reverence for human Passion and Character in every sphere, and impassioned love of Nature :—that, whilst maintaining on the whole the advances in art made since the Restoration, they renewed the half-forgotten melody and depth of tone which marked the best Elizabethan writers :—that, lastly, to what was thus inherited they added a richness in language and a variety in metre, a force and fire in narrative, a tenderness and bloom in feeling, an insight into the finer passages of the Soul and the inner meanings of the landscape, a larger and wiser Humanity—hitherto hardly attained, and perhaps unattainable even by predecessors of not inferior individual genius. In a word, the Nation which, after the Greeks in their glory, has been the most gifted of all nations for

Poetry, expressed in these men the highest strength and prodigality of its nature. They interpreted the age to itself —hence the many phases of thought and style they present : —to sympathise with each, fervently and impartially, without fear and without fancifulness, is no doubtful step in the higher education of the Soul. For, as with the Affections and the Conscience, Purity in Taste is absolutely proportionate to Strength :—and when once the mind has raised itself to grasp and to delight in Excellence, those who love most will be found to love most wisely.

166. ON FIRST LOOKING INTO CHAPMAN'S HOMER

Much have I travell'd in the realms of gold
And many goodly states and kingdoms seen ;
Round many western islands have I been
Which bards in fealty to Apollo hold.

Oft of one wide expanse had I been told
That deep-brow'd Homer ruled as his demesne :
Yet did I never breathe its pure serene
Till I heard Chapman speak out loud and bold :

—Then felt I like some watcher of the skies
When a new planet swims into his ken ;
Or like stout Cortez, when with eagle eyes

He stared at the Pacific—and all his men
Look'd at each other with a wild surmise—
Silent, upon a peak in Darien.

J. KEATS.

167. ODE ON THE POETS

Bards of Passion and of Mirth
Ye have left your souls on earth !
Have ye souls in heaven too,
Double-lived in regions new ?
—Yes, and those of heaven commune
With the spheres of sun and moon ;
With the noise of fountains wonderous
And the parle of voices thunderous ;

With the whisper of heaven's trees
And one another, in soft ease
Seated on Elysian lawns
Browsed by none but Dian's fawns ;
Underneath large blue-bells tented,
Where the daises are rose-scented,
And the rose herself has got
Perfume which on earth is not ;
Where the nightingale doth sing
Not a senseless, trancèd thing,
But divine melodious truth ;
Philosophic numbers smooth ;
Tales and golden histories
Of heaven and its mysteries.

Thus ye live on high, and then
On the earth ye live again ;
And the souls ye left behind you
Teach us, here, the way to find you
Where your other souls are joying,
Never slumber'd, never cloying.
Here, your earth-born souls still speak
To mortals, of their little week ;
Of their sorrows and delights ;
Of their passions and their spites ;
Of their glory and their shame ;
What doth strengthen and what maim :—
Thus ye teach us, every day,
Wisdom, though fled far away.

Bards of Passion and of Mirth
Ye have left your souls on earth !
Ye have souls in heaven too,
Double-lived in regions new !

J. KEATS.

168. LOVE

All thoughts, all passions, all delights,
Whatever stirs this mortal frame,
All are but ministers of Love,
    And feed his sacred flame.

Oft in my waking dreams do I
Live o'er again that happy hour,
When midway on the mount I lay
    Beside the ruin'd tower.

The moonshine stealing o'er the scene
Had blended with the lights of eve ;
And she was there, my hope, my joy,
    My own dear Genevieve !

She lean'd against the arméd man,
The statue of the arméd knight ;
She stood and listen'd to my lay,
    Amid the lingering light.

Few sorrows hath she of her own
My hope ! my joy ! my Genevieve !
She loves me best, whene'er I sing
    The songs that make her grieve.

I play'd a soft and doleful air,
I sang an old and moving story—
An old rude song, that suited well
    That ruin wild and hoary.

She listen'd with a flitting blush,
With downcast eyes and modest grace ;
For well she knew, I could not choose
    But gaze upon her face.

I told her of the Knight that wore
Upon his shield a burning brand ;
And that for ten long years he woo'd
    The Lady of the Land.

I told her how he pined : and ah !
The deep, the low, the pleading tone
With which I sang another's love
    Interpreted my own.

She listen'd with a flitting blush,
With downcast eyes, and modest grace
And she forgave me, that I gazed
    Too fondly on her face.

But when I told the cruel scorn
That crazed that bold and lovely Knight,
And that he cross'd the mountain-woods,
  Nor rested day nor night ;

That sometimes from the savage den,
And sometimes from the darksome shade,
And sometimes starting up at once
  In green and sunny glade.

There came and look'd him in the face
An angel beautiful and bright ;
And that he knew it was a Fiend,
  This miserable Knight !

And that unknowing what he did,
He leap'd amid a murderous band,
And saved from outrage worse than death
  The Lady of the Land ;

And how she wept, and clasp'd his knees ;
And how she tended him in vain ;
And ever strove to expiate
  The scorn that crazed his brain ;

And that she nursed him in a cave,
And how his madness went away,
When on the yellow forest-leaves
  A dying man he lay ;

—His dying words—but when I reach'd
That tenderest strain of all the ditty,
That faltering voice and pausing harp
  Disturb'd her soul with pity !

All impulses of soul and sense
Had thrill'd my guileless Genevieve ;
The music and the doleful tale,
  The rich and balmy eve ;

And hopes, and fears that kindle hope,
An undistinguishable throng,
And gentle wishes long subdued,
  Subdued and cherish'd long !

She wept with pity and delight,
She blush'd with love, and virgin shame ;
And like the murmur of a dream,
    I heard her breathe my name.

Her bosom heaved—she stepp'd aside,
As conscious of my look she stept—
Then suddenly, with timorous eye
    She fled to me and wept.

She half enclosed me with her arms,
She press'd me with a meek embrace ;
And bending back her head, look'd up,
    And gazed upon my face.

'Twas partly love, and partly fear,
And partly 'twas a bashful art
That I might rather feel, than see
    The swelling of her heart.

I calm'd her fears, and she was calm,
And told her love with virgin pride ;
And so I won my Genevieve,
    My bright and beauteous Bride.

                S. T. COLERIDGE.

169. ALL FOR LOVE

O talk not to me of a name great in story ;
The days of our youth are the days of our glory ;
And the myrtle and ivy of sweet two-and-twenty
Are worth all your laurels, though ever so plenty.

What are garlands and crowns to the brow that is wrinkled ?
'Tis but as a dead flower with May-dew besprinkled :
Then away with all such from the head that is hoary—
What care I for the wreaths that can only give glory ?

O Fame !—if I e'er took delight in thy praises,
'Twas less for the sake of thy high-sounding phrases,
Than to see the bright eyes of the dear one discover
She thought that I was not unworthy to love her.

There chiefly I sought thee, there only I found thee;
Her glance was the best of the rays that surround thee;
When it sparkled o'er aught that was bright in my story,
I knew it was love, and I felt it was glory.

LORD BYRON.

170. THE OUTLAW

O Brignall banks are wild and fair,
  And Greta woods are green,
And you may gather garlands there
  Would grace a summer-queen.
And as I rode by Dalton-Hall
  Beneath the turrets high,
A Maiden on the castle-wall
  Was singing merrily:
" O Brignall Banks are fresh and fair,
  And Greta woods are green;
I'd rather rove with Edmund there
  Than reign our English queen."

" If, Maiden, thou wouldst wend with me,
  To leave both tower and town,
Thou first must guess what life lead we
  That dwell by dale and down.
And if thou canst that riddle read,
  As read full well you may,
Then to the greenwood shalt thou speed
  As blithe as Queen of May."
Yet sung she " Brignall banks are fair,
  And Greta woods are green;
I'd rather rove with Edmund there
  Than reign our English queen.

" I read you by your bugle-horn
  And by your palfrey good,
I read you for a Ranger sworn
  To keep the king's greenwood."
" A Ranger, lady, winds his horn,
  And 'tis at peep of light;
His blast is heard at merry morn,
  And mine at dead of night."
Yet sung she " Brignall banks are fair
  And Greta woods are gay;

I would I were with Edmund there
  To reign his Queen of May !

" With burnish'd brand and musketoon
  So gallantly you come,
I read you for a bold Dragoon
  That lists the tuck of drum."
" I list no more the tuck of drum,
  No more the trumpet hear ;
But when the beetle sounds his hum
  My comrades take the spear.
And O ! though Brignall banks be fair
  And Greta woods be gay,
Yet mickle must the maiden dare
  Would reign my Queen of May !

" Maiden ! a nameless life I lead,
  A nameless death I'll die !
The fiend whose lantern lights the mead
  Were better mate than I !
And when I'm with my comrades met
  Beneath the greenwood bough
What once we were we all forget,
  Nor think what we are now."

Chorus

Yet Brignall banks are fresh and fair,
  And Greta woods are green,
And you may gather garlands there
  Would grace a summer-queen.
                              Sir W. Scott.

171

There be none of Beauty's daughters
  With a magic like Thee ;
And like music on the waters
  Is thy sweet voice to me :
When, as if its sound were causing
The charmèd ocean's pausing,
The waves lie still and gleaming,
And the lull'd winds seem dreaming :

And the midnight moon is weaving
  Her bright chain o'er the deep,

Whose breast is gently heaving
    As an infant's asleep :
So the spirit bows before thee
To listen and adore thee ;
With a full but soft emotion,
Like the swell of Summer's ocean.

LORD BYRON.

172. LINES TO AN INDIAN AIR

I arise from dreams of Thee
In the first sweet sleep of night,
When the winds are breathing low
And the stars are shining bright :
I arise from dreams of thee,
And a spirit in my feet
Has led me—who knows how ?
To thy chamber-window, Sweet !

The wandering airs they faint
On the dark, the silent stream—
The champak odours fail
Like sweet thoughts in a dream ;
The nightingale's complaint
It dies upon her heart,
As I must die on thine
O belovéd as thou art

O lift me from the grass !
I die, I faint, I fail !
Let thy love in kisses rain
On my lips and eyelids pale.
My cheek is cold and white, alas !
My heart beats loud and fast ;
O ! press it close to thine again
Where it will break at last.

P. B. SHELLEY.

173

She walks in beauty, like the night
Of cloudless climes and starry skies,
And all that's best of dark and bright
Meets in her aspect and her eyes,

Thus mellow'd to that tender light
Which heaven to gaudy day denies.

One shade the more, one ray the less
Had half impair'd the nameless grace
Which waves in every raven tress
Or softly lightens o'er her face,
Where thoughts serenely sweet express
How pure, how dear their dwelling-place.

And on that cheek and o'er that brow
So soft, so calm, yet eloquent,
The smiles that win, the tints that glow
But tell of days in goodness spent,—
A mind at peace with all below
A heart whose love is innocent.

LORD BYRON.

174

She was a phantom of delight
When first she gleam'd upon my sight;
A lovely apparition, sent
To be a moment's ornament;
Her eyes as stars of twilight fair;
Like Twilight's, too, her dusky hair;
But all things else about her drawn
From May-time and the cheerful dawn;
A dancing shape, an image gay,
To haunt, to startle, and waylay.

I saw her upon nearer view,
A spirit, yet a woman too!
Her household motions light and free,
And steps of virgin-liberty;
A countenance in which did meet
Sweet records, promises as sweet;
A creature not too bright or good
For human nature's daily food,
For transient sorrows, simple wiles,
Praise, blame, love, kisses, tears, and smiles.

And now I see with eye serene
The very pulse of the machine;

A being breathing thoughtful breath,
A traveller between life and death :
The reason firm, the temperate will,
Endurance, foresight, strength, and skill ;
A perfect, woman, nobly plann'd
To warn, to comfort, and command ;
And yet a Spirit still, and bright
With something of an angel-light.

                              W. WORDSWORTH.

175

She is not fair to outward view
    As many maidens be :
Her loveliness I never knew
    Until she smiled on me.
O then I saw her eye was bright,
A well of love, a spring of light.

But now her looks are coy and cold,
    To mine they ne'er reply,
And yet I cease not to behold
    The love-light in her eye :
Her very frowns are fairer far
Than smiles of other maidens are.

                              H. COLERIDGE.

176

I fear thy kisses, gentle maiden ;
Thou needest not fear mine ;
My spirit is too deeply laden
Ever to burthen thine

I fear thy mien, thy tones, thy motion ;
Thou needest not fear mine ;
Innocent is the heart's devotion
With which I worship thine.

                              P. B. SHELLEY.

177. THE LOST LOVE

She dwelt among the untrodden ways
  Beside the springs of Dove ;
A maid whom there were none to praise,
  And very few to love.

A violet by a mossy stone
  Half-hidden from the eye !
—Fair as a star, when only one
  Is shining in the sky.

She lived unknown, and few could know
When Lucy ceased to be ;
But she is in her grave, and O !
  The difference to me !

W. WORDSWORTH.

178

I travell'd among unknown men
  In lands beyond the sea ;
Nor, England ! did I know till then
  What love I bore to thee

'Tis past, that melancholy dream !
  Nor will I quit thy shore
A second time, for still I seem
  To love thee more and more.

Among thy mountains did I feel
  The joy of my desire ;
And she I cherish'd turn'd her wheel
  Beside an English fire.

Thy mornings show'd, thy nights conceal'd
  The bowers where Lucy play'd ;
And thine too is the last green field
  That Lucy's eyes survey'd.

W. WORDSWORTH.

179. THE EDUCATION OF NATURE

Three years she grew in sun and shower ;
Then Nature said, " A lovelier flower
On earth was never sown :
This child I to myself will take ;
She shall be mine, and I will make
A lady of my own.

" Myself will to my darling be
Both law and impulse : and with me
The girl, in rock and plain
In earth and heaven, in glade and bower
Shall feel an overseeing power
To kindle or restrain.

" She shall be sportive as the fawn
That wild with glee across the lawn
Or up the mountain springs ;
And hers shall be the breathing balm,
And hers the silence and the calm
Of mute insensate things.

" The floating clouds their state shall lend
To her ; for her the willow bend ;
Nor shall she fail to see
E'en in the motions of the storm
Grace that shall mould the maiden's form
By silent sympathy.

" The stars of midnight shall be dear
To her ; and she shall lean her ear
In many a secret place
Where rivulets dance their wayward round,
And beauty born of murmuring sound
Shall pass into her face.

" And vital feelings of delight
Shall rear her form to stately height,
Her virgin bosom swell ;
Such thoughts to Lucy I will give
While she and I together live
Here in this happy dell."

Thus Nature spake—The work was done—
How soon my Lucy's race was run !
She died, and left to me
This heath, this calm and quiet scene ;
The memory of what has been,
And never more will be.
                              W. WORDSWORTH.

180

A slumber did my spirit seal ;
  I had no human fears :
She seem'd a thing that could not feel
  The touch of earthly years.

No motion has she now, no force ;
  She neither hears nor sees ;
Roll'd round in earth's diurnal course
  With rocks, and stones, and trees !
                              W. WORDSWORTH.

181. LORD ULLIN'S DAUGHTER

A Chieftain to the Highlands bound
Cries " Boatman, do not tarry !
And I'll give thee a silver pound
To row us o'er the ferry ! "

" Now who be ye, would cross Lochgyle
This dark and stormy water ? "
" O I'm the chief of Ulva's isle,
And this, Lord Ullin's daughter.

" And fast before her father's men
Three days we've fled together,
For should he find us in the glen,
My blood would stain the heather.

" His horsemen hard behind us ride—
Should they our steps discover,
Then who will cheer my bonny bride
When they have slain her lover ? "

Out spoke the hardy Highland wight
" I'll go, my chief, I'm ready :
It is not for your silver bright,
But for your winsome lady :—

" And by my word ! the bonny bird
In danger shall not tarry ;
So though the waves are raging white
I'll row you o'er the ferry."

By this the storm grew loud apace,
The water-wraith was shrieking ;
And in the scowl of heaven each face
Grew dark as they were speaking.

But still as wilder blew the wind
And as the night grew drearer,
Adown the glen rode arméd men,
Their trampling sounded nearer.

" O haste thee, haste ! " the lady cries,
" Though tempests round us gather ;
I'll meet the raging of the skies,
But not an angry father."

The boat has left a stormy land,
A stormy sea before her,—
When, O ! too strong for human hand
The tempest gather'd o'er her.

And still they row'd amidst the roar
Of waters fast prevailing :
Lord Ullin reach'd that fatal shore,—
His wrath was changed to wailing.

For, sore dismay'd, through storm and shade
His child he did discover :—
One lovely hand she stretch'd for aid,
And one was round her lover.

" Come back ! come back ! " he cried in grief,
" Across this stormy water :
And I'll forgive your Highland chief,
My daughter !—O my daughter ! "

'Twas vain : the loud waves lash'd the shore,
Return or aid preventing :
The waters wild went o'er his child,
And he was left lamenting.

T. CAMPBELL.

182. JOCK O' HAZELDEAN

" Why weep ye by the tide, ladie ?
   Why weep ye by the tide ?
I'll wed ye to my youngest son,
   And ye sall he his bride :
And ye sall be his bride, ladie,
   Sae comely to be seen "—
But aye she loot the tears doon fa'
   For Jock o' Hazeldean.

" Now let this wilfu' grief be done,
   And dry that cheek so pale ;
Young Frank is chief of Errington
   And lord of Langley-dale ;
His step is first in peaceful ha',
   His sword in battle keen "—
But aye she loot the tears down fa'
   For Jock o' Hazeldean.

" A chain of gold ye sall not lack,
   Nor braid to bind your hair,
Nor mettled hound, nor managed hawk
   Nor palfrey fresh and fair ;
And you the foremost o' them a'
   Shall ride our forest queen "—
But aye she loot the tears down fa'
   For Jock o' Hazeldean.

The kirk was deck'd at morning-tide,
   The tapers glimmer'd fair ;
The priest and bridegroom wait the bride,
   And dame and knight are there :
They sought her baith by bower and ha' ;
   The ladie was not seen !
She's o'er the Border, and awa'
   Wi' Jock o' Hazeldean.

SIR W. SCOTT.

183. FREEDOM AND LOVE

How delicious is the winning
Of a kiss at love's beginning,
When two mutual hearts are sighing
For the knot there's no untying !

Yet remember, 'midst your wooing,
Love has bliss, but Love has ruing ;
Other smiles may make you fickle,
Tears for other charms may trickle.

Love he comes, and Love he tarries,
Just as fate or fancy carries ;
Longest stays, when sorest chidden ;
Laughs and flies, when press'd and bidden.

Bind the sea to slumber stilly,
Bind its odour to the lily,
Bind the aspen ne'er to quiver,
Then bind Love to last for ever.

Love's a fire that needs renewal
Of fresh beauty for its fuel :
Love's wing moults when caged and captured,
Only free, he soars enraptured.

Can you keep the bee from ranging
Or the ringdove's neck from changing ?
No ! nor fetter'd Love from dying
In the knot there's no untying.

T. CAMPBELL.

184. LOVE'S PHILOSOPHY

The fountains mingle with the river
And the rivers with the ocean,
The winds of heaven mix for ever
With a sweet emotion ;
Nothing in the world is single,
All things by a law divine
In one another's being mingle—
Why not I with thine ?

See the mountains kiss high heaven
And the waves clasp one another;
No sister-flower would be forgiven
If it disdain'd its brother:
And the sunlight clasps the earth,
And the moonbeams kiss the sea—
What are all these kissings worth,
If thou kiss not me?

P. B. SHELLEY.

185. ECHOES

How sweet the answer Echo makes
To Music at night
When, roused by lute or horn, she wakes,
And far away o'er lawns and lakes
Goes answering light!

Yet Love hath echoes truer far
And far more sweet
Than e'er, beneath the moonlight's star,
Of horn or lute or soft guitar
The songs repeat.

'Tis when the sigh,—in youth sincere
And only then,
The sigh that's breathed for one to hear—
Is by that one, that only Dear
Breathed back again.—

T. MOORE.

186. A SERENADE

Ah! County Guy, the hour is nigh,
    The sun has left the lea,
The orange-flower perfumes the bower,
    The breeze is on the sea.
The lark, his lay who trill'd all day,
    Sits hush'd his partner nigh;
Breeze, bird, and flower confess the hour,
    But where is County Guy?

The village maid steals through the shade
    Her shepherd's suit to hear;

To Beauty shy, by lattice high,
  Sings high-born Cavalier.
The star of Love, all stars above,
  Now reigns o'er earth and sky,
And high and low the influence know—
  But where is County Guy?

SIR W. SCOTT.

187. TO THE EVENING STAR

Gem of the crimson-colour'd Even,
Companion of retiring day,
Why at the closing gates of heaven,
Beloved Star, dost thou delay?

So fair thy pensile beauty burns
When soft the tear of twilight flows
So due thy plighted love returns
To chambers brighter than the rose;

To Peace, to Pleasure, and to Love
So kind a star thou seem'st to be,
Sure some enamour'd orb above
Descends and burns to meet with thee.

Thine is the breathing, blushing hour
When all unheavenly passions fly,
Chased by the soul-subduing power
Of Love's delicious witchery.

O! sacred to the fall of day
Queen of propitious stars, appear
And early rise, and long delay
When Caroline herself is here

Shine on her chosen green resort
Whose trees the sunward summit crown,
And wanton flowers, that well may court
An angel's feet to tread them down:—

Shine on her sweetly scented road
Thou star of evening's purple dome,
That lead'st the nightingale abroad,
And guid'st the pilgrim to his home.

Shine where my charmer's sweeter breath
Embalms the soft exhaling dew,
Where dying winds a sigh bequeath
To kiss the cheek of rosy hue :—

Where, winnow'd by the gentle air,
Her silken tresses darkly flow
And fall upon her brow so fair,
Like shadows on the mountain snow.

Thus, ever thus, at day's decline
In converse sweet to wander far—
O bring with thee my Caroline,
And thou shalt be my Ruling Star !

T. CAMPBELL.

188. TO THE NIGHT

Swiftly walk over the western wave,
        Spirit of Night !
Out of the misty eastern cave
Where all the long and lone daylight
Thou wovest dreams of joy and fear
Which make thee terrible and dear,—
        Swift be thy flight !

Wrap thy form in a mantle gray
        Star-inwrought !
Blind with thine hair the eyes of day,
Kiss her until she be wearied out,
Then wander o'er city, and sea, and land
Touching all with thine opiate wand—
        Come, long-sought !

When I arose and saw the dawn,
        I sigh'd for thee ;
When light rode high, and the dew was gone,
And noon lay heavy on flower and tree,
And the weary Day turn'd to his rest
Lingering like an unloved guest,
        I sigh'd for thee.

Thy brother Death came, and cried
        Wouldst thou me ?

Thy sweet child Sleep, the filmy-eyed,
　　Murmur'd like a noon-tide bee
Shall I nestle near thy side ?
Wouldst thou me ?—And I replied
　　　　No, not thee !

Death will come when thou art dead,
　　　　Soon, too soon—
Sleep will come when thou art fled ;
Of neither would I ask the boon
I ask of thee, belovéd Night—
Swift be thine approaching flight,
　　　　Come soon, soon !

　　　　　　　　　　　P. B. SHELLEY.

189. TO A DISTANT FRIEND

Why art thou silent ? Is thy love a plant
Of such weak fibre that the treacherous air
Of absence withers what was once so fair ?
Is there no debt to pay, no boon to grant ?

Yet have my thoughts for thee been vigilant,
Bound to thy service with unceasing care—
The mind's least generous wish a mendicant
For nought but what thy happiness could spare.

Speak !—though this soft warm heart, once free to hold
A thousand tender pleasures, thine and mine,
Be left more desolate, more dreary cold
Than a forsaken bird's-nest fill'd with snow
'Mid its own bush of leafless eglantine—
Speak, that my torturing doubts their end may know !

　　　　　　　　　　　W. WORDSWORTH.

190

When we two parted
In silence and tears,
Half broken-hearted,
To sever for years,
Pale grew thy cheek and cold,

Colder thy kiss;
Truly that hour foretold
Sorrow to this!

The dew of the morning
Sunk chill on my brow;
It felt like the warning
Of what I feel now.
Thy vows are all broken,
And light is thy fame:
I hear thy name spoken
And share in its shame.

They name thee before me,
A knell to mine ear;
A shudder comes o'er me—
Why wert thou so dear?
They know not I knew thee
Who knew thee too well:
Long, long shall I rue thee
Too deeply to tell.

In secret we met:
In silence I grieve
That thy heart could forget,
Thy spirit deceive.
If I should meet thee
After long years,
How should I greet thee?—
With silence and tears.

LORD BYRON.

191. HAPPY INSENSIBILITY

In a drear-nighted December
Too happy, happy Tree
Thy branches ne'er remember
Their green felicity:
The north cannot undo them
With a sleety whistle through them,
Nor frozen thawings glue them
From budding at the prime.

In a drear-nighted December
Too happy, happy Brook
Thy bubblings ne'er remember
Apollo's summer look ;
But with a sweet forgetting
They stay their crystal fretting,
Never, never petting
About the frozen time.

Ah would 'twere so with many
A gentle girl and boy !
But were there ever any
Writhed not at passéd joy ?
To know the change and feel it,
When there is none to heal it
Nor numbéd sense to steal it—
Was never said in rhyme.

                                        J. KEATS.

192

Where shall the lover rest
    Whom the fates sever
From his true maiden's breast
    Parted for ever ?
Where, through groves deep and high
    Sounds the far billow,
Where early violets die
    Under the willow.
        Eleu loro
    Soft shall be his pillow.

There, through the summer day
    Cool streams are laving :
There, while the tempests sway,
    Scarce are boughs waving ;
There thy rest shalt thou take,
    Parted for ever,
Never again to wake
    Never, O never !
        Eleu loro
    Never, O never !

Where shall the traitor rest,
  He, the deceiver,
Who could win maiden's breast,
  Ruin, and leave her?
In the lost battle,
  Borne down by the flying,
Where mingles war's rattle
  With groans of the dying;
    Eleu loro
There shall he be lying.

Her wing shall the eagle flap
  O'er the falsehearted;
His warm blood the wolf shall lap
  Ere life be parted:
Shame and dishonour sit
  By his grave ever;
Blessing shall hallow it
  Never, O never!
    Eleu loro
  Never, O never!

SIR W. SCOTT.

193. LA BELLE DAME SANS MERCI

" O what can ail thee, knight-at-arms,
  Alone and palely loitering?
The sedge has wither'd from the lake,
  And no birds sing.

" O what can ail thee, knight-at-arms,
  So haggard and so woe-begone?
The squirrel's granary is full,
  And the harvest's done.

" I see a lily on thy brow
  With anguish moist and fever-dew,
And on thy cheeks a fading rose
  Fast withereth too."

" I met a lady in the meads,
  Full beautiful—a faery's child,
Her hair was long, her foot was light,
  And her eyes were wild.

" I made a garland for her head,
    And bracelets too, and fragrant zone ;
She look'd at me as she did love,
    And made sweet moan.

" I set her on my pacing steed
    And nothing else saw all day long,
For sidelong would she bend, and sing
    A faery's song.

" She found me roots of relish sweet,
    And honey wild and manna-dew,
And sure in language strange she said
    ' I love thee true.'

" She took me to her elfin grot,
    And there she wept, and sigh'd full sore,
And there I shut her wild wild eyes
    With kisses four.

" And there she lulléd me asleep,
    And there I dream'd—Ah ! woe betide !
The latest dream I ever dream'd
    On the cold hill's side.

" I saw pale kings and princes too,
    Pale warriors, death-pale were they all ;
They cried—' La belle Dame sans Merci
    Hath thee in thrall ! '

" I saw their starved lips in the gloam
    With horrid warning gapéd wide,
And I awoke and found me here
    On the cold hill's side.

" And this is why I sojourn here
    Alone and palely loitering,
Though the sedge is wither'd from the lake
    And no birds sing."

                                        J. KEATS.

194. THE ROVER

" A weary lot is thine, fair maid,
    A weary lot is thine !

To pull the thorn thy brow to braid,
  And press the rue for wine.
A lightsome eye, a soldier's mien,
  A feather of the blue,
A doublet of the Lincoln green—
  No more of me you knew
      My Love!
No more of me you knew.

" The morn is merry June, I trow,
  The rose is budding fain;
But she shall bloom in winter snow
  Ere we two meet again."
He turn'd his charger as he spake
  Upon the river shore,
He gave the bridle-reins a shake,
  Said " Adieu for evermore
      My Love!
And adieu for evermore."

SIR W. SCOTT.

195. THE FLIGHT OF LOVE

When the lamp is shatter'd
The light in the dust lies dead—
When the cloud is scatter'd,
The rainbow's glory is shed.
When the lute is broken,
Sweet tones are remember'd not;
When the lips have spoken,
Loved accents are soon forgot.

As music and splendour
Survive not the lamp and the lute,
The heart's echoes render
No song when the spirit is mute—
No song but sad dirges,
Like the wind through a ruin'd cell,
Or the mournful surges
That ring the dead seaman's knell.

When hearts have once mingled,
Love first leaves the well-built nest;

The weak one is singled
To endure what it once possesst.
O Love ! who bewailest
The frailty of all things here,
Why choose you the frailest
For your cradle, your home, and your bier ?

Its passions will rock thee
As the storms rock the ravens on high ;
Bright reason will mock thee
Like the sun from a wintry sky.
From thy nest every rafter
Will rot, and thine eagle home
Leave thee naked to laughter,
When leaves fall and cold winds come.

P. B. SHELLEY.

196. THE MAID OF NEIDPATH

O lovers' eyes are sharp to see,
  And lovers' ears in hearing ;
And love, in life's extremity
  Can lend an hour of cheering.
Disease had been in Mary's bower
  And slow decay from mourning,
Though now she sits on Neidpath's tower
  To watch her Love's returning.

All sunk and dim her eyes so bright,
  Her form decay'd by pining,
Till through her wasted hand, at night,
  You saw the taper shining.
By fits a sultry hectic hue
  Across her cheek was flying ;
By fits so ashy pale she grew
  Her maidens thought her dying.

Yet keenest powers to see and hear
  Seem'd in her frame residing ;
Before the watch-dog prick'd his ear
  She heard her lover's riding ;
Ere scarce a distant form was kenn'd
  She knew and waved to greet him,
And o'er the battlement did bend
  As on the wing to meet him.

He came—he pass'd—an heedless gaze
    As o'er some stranger glancing ;
Her welcome, spoke in faltering phrase,
    Lost in his courser's prancing—
The castle-arch, whose hollow tone
    Returns each whisper spoken,
Could scarcely catch the feeble moan
    Which told her heart was broken.

Sir W. Scott.

197. THE MAID OF NEIDPATH

Earl March look'd on his dying child,
    And smit with grief to view her—
The youth, he cried, whom I exiled
    Shall be restored to woo her.

She's at the window many an hour
    His coming to discover :
And he look'd up to Ellen's bower
    And she look'd on her lover—

But ah ! so pale, he knew her not,
    Though her smile on him was dwelling—
And am I then forgot—forgot ?
    It broke the heart of Ellen.

In vain he weeps, in vain he sighs,
    Her cheek is cold as ashes ;
Nor love's own kiss shall wake those eyes
    To lift their silken lashes.

T. Campbell.

198

Bright Star ! would I were steadfast as thou art—
Not in lone splendour hung aloft the night,
And watching, with eternal lids apart,
Like nature's patient sleepless Eremite,

The moving waters at their priestlike task
Of pure ablution round earth's human shores,
Or gazing on the new soft fallen mask
Of snow upon the mountains and the moors :—

No—yet still steadfast, still unchangeable,
Pillow'd upon my fair Love's ripening breast
To feel for ever its soft fall and swell,
Awake for ever in a sweet unrest ;

Still, still to hear her tender-taken breath,
And so live ever,—or else swoon to death.

J. KEATS.

199. THE TERROR OF DEATH

When I have fears that I may cease to be
Before my pen has glean'd my teeming brain,
Before high-pilèd books, in charact'ry
Hold like rich garners the full-ripen'd grain ;

When I behold, upon the night's starr'd face,
Huge cloudy symbols of a high romance,
And think that I may never live to trace
Their shadows, with the magic hand of chance ;

And when I feel, fair Creature of an hour !
That I shall never look upon thee more,
Never have relish in the fairy power
Of unreflecting love—then on the shore

Of the wide world I stand alone, and think
Till Love and Fame to nothingness do sink.

J. KEATS.

200. DESIDERIA

Surprised by joy—impatient as the wind—
I turn'd to share the transport—Oh, with whom
But Thee—deep buried in the silent tomb,
That spot which no vicissitude can find ?

Love, faithful love recall'd thee to my mind—
But how could I forget thee ? Through what power
Even for the least division of an hour
Have I been so beguiled as to be blind

To my most grievous loss ?—That thought's return
Was the worst pang that sorrow ever bore
Save one, one only, when I stood forlorn,

Knowing my heart's best treasure was no more ;
That neither present time, nor years unborn
Could to my sight that heavenly face restore.

W. WORDSWORTH.

201

At the mid hour of night, when stars are weeping, I fly
To the lone vale we loved, when life shone warm in thine
    eye ;
And I think oft, if spirits can steal from the regions of air
To revisit past scenes of delight, thou wilt come to me there
And tell me our love is remember'd, even in the sky !

Then I sing the wild song it once was rapture to hear
When our voices, commingling, breathed like one on the
    ear ;
And as Echo far off through the vale my sad orison rolls,
I think, O my Love ! 'tis thy voice, from the Kingdom of
    Souls
Faintly answering still the notes that once were so dear.

T. MOORE.

202. ELEGY ON THYRZA

And thou art dead, as young and fair
    As aught of mortal birth ;
And forms so soft and charms so rare
    Too soon return'd to Earth !
Though Earth received them in her bed,
And o'er the spot the crowd may tread
    In carelessness or mirth,
There is an eye which could not brook
A moment on that grave to look.

I will not ask where thou liest low
Nor gaze upon the spot ;
There flowers or weeds at will may grow
So I behold them not :
It is enough for me to prove
That what I loved and long must love
    Like common earth can rot ;
To me there needs no stone to tell
'Tis Nothing that I loved so well.

Yet did I love thee to the last,
  As fervently as thou
Who didst not change through all the past
  And canst not alter now.
The love where Death has set his seal
Nor age can chill, nor rival steal,
  Nor falsehood disavow :
And, what were worse, thou canst not see
Or wrong, or change, or fault in me.

The better days of life were ours ;
  The worst can be but mine :
The sun that cheers, the storm that lours
  Shall never more be thine.
The silence of that dreamless sleep
I envy now too much to weep ;
  Nor need I to repine
That all those charms have pass'd away
I might have watch'd through long decay.

The flower in ripen'd bloom unmatch'd
  Must fall the earliest prey ;
Though by no hand untimely snatch'd,
  The leaves must drop away.
And yet it were a greater grief
To watch it withering, leaf by leaf,
  Than see it pluck'd to-day ;
Since earthly eye but ill can bear
To trace the change to foul from fair.

I know not if I could have borne
  To see thy beauties fade ;
The night that follow'd such a morn
  Had worn a deeper shade :
Thy day without a cloud hath past,
And thou wert lovely to the last,
  Extinguish'd, not decay'd ;
As stars that shoot along the sky
Shine brightest as they fall from high.

As once I wept if I could weep,
  My tears might well be shed
To think I was not near, to keep
  One vigil o'er thy bed ;

G.T.   *Where shall the Lover Rest*

"In the lost battle borne down by the flying."

To gaze, how fondly! on thy face,
To fold thee in a faint embrace,
   Uphold thy drooping head;
And show that love, however vain,
Nor thou nor I can feel again.

Yet how much less it were to gain,
   Though thou hast left me free,
The loveliest things that still remain
   Than thus remember thee!
The all of thine that cannot die
Through dark and dread Eternity
   Returns again to me,
And more thy buried love endears
Than aught except its living years.

                 LORD BYRON.

203

One word is too often profaned
   For me to profane it,
One feeling too falsely disdain'd
   For thee to disdain it.
One hope is too like despair
   For prudence to smother,
And Pity from thee more dear
   Than that from another.

I can give not what men call love;
   But wilt thou accept not
The worship the heart lifts above
   And the Heavens reject not:
The desire of the moth for the star,
   Of the night for the morrow,
The devotion to something afar
   From the sphere of our sorrow?

                 P. B. SHELLEY.

204. GATHERING SONG OF DONALD THE BLACK

    Pibroch of Donuil Dhu
     Pibroch of Donuil

Wake thy wild voice anew,
  Summon Clan Conuil.
Come away, come away,
  Hark to the summons !
Come in your war-array,
  Gentles and commons.

Come from deep glen, and
  From mountain so rocky ;
The war-pipe and pennon
  Are at Inverlochy.
Come every hill-plaid, and
  True heart that wears one,
Come every steel blade, and
Strong hand that bears one.

Leave untended the herd,
  The flock without shelter ;
Leave the corpse uninterr'd,
  The bride at the altar ;
Leave the deer, leave the steer
  Leave nets and barges :
Come with your fighting gear,
  Broadswords and targes.

Come as the winds come, when
  Forests are rended,
Come as the waves come, when
  Navies are stranded :
Faster come, faster come,
  Faster and faster,
Chief, vassal, page and groom,
  Tenant and master.

Fast they come, fast they come ;
  See how they gather !
Wide waves the eagle plume
  Blended with heather.
Cast your plaids, draw your blades,
  Forward each man set !
Pibroch of Donuil Dhu
  Knell for the onset !

Sir W. Scott.

205

A wet sheet and a flowing sea
　A wind that follows fast
And fills the white and rustling sail
　And bends the gallant mast ;
And bends the gallant mast, my boys
　While like the eagle free
Away the good ship flies, and leaves
　Old England on the lee.

O for a soft and gentle wind !
　I heard a fair one cry :
But give to me the snoring breeze
　And white waves heaving high ;
And white waves heaving high, my lads,
　The good ship tight and free—
The world of waters is our home,
　And merry men are we.

There's tempest in yon hornéd moon,
　And lightning in yon cloud ;
But hark the music, mariners !
　The wind is piping loud ;
The wind is piping loud, my boys,
　The lightning flashes free—
While the hollow oak our palace is,
　Our heritage the sea.

A. CUNNINGHAM.

206

Ye Mariners of England
That guard our native seas !
Whose flag has braved, a thousand years,
The battle and the breeze !
Your glorious standard launch again
To match another foe :
And sweep through the deep,
While the stormy winds do blow ;
While the battle rages loud and long
And the stormy winds do blow.

The spirits of your fathers
Shall start from every wave—
For the deck it was their field of fame,
And Ocean was their grave :
Where Blake and mighty Nelson fell
Your manly hearts shall glow,
As ye sweep through the deep,
While the stormy winds do blow ;
While the battle rages loud and long
And the stormy winds do blow.

Britannia needs no bulwarks,
No towers along the steep ;
Her march is o'er the mountain waves,
Her home is on the deep.
With thunders from her native oak
She quells the floods below—
As they roar on the shore,
When the stormy winds do blow ;
When the battle rages loud and long
And the stormy winds do blow.

The meteor flag of England
Shall yet terrific burn ;
Till danger's troubled night depart
And the star of peace return.
Then, then, ye ocean-warriors !
Our song and feast shall flow
To the fame of your name,
When the storm has ceased to blow ;
When the fiery fight is heard no more,
And the storm has ceased to blow.

T. CAMPBELL.

207. BATTLE OF THE BALTIC

Of Nelson and the North
Sing the glorious day's renown
When to battle fierce came forth
All the might of Denmark's crown,
And her arms along the deep proudly shone ;
By each gun the lighted brand
In a bold determined hand,
And the Prince of all the land
Led them on.

Like leviathans afloat
Lay their bulwarks on the brine ;
While the sign of battle flew
On the lofty British line :
It was ten of April morn by the chime :
As they drifted on their path
There was silence deep as death ,
And the boldest held his breath
For a time.

But the might of England flush'd
To anticipate the scene ;
And her van the fleeter rush'd
O'er the deadly space between
" Hearts of oak ! " our captains cried, when each gun
From its adamantine lips
Spread a death-shade round the ships,
Like the hurricane eclipse
Of the sun.

Again ! again ! again !
And the havoc did not slack,
Till a feeble cheer the Dane
To our cheering sent us back ;—
Their shots along the deep slowly boom :—
Then ceased—and all is wail,
As they strike the shatter'd sail ;
Or in conflagration pale
Light the gloom.

Out spoke the victor then
As he hail'd them o'er the wave,
" Ye are brothers ! ye are men !
And we conquer but to save :—
So peace instead of death let us bring :
But yield, proud foe, thy fleet
With the crews, at England's feet,
And make submission meet
To our King."

Then Denmark blest our chief
That he gave her wounds repose ;
And the sounds of joy and grief
From her people wildly rose,

As death withdrew his shades from the day :
While the sun look'd smiling bright
O'er a wide and woeful sight,
Where the fires of funeral light
Died away.

Now joy, old England, raise !
For the tidings of thy might,
By the festal cities' blaze,
Whilst the wine-cup shines in light ;
And yet amidst that joy and uproar,
Let us think of them that sleep
Full many a fathom deep
By thy wild and stormy steep,
Elsinore !

Brave hearts ! to Britain's pride
Once so faithful and so true,
On the deck of fame that died
With the gallant good Riou :
Soft sigh the winds of heaven o'er their grave !
While the billow mournful rolls
And the mermaid's song condoles
Singing glory to the souls
Of the brave !

T. CAMPBELL.

208. ODE TO DUTY

Stern Daughter of the voice of God !
O Duty ! if that name thou love
Who art a light to guide, a rod
To check the erring, and reprove ;
Thou who art victory and law
With empty terrors overawe ;
From vain temptations dost set free,
And calm'st the weary strife of frail humanity !

There are who ask not if thine eye
Be on them ; who, in love and truth
Where no misgiving is, rely
Upon the genial sense of youth :
Glad hearts ! without reproach or blot,
Who do thy work, and know it not :

Oh ! if through confidence misplaced
They fail, thy saving arms, dread Power ! around them
    cast.

Serene will be our days and bright
And happy will our nature be
When love is an unerring light,
And joy its own security.
And they a blissful course may hold
Ev'n now who, not unwisely bold,
Yet find that other strength, according to their need.

I, loving freedom, and untried,
No sport of every random gust,
Yet being to myself a guide,
Too blindly have reposed my trust :
And oft, when in my heart was heard
Thy timely mandate, I deferr'd
The task, in smoother walks to stray ;
But thee I now would serve more strictly, if I may.

Through no disturbance of my soul
Or strong compunction in me wrought,
I supplicate for thy controul,
But in the quietness of thought :
Me this uncharter'd freedom tires ;
I feel the weight of chance desires :
My hopes no more must change their name ;
I long for a repose which ever is the same.

Stern lawgiver ! yet thou dost wear
The Godhead's most benignant grace ;
Nor know we anything so fair
As is the smile upon thy face :
Flowers laugh before thee on their beds,
And fragrance in thy footing treads ;
Thou dost preserve the Stars from wrong ;
And the most ancient Heavens, through thee, are fresh
    and strong.

To humbler functions, awful Power !
I call thee : I myself commend
Unto thy guidance from this hour ;
O let my weakness have an end !

Give unto me, made lowly wise,
The spirit of self-sacrifice ;
The confidence of reason give ;
And in the light of Truth thy bondman let me live.
W. WORDSWORTH.

209. ON THE CASTLE OF CHILLON

Eternal Spirit of the chainless Mind !
Brightest in dungeons, Liberty, thou art—
For there thy habitation is the heart—
The heart which love of Thee alone can bind ;

And when thy sons to fetters are consign'd,
To fetters, and the damp vault's dayless gloom,
Their country conquers with their martyrdom
And Freedom's fame finds wings on every wind.

Chillon ! thy prison is a holy place
And thy sad floor an altar, for 'twas trod,
Until his very steps have left a trace

Worn as if thy cold pavement were a sod,
By Bonnivard ! May none those marks efface !
For they appeal from tyranny to God.
LORD BYRON.

210. ENGLAND AND SWITZERLAND
1802

Two Voices are there ; one is of the Sea,
One of the Mountains ; each a mighty voice :
In both from age to age thou didst rejoice,
They were thy chosen music, Liberty !

There came a tyrant, and with holy glee
Thou fought'st against him,—but hast vainly striven :
Thou from thy Alpine holds at length art driven
Where not a torrent murmurs heard by thee.

—Of one deep bliss thine ear hath been bereft ;
Then cleave, O cleave to that which still is left—
For, high-soul'd Maid, what sorrow would it be

That Mountain floods should thunder as before,
And Ocean bellow from his rocky shore,
And neither awful Voice be heard by Thee !
                                        W. WORDSWORTH.

211. ON THE EXTINCTION OF THE VENETIAN REPUBLIC

Once did She hold the gorgeous East in fee
And was the safeguard of the West ; the worth
Of Venice did not fall below her birth,
Venice, the eldest child of liberty.

She was a maiden city, bright and free ;
No guile seduced, no force could violate ;
And when she took unto herself a mate,
She must espouse the everlasting Sea.

And what if she had seen those glories fade,
Those titles vanish, and that strength decay,—
Yet shall some tribute of regret be paid

When her long life hath reach'd its final day :
Men are we, and must grieve when even the shade
Of that which once was great has pass'd away.
                                        W. WORDSWORTH.

212. LONDON, MDCCCII

O friend ! I know not which way I must look
For comfort, being, as I am, opprest
To think that now our life is only drest
For show ; mean handiwork of craftsman, cook,

Or groom !—We must run glittering like a brook
In the open sunshine, or we are unblest ;
The wealthiest man among us is the best :
No grandeur now in Nature or in book

Delights us. Rapine, avarice, expense,
This is idolatry ; and these we adore :
Plain living and high thinking are no more :

The homely beauty of the good old cause
Is gone ; our peace, our fearful innocence,
And pure religion breathing household laws.

W. WORDSWORTH.

213. THE SAME

Milton ! thou shouldest be living at this hour :
England hath need of thee : she is a fen
Of stagnant waters : altar, sword, and pen,
Fireside, the heroic wealth of hall and bower,

Have forfeited their ancient English dower
Of inward happiness. We are selfish men :
O ! raise us up, return to us again ;
And give us manners, virtue, freedom, power.

Thy soul was like a Star, and dwelt apart :
Thou hadst a voice whose sound was like the sea,
Pure as the naked heavens, majestic, free ;

So didst thou travel on life's common way
In cheerful godliness ; and yet thy heart
The lowliest duties on herself did lay.

W. WORDSWORTH.

214

When I have borne in memory what has tamed
Great nations ; how ennobling thoughts depart
When men change swords for ledgers, and desert
The student's bower for gold,—some fears unnamed

I had, my Country !—am I to be blamed ?
But when I think of thee, and what thou art,
Verily, in the bottom of my heart
Of those unfilial fears I am ashamed.

For dearly must we prize thee ; we who find
In thee a bulwark of the cause of men ;
And I by my affection was beguiled :

What wonder if a Poet now and then,
Among the many movements of his mind,
Felt for thee as a lover or a child !

W. WORDSWORTH.

215. HOHENLINDEN

On Linden, when the sun was low,
All bloodless lay the untrodden snow;
And dark as winter was the flow
    Of Iser, rolling rapidly.

But Linden saw another sight,
When the drum beat at dead of night
Commanding fires of death to light
    The darkness of her scenery.

By torch and trumpet fast array'd
Each horseman drew his battle blade,
And furious every charger neigh'd
    To join the dreadful revelry.

Then shook the hills with thunder riven;
Then rush'd the steed, to battle driven
And louder than the bolts of Heaven
    Far flash'd the red artillery.

But redder yet that light shall glow
On Linden's hills of stainéd snow;
And bloodier yet the torrent flow
    Of Iser, rolling rapidly.

'Tis morn; but scarce yon level sun
Can pierce the war-clouds, rolling dun,
Where furious Frank and fiery Hun
    Shout in their sulphurous canopy.

The combat deepens. On, ye Brave
Who rush to glory, or the grave!
Wave, Munich, all thy banners wave,
    And charge with all thy chivalry!

Few, few shall part, where many meet!
The snow shall be their winding-sheet,
And every turf beneath their feet
    Shall be a soldier's sepulchre.

                    T. CAMPBELL.

216. AFTER BLENHEIM

It was a summer evening,
  Old Kaspar's work was done,
And he before his cottage door
  Was sitting in the sun ;
And by him sported on the green
His little grandchild Wilhelmine.

She saw her brother Peterkin
  Roll something large and round
Which he beside the rivulet
  In playing there had found ;
He came to ask what he had found
That was so large and smooth and round

Old Kaspar took it from the boy
  Who stood expectant by ;
And then the old man shook his head,
  And with a natural sigh
" 'Tis some poor fellow's skull," said he,
  " Who fell in the great victory.

" I find them in the garden,
  For there's many here about ;
And oft when I go to plough
  The ploughshare turns them out.
For many thousand men," said he,
  " Were slain in that great victory."

" Now tell us what 'twas all about,"
  Young Peterkin he cries ;
And little Wilhelmine looks up
  With wonder-waiting eyes ;
" Now tell us all about the war,
  And what they fought each other for."

" It was the English," Kaspar cried,
  " Who put the French to rout ;
But what they fought each other for
  I could not well make out.
But every body said," quoth he,
  " That 'twas a famous victory

" My father lived at Blenheim then,
    Yon little stream hard by ;
They burnt his dwelling to the ground,
    And he was forced to fly :
So with his wife and child he fled,
Nor had he where to rest his head.

" With fire and sword the country round
    Was wasted far and wide,
And many a childing mother then
    And newborn baby died :
But things like that, you know, must be
At every famous victory.

" They say it was a shocking sight
    After the field was won ;
For many thousand bodies here
    Lay rotting in the sun :
But things like that, you know, must be
After a famous victory.

" Great praise the Duke of Marlbro' won
    And our good Prince Eugene " ;
" Why 'twas a very wicked thing ! "
    Said little Wilhelmine ;
" Nay—nay—my little girl," quoth he,
" It was a famous victory.

" And every body praised the Duke
    Who this great fight did win."
" But what good came of it at last ? "
    Quoth little Peterkin :—
" Why that I cannot tell," said he,
" But 'twas a famous victory."

R. SOUTHEY.

217. PRO PATRIA MORI

When he who adores thee has left but the name
    Of his fault and his sorrows behind,
O ! say wilt thou weep, when they darken the fame
    Of a life that for thee was resign'd !

Yes, weep, and however my foes may condemn,
    Thy tears shall efface their decree ;
For, Heaven can witness, though guilty to them,
    I have been but too faithful to thee.

With thee were the dreams of my earliest love ;
    Every thought of my reason was thine :
In my last humble prayer to the Spirit above
    Thy name shall be mingled with mine !
O ! blest are the lovers and friends who shall live
    The days of thy glory to see ;
But the next dearest blessing that Heaven can give
    Is the pride of thus dying for thee.

T. MOORE.

218. THE BURIAL OF SIR JOHN MOORE
AT CORUNNA

Not a drum was heard, not a funeral note,
    As his corpse to the rampart we hurried ;
Not a soldier discharged his farewell shot
    O'er the grave where our hero we buried.

We buried him darkly at dead of night,
    The sods with our bayonets turning ;
By the struggling moonbeam's misty light
    And the lantern dimly burning.

No useless coffin enclosed his breast,
    Not in sheet or in shroud we wound him :
But he lay like a warrior taking his rest,
    With his martial cloak around him.

Few and short were the prayers we said
    And we spoke not a word of sorrow,
But we steadfastly gazed on the face that was dead,
    And we bitterly thought of the morrow.

We thought as we hollow'd his narrow bed
    And smoothed down his lonely pillow,
That the foe and the stranger would tread o'er his head,
And we far away on the billow !

Lightly they'll talk of the spirit that's gone
    And o'er his cold ashes upbraid him,—
But little he'll reck, if they let him sleep on
    In the grave where a Briton has laid him.

But half of our heavy task was done
    When the clock struck the hour for retiring,
And we heard the distant and random gun
    That the foe was sullenly firing.

Slowly and sadly we laid him down,
    From the field of his fame fresh and gory;
We carved not a line, and we raised not a stone—
    But we left him alone with his glory.
                        C. WOLFE.

219. SIMON LEE THE OLD HUNTSMAN

In the sweet shire of Cardigan,
Not far from pleasant Ivor Hall,
An old man dwells, a little man,
I've heard he once was tall.
Full five-and-thirty years he lived
A running huntsman merry;
And still the centre of his cheek
Is red as a ripe cherry.

No man like him the horn could sound,
And hill and valley rang with glee,
When Echo bandied round and round
The halloo of Simon Lee.
In those proud days he little cared
For husbandry or tillage;
To blither tasks did Simon rouse
The sleepers of the village.

He all the country could outrun,
Could leave both man and horse behind;
And often, ere the chase was done,
He reel'd and was stone-blind.
And still there's something in the world
At which his heart rejoices;
For when the chiming hounds are out,
He dearly loves their voices.

But O the heavy change !—bereft
Of health, strength, friends and kindred, see
Old Simon to the world is left
In liveried poverty :
His master's dead, and no one now
Dwells in the Hall of Ivor ;
Men, dogs, and horses, all are dead ;
He is the sole survivor.

And he is lean and he is sick
His body dwindled and awry
Rests upon ankles swoln and thick ;
His legs are thin and dry.
He has no son, he has no child ;
His wife, an aged woman,
Lives with him, near the waterfall,
Upon the village common.

Beside their moss-grown hut of clay,
Not twenty paces from the door,
A scrap of land they have, but they
Are poorest of the poor.
This scrap of land he from the heath
Enclosed when he was stronger :
But what avails the land to them
Which he can till no longer ?

Oft, working by her husband's side,
Ruth does what Simon cannot do ;
For she, with scanty cause for pride,
Is stouter of the two.
And, though you with your utmost skill
From labour could not wean them,
'Tis little, very little, all
That they can do between them

Few months of life has he in store
As he to you will tell,
For still, the more he works, the more
Do his weak ankles swell.
My gentle reader, I perceive
How patiently you've waited,
And now I fear that you expect
Some tale will be related.

O reader ! had you in your mind
Such stores as silent thought can bring,
O gentle reader ! you would find
A tale in everything.
What more I have to say is short,
And you must kindly take it ;
It is no tale ; but, should you think,
Perhaps a tale you'll make it.

One summer-day I chanced to see
This old man doing all he could
To unearth the root of an old tree,
A stump of rotten wood.
The mattock totter'd in his hand ;
So vain was his endeavour
That at the root of the old tree
He might have work'd for ever.

" You're overtask'd, good Simon Lee,
Give me your tool," to him I said ;
And at the word right gladly he
Received my proffer'd aid.
I struck, and with a single blow
The tangled root I sever'd,
At which the poor old man so long
And vainly had endeavour'd.

The tears into his eyes were brought,
And thanks and praises seem'd to run
So fast out of his heart, I thought
They never would have done.
—I've heard of hearts unkind, kind deeds
With coldness still returning ;
Alas ! the gratitude of men
Has oftener left me mourning.

W. WORDSWORTH.

220. THE OLD FAMILIAR FACES

I have had playmates, I have had companions
In my days of childhood, in my joyful school-days ;
All, all, are gone, the old familiar faces.

I have been laughing, I have been carousing,
Drinking late, sitting late, with my bosom cronies ;
All, all are gone, the old familiar faces.

I loved a Love once, fairest among women :
Closed are her doors on me, I must not see her—
All, all are gone, the old familiar faces.

I have a friend, a kinder friend has no man :
Like an ingrate, I left my friend abruptly ;
Left him, to muse on the old familiar faces.

Ghost-like I paced round the haunts of my childhood,
Earth seem'd a desert I was bound to traverse,
Seeking to find the old familiar faces.

Friend of my bosom, thou more than a brother,
Why wert not thou born in my father's dwelling ?
So might we talk of the old familiar faces,

How some they have died, and some they have left me,
And some are taken from me ; all are departed ;
All, all are gone, the old familiar faces.

C. LAMB.

221. THE JOURNEY ONWARDS

As slow our ship her foamy track
    Against the wind was cleaving,
Her trembling pennant still look'd back
    To that dear isle 'twas leaving.
So loth we part from all we love,
    From all the links that bind us ;
So turn our hearts, as on we rove,
    To those we've left behind us !

When, round the bowl, of vanish'd years
    We talk with joyous seeming—
With smiles that might as well be tears,
    So faint, so sad their beaming ;
While memory brings us back again
    Each early tie that twined us,
Oh, sweet's the cup that circles then
    To those we've left behind us !

And when in other climes, we meet
　　Some isle or vale enchanting,
Where all looks flowery wild and sweet,
　　And nought but love is wanting;
We think how great had been our bliss
　　If Heaven had but assign'd us
To live and die in scenes like this,
　　With some we've left behind us!

As travellers oft look back at eve
　　When eastward darkly going,
To gaze upon that light they leave
　　Still faint behind them glowing,—
So, when the close of pleasure's day
　　To gloom hath near consign'd us,
We turn to catch our fading ray
　　Of joy that's left behind us.

T. MOORE.

222. YOUTH AND AGE

There's not a joy the world can give like that it takes away
When the glow of early thought declines in feeling's dull
　　decay;
'Tis not on youth's smooth cheek the blush alone which
　　fades so fast,
But the tender bloom of heart is gone, ere youth itself be
　　past.

Then the few whose spirits float above the wreck of
　　happiness
Are driven o'er the shoals of guilt or ocean of excess:
The magnet of their course is gone, or only points in vain
The shore to which their shiver'd sail shall never stretch
　　again.

Then the mortal coldness of the soul like death itself come
　　down;
It cannot feel for others' woes, it dare not dream its own;
That heavy chill has frozen o'er the fountain of our tears,
And though the eye may sparkle still, 'tis where the ice
　　appears.

Though wit may flash from fluent lips, and mirth distract
　　the breast,
Through midnight hours that yield no more their former
　　hope of rest;

'Tis but as ivy-leaves around the ruin'd turret wreathe,
All green and wildly fresh without, but worn and gray
    beneath.

O could I feel as I have felt, or be what I have been,
Or weep as I could once have wept o'er many a vanish'd
    scene,—
As springs in deserts found seem sweet, all brackish though
    they be,
So midst the wither'd waste of life, those tears would flow
    to me !

                 LORD BYRON.

223. A LESSON

There is a flower, the Lesser Celandine,
That shrinks like many more from cold and rain,
And the first moment that the sun may shine,
Bright as the sun himself, 'tis out again !

When hailstones have been falling, swarm on swarm,
Or blasts the green field and the trees distrest,
Oft have I seen it muffled up from harm
In close self-shelter, like a thing at rest.

But lately, one rough day, this flower I past,
And recognised it, though an alter'd form,
Now standing forth an offering to the blast,
And buffeted at will by rain and storm.

I stopp'd and said, with inly-mutter'd voice,
" It doth not love the shower, nor seek the cold ;
This neither is its courage nor its choice,
But its necessity in being old.

" The sunshine may not cheer it, nor the dew ;
It cannot help itself in its decay ;
Stiff in its members, wither'd, changed of hue,"
And, in my spleen, I smiled that it was gray.

To be a prodigal's favourite—then, worse truth,
A miser's pensioner—behold our lot !
O Man ! that from thy fair and shining youth
Age might but take the things Youth needed not !
              W. WORDSWORTH.

224. PAST AND PRESENT

I remember, I remember
The house where I was born,
The little window where the sun
Came peeping in at morn ;
He never came a wink too soon
Nor brought too long a day ;
But now, I often wish the night
Had borne my breath away.

I remember, I remember
The roses, red and white,
The violets, and the lily-cups—
Those flowers made of light !
The lilacs where the robin built,
And where my brother set
The laburnum on his birthday,—
The tree is living yet !

I remember, I remember
Where I was used to swing,
And thought the air must rush as fresh
To swallows on the wing ;
My spirit flew in feathers then
That is so heavy now,
And summer pools could hardly cool
The fever on my brow.

I remember, I remember
The fir trees dark and high ;
I used to think their slender tops
Were close against the sky :
It was a childish ignorance,
But now 'tis little joy
To know I'm farther off from Heaven
Than when I was a boy.

T. Hood.

225. THE LIGHT OF OTHER DAYS

Oft in the stilly night
  Ere slumber's chain has bound me,
Fond Memory brings the light
  Of other days around me :
    The smiles, the tears
    Of boyhood's years,
  The words of love then spoken ;
    The eyes that shone,
    Now dimm'd and gone,
  The cheerful hearts now broken !
Thus in the stilly night
  Ere slumber's chain has bound me,
Sad Memory brings the light
  Of other days around me.

When I remember all
  The friends so link'd together
I've seen around me fall
  Like leaves in wintry weather,
    I feel like one
    Who treads alone
  Some banquet-hall deserted,
    Whose lights are fled,
    Whose garlands dead,
  And all but he departed !
Thus in the stilly night
  Ere slumber's chain has bound me,
Sad Memory brings the light
  Of other days around me.

                                        T. MOORE.

226. INVOCATION

Rarely, rarely, comest thou,
  Spirit of Delight !
Wherefore hast thou left me now
  Many a day and night ?
Many a weary night and day
'Tis since thou art fled away.

How shall ever one like me
  Win thee back again ?

With the joyous and the free
   Thou wilt scoff at pain.
Spirit false ! thou hast forgot
All but those who need thee not.

As a lizard with the shade
   Of a trembling leaf,
Thou with sorrow art dismay'd ;
   Even the sighs of grief
Reproach thee, that thou art not near,
And reproach thou wilt not hear.

Let me set my mournful ditty
   To a merry measure ;—
Thou wilt never come for pity,
   Thou wilt come for pleasure ;—
Pity then will cut away
Those cruel wings, and thou wilt stay.

I love all that thou lovest,
   Spirit of Delight !
The fresh Earth in new leaves drest
   And the starry night ;
Autumn evening, and the morn
When the golden mists are born.

I love snow and all the forms
   Of the radiant frost ;
I love waves, and winds, and storms,
   Everything almost
Which is Nature's, and may be
Untainted by man's misery.

I love tranquil solitude,
   And such society
As is quiet, wise, and good ;
   Between thee and me
What difference ? but thou dost possess
The things I seek, not love them less.

I love Love—though he has wings,
   And like light can flee,
But above all other things
   Spirit, I love thee—
Thou art love and life ! O come !
Make once more my heart thy home !

                      P. B. SHELLEY.

227. STANZAS WRITTEN IN DEJECTION NEAR NAPLES

The sun is warm, the sky is clear,
The waves are dancing fast and bright,
Blue isles and snowy mountains wear
The purple noon's transparent light :
The breath of the moist air is light
Around its unexpanded buds ;
Like many a voice of one delight—
The winds', the birds', the ocean-floods'—
The City's voice itself is soft like Solitude's.

I see the Deep's untrampled floor
With green and purple sea-weeds strown ;
I see the waves upon the shore
Like light dissolved in star-showers thrown ;
I sit upon the sands alone ;
The lightning of the noon-tide ocean
Is flashing round me, and a tone
Arises from its measured motion—
How sweet ! did any heart now share in my emotion

Alas ! I have not hope nor health,
Nor peace within nor calm around,
Nor that Content, surpassing wealth,
The sage in meditation found,
And walk'd with inward glory crown'd—
Nor fame, nor power, nor love, nor leisure ;
Others I see whom these surround—
Smiling they live, and call life pleasure ;
To me that cup has been dealt in another measure.

Yet now despair itself is mild
Even as the winds and waters are ;
I could lie down like a tired child,
And weep away the life of care
Which I have borne, and yet must bear,
Till death like sleep might steal on me,
And I might feel in the warm air
My cheek grow cold, and hear the sea
Breathe o'er my dying brain its last monotony.

P. B. SHELLEY.

228. THE SCHOLAR

My days among the Dead are past ;
Around me I behold,
Where'er these casual eyes are cast,
The mighty minds of old :
My never-failing friends are they,
With whom I converse day by day.

With them I take delight in weal
And seek relief in woe ;
And while I understand and feel
How much to them I owe,
My cheeks have often been bedew'd
With tears of thoughtful gratitude.

My thoughts are with the Dead ; with them
I live in long-past years,
Their virtues love, their faults condemn,
Partake their hopes and fears,
And from their lessons seek and find
Instruction with an humble mind.

My hopes are with the Dead ; anon
My place with them will be,
And I with them shall travel on
Through all Futurity ;
Yet leaving here a name, I trust,
That will not perish in the dust.

                              R. SOUTHEY.

229. THE MERMAID TAVERN

Souls of Poets dead and gone
What Elysium have ye known,
Happy field or mossy cavern,
Choicer than the Mermaid Tavern ?
Have ye tippled drink more fine
Than mine host's Canary wine ?
Or are fruits of Paradise
Sweeter than those dainty pies
Of Venison ? O generous food !
Drest as though bold Robin Hood
Would, with his Maid Marian,
Sup and bowse from horn and can.

I have heard that on a day
Mine host's signboard flew away
Nobody knew whither, till
An astrologer's old quill
To a sheepskin gave the story—
Said he saw you in your glory
Underneath a new-old Sign
Sipping beverage divine,
And pledging with contented smack
The Mermaid in the Zodiac !
  Souls of Poets dead and gone
What Elysium have ye known—
Happy field or mossy cavern—
Choicer than the Mermaid Tavern ?

J. KEATS.

230. THE PRIDE OF YOUTH

Proud Maisie is in the wood,
   Walking so early ;
Sweet Robin sits on the bush
   Singing so rarely.

" Tell me, thou bonny bird,
   When shall I marry me ? "
—" When six braw gentlemen
   Kirkward shall carry ye."

" Who makes the bridal bed,
   Birdie, say truly ? "
—" The gray-headed sexton
   That delves the grave duly.

" The glowworm o'er grave and stone
   Shall light thee steady ;
The owl from the steeple sing
   Welcome, proud lady."

SIR W. SCOTT.

231. THE BRIDGE OF SIGHS

One more Unfortunate
Weary of breath
Rashly importunate
Gone to her death !

Take her up tenderly,
Lift her with care ;
Fashion'd so slenderly,
Young, and so fair !

Look at her garments
Clinging like cerements ;
Whilst the wave constantly
Drips from her clothing ;
Take her up instantly,
Loving, not loathing.

Touch her not scornfully ;
Think of her mournfully ;
Gently and humanly ;
Not of the stains of her—
All that remains of her
Now is pure womanly.

Make no deep scrutiny
Into her mutiny
Rash and undutiful :
Past all dishonour,
Death has left on her
Only the beautiful.

Still, for all slips of hers,
One of Eve's family—
Wipe those poor lips of hers
Oozing so clammily.

Loop up her tresses
Escaped from the comb,
Her fair auburn tresses ;
Whilst wonderment guesses
Where was her home ?

Who was her father ?
Who was her mother ?
Had she a sister ?
Had she a brother ?
Or was there a dearer one
Still, and a nearer one
Yet, than all other ?

Alas ! for the rarity
Of Christian charity
Under the sun !
O ! it was pitiful !
Near a whole city full,
Home she had none.

Sisterly, brotherly,
Fatherly, motherly
Feelings had changed :
Love, by harsh evidence,
Thrown from its eminence ;
Even God's providence
Seeming estranged.

Where the lamps quiver
So far in the river,
With many a light
From window and casement,
From garret to basement,
She stood, with amazement,
Houseless by night.

The bleak wind of March
Made her tremble and shiver ;
But not the dark arch,
Of the black flowing river :
Mad from life's history,
Glad to death's mystery
Swift to be hurl'd—
Any where, any where
Out of the world !

Is she plunged boldly,
No matter how coldly
The rough river ran,
Over the brink of it,—

Picture it, think of it,
Dissolute Man !
Lave in it, drink of it
Then, if you can !

Take her up tenderly,
Lift her with care ;
Fashion'd so slenderly,
Young, and so fair !

Ere her limbs frigidly
Stiffen too rigidly,
Decently, kindly,
Smooth and compose them ;
And her eyes, close them,
Staring so blindly !

Dreadfully staring
Thro' muddy impurity,
As when with the daring
Last look of despairing
Fix'd on futurity.

Perishing gloomily
Spurr'd by contumely,
Cold inhumanity,
Burning insanity,
Into her rest.
—Cross her hands humbly
As if praying dumbly,
Over her breast !

Owning her weakness,
Her evil behaviour,
And leaving, with meekness,
Her sins to her Saviour !

                                    T. HOOD.

232. ELEGY

O snatch'd away in beauty'd bloom !
On thee shall press no ponderous tomb ;
But on thy turf shall roses rear
Their leaves, the earliest of the year,
And the wild cypress wave in tender gloom :

And oft by yon blue gushing stream
Shall Sorrow lean her drooping head,
And feed deep thought with many a dream,
And lingering pause and lightly tread ;
Fond wretch ! as if her step disturb'd the dead !

Away ! we know that tears are vain,
That Death nor heeds nor hears distress :
Will this unteach us to complain ?
Or make one mourner weep the less ?
And thou, who tell'st me to forget,
Thy looks are wan, thine eyes are wet.

LORD BYRON.

233. HESTER

When maidens such as Hester die
Their place ye may not well supply,
Though ye among a thousand try
  With vain endeavour.
A month or more hath she been dead,
Yet cannot I by force be led
To think upon the wormy bed
  And her together.
A springy motion in her gait,
A rising step, did indicate
Of pride and joy no common rate
  That flush'd her spirit :
I know not by what name beside
I shall it call ; if 'twas not pride,
It was a joy to that allied
  She did inherit.

Her parents held the Quaker rule
Which doth the human feeling cool ;
But she was train'd in Nature's school,
  Nature had blest her.
A waking eye, a prying mind,
A heart that stirs, is hard to bind ;
A hawk's keen sight ye cannot blind,
  Ye could not Hester.

My sprightly neighbour ! gone before
To that unknown and silent shore,

Shall we not meet, as heretofore
    Some summer morning—
When from thy cheerful eyes a ray
Hath struck a bliss upon the day,
A bliss that would not go away,
    A sweet fore-warning ?

                     C. LAMB.

234. CORONACH

He is gone on the mountain,
    He is lost to the forest,
Like a summer-dried fountain,
    When our need was the sorest.
The fount reappearing
    From the raindrops shall borrow,
But to us comes no cheering,
    To Duncan no morrow !

The hand of the reaper
    Take the ears that are hoary,
But the voice of the weeper
    Wails manhood in glory.
The autumn winds rushing
    Waft the leaves that are serest,
But our flower was in flushing
    When blighting was nearest.

Fleet foot on the correi,
    Sage counsel in cumber,
Red hand in the foray,
    How sound is thy slumber !
Like the dew on the mountain,
    Like the foam on the river,
Like the bubble on the fountain,
    Thou art gone, and for ever !

               SIR W. SCOTT.

235. THE DEATH BED

We watch'd her breathing thro' the night,
    Her breathing soft and low,
As in her breast the wave of life
    Kept heaving to and fro.

But when the morn came dim and sad
  And chill with early showers,
Her quiet eyelids closed—she had
  Another morn than ours.

T. Hood.

236. ROSABELLE

O listen, listen, ladies gay !
  No haughty feat of arms I tell ;
Soft is the note, and sad the lay
  That mourns the lovely Rosabelle.

" Moor, moor the barge, ye gallant crew,
  And, gentle lady, deign to stay !
Rest thee in Castle Ravensheuch,
  Nor tempt the stormy firth to-day.

" The blackening wave is edged with white ;
  To inch and rock the sea-mews fly ;
The fishers have heard the Water-Sprite,
  Whose screams forbode that wreck is nigh.

" Last night the gifted Seer did view
  A wet shroud swathed round lady gay ;
Then stay thee, Fair, in Ravensheuch ;
  Why cross the gloomy firth to-day ? "

" 'Tis not because Lord Lindesay's heir
  To-night at Roslin leads the ball,
But that my lady-mother there
  Sits lonely in her castle-hall.

" 'Tis not because the ring they ride,
  And Lindesay at the ring rides well,
But that my sire the wine will chide
  If 'tis not fill'd by Rosabelle."

—O'er Roslin all that dreary night
  A wondrous blaze was seen to gleam ;
'Twas broader than the watch-fire's light,
  And redder than the bright moonbeam.

It glared on Roslin's castled rock,
  It ruddied all the copse-wood glen ;
'Twas seen from Dryden's grove of oak,
  And seen from cavern'd Hawthornden.

Seem'd all on fire that chapel proud
  Where Roslin's chiefs uncoffin'd lie,
Each Baron, for a sable shroud,
  Sheath'd in his iron panoply.

Seem'd all on fire within, around,
  Deep sacristy and altar's pale ;
Shone every pillar foliage-bound,
  And glimmer'd all the dead men's mail.

Blazed battlement and pinnet high,
  Blazed every rose-carved buttress fair—
So still they blaze, when fate is nigh
  The lordly line of high Saint Clair.

There are twenty of Roslin's barons bold
  Lie buried within that proud chapelle ;
Each one the holy vault doth hold,
  But the sea holds lovely Rosabelle !

And each Saint Clair was buried there
  With candle, with book, and with knell ;
But the sea-caves rung, and the wild winds sung
  The dirge of lovely Rosabelle.

                                        SIR W. SCOTT.

237. ON AN INFANT DYING AS SOON AS BORN

I saw where in the shroud did lurk
A curious frame of Nature's work ;
A flow'ret crushéd in the bud,
A nameless piece of Babyhood
Was in her cradle-coffin lying ;
Extinct, with scarce the sense of dying :
So soon to exchange the imprisoning womb
For darker closets of the tomb !
She did but ope an eye, and put
A clear beam forth, then straight up shut
For the long dark : ne'er more to see
Through glasses of mortality.
Riddle of destiny, who can show
What thy short visit meant, or know

What thy errand here below ?
Shall we say, that Nature blind
Check'd her hand, and changed her mind
Just when she had exactly wrought
A finish'd pattern without fault ?
Could she flag, or could she tire,
Or lack'd she the Promethean fire
(With her nine moons' long workings sicken'd)
That should thy little limbs have quicken'd ?
Limbs so firm, they seem'd to assure
Life of health, and days mature :
Woman's self in miniature !
Limbs so fair, they might supply
(Themselves now but cold imagery)
The sculptor to make Beauty by.
Or did the stern-eyed Fate descry
That babe or mother, one must die ;
So in mercy left the stock
And cut the branch ; to save the shock
Of young years widow'd, and the pain
When Single State comes back again
To the lone man who, reft of wife,
Thenceforward drags a maiméd life ?
The economy of Heaven is dark,
And wisest clerks have miss'd the mark
Why human buds, like this, should fall,
More brief than fly ephemeral
That has his day ; while shrivell'd crones
Stiffen with age to stocks and stones ;
And crabbéd use the conscience sears
In sinners of an hundred years.
—Mother's prattle, mother's kiss,
Baby fond, thou ne'er wilt miss :
Rites, which custom does impose,
Silver bells, and baby clothes ;
Coral redder than those lips
Which pale death did late eclipse ;
Music framed for infants' glee,
Whistle never tuned for thee ;
Though thou want'st not, thou shalt have them,
Loving hearts were they which gave them.
Let not one be missing ; nurse,
See them laid upon the hearse
Of infant slain by doom perverse.

Why should kings and nobles have
Pictured trophies to their grave,
And we, churls, to thee deny
Thy pretty toys with thee to lie—
A more harmless vanity?

C. LAMB.

238. THE AFFLICTION OF MARGARET

Where art thou, my beloved Son,
Where art thou, worse to me than dead!
O find me, prosperous or undone!
Or if the grave be now thy bed,
Why am I ignorant of the same
That I may rest; and neither blame
Nor sorrow may attend thy name?

Seven years, alas! to have received
No tidings of an only child—
To have despair'd, have hoped, believed,
And be for evermore beguiled,—
Sometimes with thoughts of very bliss!
I catch at them, and then I miss;
Was ever darkness like to this?

He was among the prime in worth,
An object beauteous to behold;
Well born, well bred; I sent him forth
Ingenuous, innocent, and bold:
If things ensued that wanted grace
As hath been said, they were not base;
And never blush was on my face.

Ah! little doth the young-one dream
When full of play and childish cares,
What power is in his wildest scream
Heard by his mother unawares!
He knows it not, he cannot guess;
Years to a mother bring distress;
But do not make her love the less.

Neglect me! no, I suffer'd long
From that ill thought; and being blind
Said " Pride shall help me in my wrong:

Kind mother have I been, as kind
As ever breathed " : and that is true ;
I've wet my path with tears like dew,
Weeping for him when no one knew.

My Son, if thou be humbled, poor,
Hopeless of honour and of gain,
O ! do not dread thy mother's door,
Think not of me with grief and pain :
I now can see with better eyes ;
And worldly grandeur I despise
And fortune with her gifts and lies.

Alas ! the fowls of heaven have wings
And blasts of heaven will aid their flight ;
They mount—how short a voyage brings
The wanderers back to their delight !
Chains tie us down by land and sea ;
And wishes, vain as mine, may be
All that is left to comfort thee.

Perhaps some dungeon hears thee groan
Maim'd, mangled by inhuman men ;
Or thou upon a desert thrown
Inheritest the lion's den ;
Or hast been summon'd to the deep
Thou, thou, and all thy mates, to keep
An incommunicable sleep.

I look for ghosts : but none will force
Their way to me ; 'tis falsely said
That there was ever intercourse
Between the living and the dead ;
For surely then I should have sight
Of him I wait for day and night
With love and longings infinite.

My apprehensions come in crowds ;
I dread the rustling of the grass ;
The very shadows of the clouds
Have power to shake me as they pass ;
I question things, and do not find
One that will answer to my mind ;
And all the world appears unkind.

Beyond participation lie
My troubles, and beyond relief:
If any chance to heave a sigh
They pity me, and not my grief.
Then come to me, my Son, or send
Some tidings that my woes may end!
I have no other earthly friend.

W. WORDSWORTH.

239. HUNTING SONG

Waken, lords and ladies gay,
On the mountain dawns the day;
All the jolly chase is here
With hawk and horse and hunting-spear;
Hounds are in their couples yelling,
Hawks are whistling, horns are knelling,
Merrily merrily mingle they
"Waken, lords and ladies gay."

Waken, lords and ladies gay,
The mist has left the mountain gray,
Springlets in the dawn are steaming,
Diamonds on the brake are gleaming,
And foresters have busy been
To track the buck in thicket green;
Now we come to chant our lay
"Waken, lords and ladies gay."

Waken, lords and ladies gay,
To the greenwood haste away;
We can show you where he lies,
Fleet of foot and tall of size;
We can show the marks he made
When 'gainst the oak his antlers fray'd;
You shall see him brought to bay;
"Waken, lords and ladies gay."

Louder, louder chant the lay
Waken, lords and ladies gay!
Tell them youth and mirth and glee
Run a course as well as we;

> Time, stern huntsman ! who can baulk,
> Stanch as hound and fleet as hawk ;
> Think of this, and rise with day
> Gentle lords and ladies gay !
>
> SIR W. SCOTT.

240. TO THE SKYLARK

Ethereal minstrel ! pilgrim of the sky !
Dost thou despise the earth where cares abound ?
Or while the wings aspire, are heart and eye
Both with thy nest upon the dewy ground ?
Thy nest which thou canst drop into at will,
Those quivering wings composed, that music still !

To the last point of vision, and beyond
Mount, daring warbler !—that love-prompted strain
—'Twixt thee and thine a never-failing bond—
Thrills not the less the bosom of the plain :
Yet might'st thou seem, proud privilege ! to sing
All independent of the leafy Spring.

Leave to the nightingale her shady wood ;
A privacy of glorious light is thine,
Whence thou dost pour upon the world a flood
Of harmony, with instinct more divine ;
Type of the wise, who soar, but never roam—
True to the kindred points of Heaven and Home !

W. WORDSWORTH.

241. TO A SKYLARK

Hail to thee, blithe Spirit !
    Bird thou never wert,
That from heaven, or near it
    Pourest thy full heart
In profuse strains of unpremeditated art.

Higher still and higher
    From the earth thou springest,
Like a cloud of fire ;
    The blue deep thou wingest,
And singing still dost soar, and soaring ever singest.

In the golden lightning
  Of the sunken sun
O'er which clouds are brightening,
  Thou dost float and run,
Like an unbodied joy whose race is just begun.

The pale purple even
  Melts around thy flight;
Like a star of heaven
  In the broad daylight
Thou art unseen, but yet I hear thy shrill delight:

Keen as are the arrows
  Of that silver sphere,
Whose intense lamp narrows
  In the white dawn clear
Until we hardly see, we feel that it is there.

All the earth and air
  With thy voice is loud,
As, when night is bare,
  From one lonely cloud
The moon rains out her beams, and heaven is overflow'd.

What thou art we know not;
  What is most like thee?
From rainbow clouds there flow not
  Drops so bright to see
As from thy presence showers a rain of melody.

Like a poet hidden
  In the light of thought,
Singing hymns unbidden,
  Till the world is wrought
To sympathy with hopes and fears it heeded not:

Like a high-born maiden
  In a palace tower,
Soothing her love-laden
  Soul in secret hour
With music sweet as love, which overflows her bower:

Like a glow-worm golden
  In a dell of dew,

   Scattering unbeholden
    Its aerial hue
Among the flowers and grass, which screen it from the
     view :

   Like a rose embower'd
    In its own green leaves,
   By warm winds deflower'd,
    Till the scent it gives
Makes faint with too much sweet these heavy-wingéd
     thieves.

   Sound of vernal showers
    On the twinkling grass,
   Rain-awaken'd flowers,
    All that ever was
Joyous, and clear, and fresh, thy music doth surpass.

   Teach us, sprite or bird,
    What sweet thoughts are thine
   I have never heard
    Praise of love or wine
That panted forth a flood of rapture so divine.

   Chorus hymeneal
    Or triumphal chaunt
   Match'd with thine, would be all
    But an empty vaunt—
A thing wherein we feel there is some hidden want.

   What objects are the fountains
    Of thy happy strain ?
   What fields, or waves, or mountains ?
    What shapes of sky or plain ?
What love of thine own kind ? what ignorance of pain ?

   With thy clear keen joyance
    Languor cannot be :
   Shadow of annoyance
    Never came near thee :
Thou lovest ; but ne'er knew love's sad satiety.

   Waking or asleep
    Thou of death must deem
   Things more true and deep
    Than we mortals dream,
Or how could thy notes flow in such a crystal stream ?

We look before and after
   And pine for what is not
Our sincerest laughter
   With some pain is fraught ;
Our sweetest songs are those that tell of saddest thought.

Yet if we could scorn
   Hate, and pride, and fear ;
If we were things born
   Not to shed a tear,
I know not how thy joy we ever should come near.

Better than all measures
   Of delightful sound,
Better than all treasures
   That in books are found,
Thy skill to poet were, thou scorner of the ground !

Teach me half the gladness
   That thy brain must know,
Such harmonious madness
   From my lips would flow
The world should listen then, as I am listening now !
                  P. B. SHELLEY.

242. THE GREEN LINNET

Beneath these fruit-tree boughs that shed
Their snow-white blossoms on my head,
With brightest sunshine round me spread
   Of Spring's unclouded weather,
In this sequester'd nook how sweet
To sit upon my orchard-seat !
And flowers and birds once more to greet,
   My last year's friends together.

One have I mark'd, the happiest guest
In all this covert of the blest :
Hail to Thee, far above the rest
   In joy of voice and pinion !
Thou, Linnet ! in thy green array
Presiding Spirit here to-day
Dost lead the revels of the May,
   And this is thy dominion.

While birds, and butterflies, and flowers
Make all one band of paramours,
Thou, ranging up and down the bowers,
Art sole in thy employment ;
A Life, a Presence like the air,
Scattering thy gladness without care,
Too blest with any one to pair,
Thyself thy own enjoyment.

Amid yon tuft of hazel trees
That twinkle to the gusty breeze,
Behold him perch'd in ecstasies
Yet seeming still to hover ;
There, where the flutter of his wings
Upon his back and body flings
Shadows and sunny glimmerings,
That cover him all over.

My dazzled sight he oft deceives—
A brother of the dancing leaves ;
Then flits, and from the cottage-eaves
Pours forth his song in gushes,
As if by that exulting strain
He mock'd and treated with disdain
The voiceless Form he chose to feign
While fluttering in the bushes.

W. WORDSWORTH.

243. TO THE CUCKOO

O blithe new-comer ! I have heard,
I hear thee and rejoice :
O Cuckoo ! shall I call thee bird,
Or but a wandering Voice ?

While I am lying on the grass
Thy twofold shout I hear ;
From hill to hill it seems to pass,
At once far off and near.

Though babbling only to the vale
Of sunshine and of flowers,
Thou bringest unto me a tale
Of visionary hours.

Thrice welcome, darling of the Spring !
Even yet thou art to me
No bird, but an invisible thing,
A voice, a mystery ;

The same whom in my school-boy days
I listen'd to ; that Cry
Which made me look a thousand ways
In bush, and tree, and sky.

To seek thee did I often rove
Through woods and on the green ;
And thou wert still a hope, a love ;
Still long'd for, never seen !

And I can listen to thee yet ;
Can lie upon the plain
And listen, till I do beget
That golden time again.

O blessèd bird ! the earth we pace
Again appears to be
An unsubstantial, fairy place,
That is fit home for Thee !

W. WORDSWORTH.

244. ODE TO A NIGHTINGALE

My heart aches, and a drowsy numbness pains
  My sense, as though of hemlock I had drunk,
Or emptied some dull opiate to the drains
  One minute past, and Lethe-wards had sunk :
'Tis not through envy of thy happy lot,
  But being too happy in thy happiness,—
    That thou, light-wingèd Dryad of the trees,
      In some melodious plot
Of beechen green, and shadows numberless,
  Singest of summer in full-throated ease.

O for a draught of vintage, that hath been
  Cool'd a long age in the deep delvèd earth,
Tasting of Flora and the country-green,
  Dance, and Provencal song, and sun-burnt mirth !

O for a beaker full of the warm South,
  Full of the true, the blushful Hippocrene,
    With beaded bubbles winking at the brim
      And purple-stainéd mouth ;
That I might drink, and leave the world unseen,
  And with thee fade away into the forest dim :

Fade far away, dissolve, and quite forget
  What thou among the leaves hast never known,
The weariness, the fever, and the fret
  Here, where men sit and hear each other groan ;
Where palsy shakes a few, sad, last gray hairs,
  Where youth grows pale, and spectre-thin, and dies ;
    Where but to think is to be full of sorrow
      And leaden-eyed despairs ;
Where Beauty cannot keep her lustrous eyes,
  Or new Love pine at them beyond to-morrow.

Away ! away ! for I will fly to thee,
  Not charioted by Bacchus and his pards,
But on the viewless wings of Poesy,
  Though the dull brain perplexes and retards :
Already with thee ! tender is the night,
  And haply the Queen-Moon is on her throne,
    Cluster'd around by all her starry Fays ;
      But here there is no light
Save what from heaven is with the breezes blown
  Through verdurous glooms and winding mossy ways.

I cannot see what flowers are at my feet,
  Nor what soft incense hangs upon the boughs,
But, in embalméd darkness, guess each sweet
  Wherewith the seasonable month endows
The grass, the thicket, and the fruit-tree wild ;
  White hawthorn, and the pastoral eglantine ;
    Fast-fading violets cover'd up in leaves ;
      And mid-May's eldest child
The coming musk-rose, full of dewy wine,
  The murmurous haunt of flies on summer eves.

Darkling I listen ; and for many a time
  I have been half in love with easeful Death,
Call'd him soft names in many a muséd rhyme,
  To take into the air my quiet breath ;

Now more than ever seems it rich to die,
  To cease upon the midnight with no pain,
    While thou art pouring forth thy soul abroad
      In such an ecstasy !
Still wouldst thou sing, and I have ears in vain—
  To thy high requiem become a sod.

Thou wast not born for death, immortal Bird !
  No hungry generations tread thee down ;
The voice I hear this passing night was heard
  In ancient days by emperor and clown :
Perhaps the self-same song that found a path
  Through the sad heart of Ruth, when, sick for home,
    She stood in tears amid the alien corn ;
      The same that oft-times hath
Charm'd magic casements, opening on the foam
  Of perilous seas, in faery lands forlorn.

Forlorn ! the very word is like a bell
  To toll me back from thee to my sole self !
Adieu ! the fancy cannot cheat so well
  As she is famed to do, deceiving elf.
Adieu ! adieu ! thy plaintive anthem fades
  Past the near meadows, over the still stream,
  Up the hill-side ; and now 'tis buried deep
    In the next valley-glades :
Was it a vision, or a waking dream ?
  Fled is that music :—do I wake or sleep ?

                        J. KEATS.

245. UPON WESTMINSTER BRIDGE
Sept. 3, 1802

Earth has not anything to show more fair :
Dull would he be of soul who could pass by
A sight so touching in its majesty :
This City now doth like a garment wear.

The beauty of the morning : silent, bare,
Ships, towers, domes, theatres, and temples lie
Open unto the fields, and to the sky,
All bright and glittering in the smokeless air.

Never did sun more beautifully steep
In his first splendour valley, rock, or hill ;
Ne'er saw I, never felt, a calm so deep !

The river glideth at his own sweet will :
Dear God ! the very houses seem asleep ;
And all that mighty heart is lying still !

W. WORDSWORTH.

246. OZYMANDIAS OF EGYPT

I met a traveller from an antique land
Who said : Two vast and trunkless legs of stone
Stand in the desert. Near them on the sand
Half sunk, a shatter'd visage lies, whose frown
And wrinkled lip and sneer of cold command
Tell that its sculptor well those passions read
Which yet survive, stamp'd on these lifeless things,
The hand that mock'd them and the heart that fed ;
And on the pedestal these words appear :
" My name is Ozymandias, king of kings :
Look on my works, ye Mighty, and despair ! "
Nothing beside remains. Round the decay
Of that colossal wreck, boundless and bare,
The lone and level sands stretch far away.

P. B. SHELLEY.

247. COMPOSED AT NEIDPATH CASTLE, THE PROPERTY OF LORD QUEENSBERRY, 1803

Degenerate Douglas ! O the unworthy lord !
Whom mere despite of heart could so far please
And love of havoc (for with such disease
Fame taxes him) that he could send forth word

To level with the dust a noble horde,
A brotherhood of venerable trees,
Leaving an ancient dome, and towers like these
Beggar'd and outraged !—Many hearts deplored

The fate of those old trees ; and oft with pain
The traveller at this day will stop and gaze
On wrongs, which Nature scarcely seems to heed :

For shelter'd places, bosoms, nooks, and bays,
And the pure mountains, and the gentle Tweed,
And the green silent pastures, yet remain.

W. WORDSWORTH.

248. ADMONITION TO A TRAVELLER

Yes, there is holy pleasure in thine eye !
—The lovely cottage in the guardian nook
Hath stirr'd thee deeply ; with its own dear brook,
Its own small pasture, almost its own sky !

But covet not the abode—O do not sigh
As many do, repining while they look ;
Intruders who would tear from Nature's book
This precious leaf with harsh impiety :

—Think what the home would be if it were thine,
Even thine, though few thy wants !—Roof, window,
    door,
The very flowers are sacred to the Poor,

The roses to the porch which they entwine :
Yea, all that now enchants thee, from the day
On which it should be touch'd would melt away !
                                        W. WORDSWORTH.

249. TO THE HIGHLAND GIRL OF INVERSNEYDE

Sweet Highland Girl, a very shower
Of beauty is thy earthly dower !
Twice seven consenting years have shed
Their utmost bounty on thy head :
And these gray rocks, this household lawn,
These trees—a veil just half withdrawn,
This fall of water that doth make
A murmur near the silent lake,
This little bay, a quiet road
That holds in shelter thy abode ;
In truth together ye do seem
Like something fashion'd in a dream ;
Such forms as from their covert peep
When earthly cares are laid asleep
But O fair Creature ! in the light
Of common day, so heavenly bright,
I bless Thee, Vision as thou art,
I bless thee with a human heart :
God shield thee to thy latest years !

I neither know thee nor thy peers :
And yet my eyes are fill'd with tears.

With earnest feeling I shall pray
For thee when I am far away ;
For never saw I mien or face
In which more plainly I could trace
Benignity and home-bred sense
Ripening in perfect innocence.
Here scatter'd like a random seed,
Remote from men, Thou dost not need
The embarrass'd look of shy distress,
And maidenly shamefacedness :
Thou wear'st upon thy forehead clear
The freedom of a mountaineer :
A face with gladness overspread,
Soft smiles, by human kindness bred ;
And seemliness complete, that sways
Thy courtesies, about thee plays ;
With no restraint, but such as springs
From quick and eager visitings
Of thoughts that lie beyond the reach
Of thy few words of English speech :
A bondage sweetly brook'd, a strife
That gives thy gestures grace and life !
So have I, not unmoved in mind,
Seen birds of tempest-loving kind,
Thus beating up against the wind.

What hand but would a garland cull
For thee who art so beautiful ?
O happy pleasure ! here to dwell
Beside thee in some healthy dell ;
Adopt your homely ways and dress,
A shepherd, thou a shepherdess !
But I could frame a wish for thee
More like a grave reality :
Thou art to me but as a wave
Of the wild sea : and I would have
Some claim upon thee, if I could,
Though but of common neighbourhood.
What joy to hear thee, and to see !
Thy elder brother I would be,
Thy father, anything to thee.

Now thanks to Heaven ! that of its grace
Hath led me to this lonely place ;
Joy have I had ; and going hence
I bear away my recompense.
In spots like these it is we prize
Our memory, feel that she hath eyes ;
Then why should I be loth to stir ?
I feel this place was made for her ;
To give new pleasure like the past,
Continued long as life shall last.
Nor am I loth, though pleased at heart,
Sweet Highland Girl ! from thee to part ;
For I, methinks, till I grow old
As fair before me shall behold
As I do now, the cabin small,
The lake, the bay, the waterfall
And Thee, the spirit of them all !

W. WORDSWORTH.

250. THE REAPER

Behold her, single in the field,
Yon solitary Highland Lass !
Reaping and singing by herself ;
Stop here, or gently pass !
Alone she cuts and binds the grain,
And sings a melancholy strain ;
O listen ! for the vale profound
Is overflowing with the sound.

No nightingale did ever chaunt
More welcome notes to weary bands
Of travellers in some shady haunt,
Among Arabian sands :
No sweeter voice was ever heard
In spring-time from the cuckoo-bird,
Breaking the silence of the seas
Among the farthest Hebrides.

Will no one tell me what she sings ?
Perhaps the plaintive numbers flow
For old, unhappy, far-off things,
And battles long ago :

Or is it some more humble lay,
Familiar matter of to-day?
Some natural sorrow, loss, or pain,
That has been, and may be again!

Whate'er the theme, the maiden sang
As if her song could have no ending;
I saw her singing at her work,
And o'er the sickle bending;
I listen'd till I had my fill;
And, as I mounted up the hill,
The music in my heart I bore
Long after it was heard no more.

W. WORDSWORTH.

251. THE REVERIE OF POOR SUSAN

At the corner of Wood Street, when daylight appears
Hangs a Thrush that sings loud, it has sung for three years:
Poor Susan has pass'd by the spot, and has heard
In the silence of morning the song of the bird.

'Tis a note of enchantment; what ails her? She sees
A mountain ascending, a vision of trees;
Bright volumes of vapour through Lothbury glide,
And a river flows on through the vale of Cheapside.

Green pastures she views in the midst of the dale
Down which she so often has tripp'd with her pail;
And a single small cottage, a nest like a dove's,
The one only dwelling on earth that she loves.

She looks, and her heart is in heaven: but they fade
The mist and the river, the hill and the shade;
The stream will not flow, and the hill will not rise,
And the colours have all pass'd away from her eyes!

W. WORDSWORTH.

252. TO A LADY, WITH A GUITAR

Ariel to Miranda :—Take
This slave of music, for the sake
Of him, who is the slave of thee;

And teach it all the harmony
In which thou canst, and only thou,
Make the delighted spirit glow,
Till joy denies itself again
And, too intense, is turn'd to pain.
For by permission and command
Of thine own Prince Ferdinand,
Poor Ariel sends this silent token
Of more than ever can be spoken;
Your guardian spirit, Ariel, who
From life to life must still pursue
Your happiness, for thus alone
Can Ariel ever find his own;
From Prospero's enchanted cell,
As the mighty verses tell,
To the throne of Naples he
Lit you o'er the trackless sea,
Flitting on, your prow before,
Like a living meteor.
When you die, the silent Moon
In her interlunar swoon
Is not sadder in her cell
Than deserted Ariel;
When you live again on earth,
Like an unseen Star of birth
Ariel guides you o'er the sea
Of life from your nativity :—
Many changes have been run
Since Ferdinand and you begun
Your course of love, and Ariel still
Has track'd your steps and served your will.
Now in humbler, happier lot,
This is all remember'd not;
And now, alas! the poor sprite is
Imprison'd for some fault of his
In a body like a grave—
From you he only dares to crave
For his service and his sorrow
A smile to-day, a song to-morrow.

The artist who this viol wrought
To echo all harmonious thought,
Fell'd a tree, while on the steep
The woods were in their winter sleep,

Rock'd in that repose divine
On the wind-swept Apennine ;
And dreaming, some of autumn past,
And some of spring approaching fast,
And some of April buds and showers,
And some of songs in July bowers,
And all of love ; and so this tree,—
O that such our death may be !—
Died in sleep, and felt no pain,
To live in happier form again :
From which, beneath Heaven's fairest star,
The artist wrought this loved Guitar ;
And taught it justly to reply
To all who question skilfully
In language gentle as thine own ;
Whispering in enamour'd tone
Sweet oracles of woods and dells,
And summer winds in sylvan cells ;
—For it had learnt all harmonies
Of the plains and of the skies,
Of the forests and the mountains,
And the many-voicéd fountains ;
The clearest echoes of the hills,
The softest notes of falling rills,
The melodies of birds and bees,
The murmuring of summer seas,
And pattering rain ; and breathing dew,
And airs of evening ; and it knew
That seldom-heard mysterious sound
Which, driven on its diurnal round,
As it floats through boundless day,
Our world enkindles on its way :
—All this it knows, but will not tell
To those who cannot question well
The spirit that inhabits it ;
It talks according to the wit
Of its companions ; and no more
Is heard than has been felt before
By those who tempt it to betray
These secrets of an elder day.
But, sweetly as its answers will
Flatter hands of perfect skill,
It keeps its highest holiest tone
For one beloved Friend alone.   P. B. SHELLEY.

253. THE DAFFODILS

I wander'd lonely as a cloud
That floats on high o'er vales and hills,
When all at once I saw a crowd,
A host of golden daffodils,
Beside the lake, beneath the trees
Fluttering and dancing in the breeze.

Continuous as the stars that shine
And twinkle on the milky way,
They stretch'd in never-ending line
Along the margin of a bay :
Ten thousand saw I at a glance
Tossing their heads in sprightly dance.

The waves beside them danced, but they
Out-did the sparkling waves in glee :—
A Poet could not but be gay
In such a jocund company !
I gazed—and gazed—but little thought
What wealth the show to me had brought ;

For oft, when on my couch I lie
In vacant or in pensive mood,
They flash upon that inward eye
Which is the bliss of solitude ;
And then my heart with pleasure fills,
And dances with the daffodils.

W. WORDSWORTH.

254. TO THE DAISY

With little here to do or see
Of things that in the great world be,
Sweet Daisy ! oft I talk to thee
      For thou art worthy,
Thou unassuming commonplace
Of Nature, with that homely face,
And yet with something of a grace
      Which love makes for thee !

Oft on the dappled turf at ease
I sit and play with similes,
Loose types of things through all degrees,
  Thoughts of thy raising;
And many a fond and idle name
I give to thee, for praise or blame
As is the humour of the game,
  While I am gazing.

A nun demure, of lowly port;
Or sprightly maiden, of Love's court,
In thy simplicity the sport
  Of all temptations;
A queen in crown of rubies drest;
A starveling in a scanty vest;
Are all, as seems to suit thee best,
  Thy appellations.

A little Cyclops, with one eye
Staring to threaten and defy,
That thought comes next—and instantly
  The freak is over,
The shape will vanish, and behold!
A silver shield with boss of gold
That spreads itself, some fairy bold
  In fight to cover.

I see thee glittering from afar—
And then thou art a pretty star,
Not quite so fair as many are
  In heaven above thee!
Yet like a star, with glittering crest,
Self-poised in air thou seem'st to rest;—
May peace come never to his nest
  Who shall reprove thee!

Sweet Flower! for by that name at last
When all my reveries are past
I call thee and to that cleave fast,
  Sweet silent Creature!
Thou breath'st with me in sun and air,
Do thou, as thou art won't, repair
My heart with gladness, and a share
  Of thy meek nature!

W. WORDSWORTH.

255. ODE TO AUTUMN

Season of mists and mellow fruitfulness !
Close bosom-friend of the maturing sun ;
Conspiring with him how to load and bless
With fruit the vines that round the thatch-eaves run ;
To bend with apples the moss'd cottage-trees,
And fill all fruit with ripeness to the core ;
To swell the gourd, and plump the hazel shells
With a sweet kernel ; to set budding more
And still more, later flowers for the bees,
Until they think warm days will never cease ;
For Summer has o'erbrimm'd their clammy cells.

Who hath not seen Thee oft amid thy store ?
Sometimes whoever seeks abroad may find
Thee sitting careless on a granary floor,
Thy hair soft-lifted by the winnowing wind ;
Or on a half-reap'd furrow sound asleep,
Drowsed with the fume of poppies, while thy hook
Spares the next swath and all its twinéd flowers ;
And sometime like a gleaner thou dost keep
Steady thy laden head across a brook
Or by a cider-press, with patient look
Thou watchest the last oozings, hours by hours.

Where are the songs of Spring ? Ay, where are they
Think not of them,—thou hast thy music too,
While barréd clouds bloom the soft-dying day
And touch the stubble-plains with rosy hue ;
Then in a wailful choir the small gnats mourn
Among the river-sallows, borne aloft
Or sinking as the light wind lives or dies ;
And full-grown lambs loud bleat from hilly bourn ;
Hedge-crickets sing, and now with treble soft
The redbreast whistles from a garden croft ;
And gathering swallows twitter in the skies.

J. KEATS.

256. ODE TO WINTER
Germany, December, 1800

When first the fiery-mantled Sun
His heavenly race began to run,
Round the earth and ocean blue
His children four the Seasons flew :—
   First, in green apparel dancing,
The young Spring smiled with angel-grace ;
   Rosy Summer next advancing,
Rush'd into her sire's embrace—
Her bright-hair'd sire, who bade her keep
   For ever nearest to his smiles,
On Calpe's olive-shaded steep
   Or India's citron-cover'd isles.
More remote, and buxom-brown,
   The Queen of vintage bow'd before his throne ;
A rich pomegranate gemm'd her crown,
   A ripe sheaf bound her zone.

But howling Winter fled afar
To hills that prop the polar star ;
And loves on deer-borne car to ride
With barren darkness at his side
Round the shore where loud Lofoden
   Whirls to death the roaring whale,
Round the hall where Runic Odin
   Howls his war-song to the gale—
Save when adown the ravaged globe
   He travels on his native storm,
Deflowering Nature's grassy robe
   And trampling on her faded form ;
Till light's returning Lord assume
   The shaft that drives him to his northern fields,
Of power to pierce his raven plume
   And crystal-cover'd shield.

O sire of storms ! whose savage ear
The Lapland drum delights to hear,
When Frenzy with her bloodshot eye
Implores thy dreadful deity—
Archangel ! Power of desolation !
   Fast descending as thou art,
Say, hath mortal invocation
   Spells to touch thy stony heart :

Then, sullen Winter ! hear my prayer,
And gently rule the ruin'd year ;
Nor chill the wanderer's bosom bare
Nor freeze the wretch's falling tear :
To shuddering Want's unmantled bed
  Thy horror-breathing agues cease to lend,
And gently on the orphan head
  Of Innocence descend.

But chiefly spare, O kings of clouds !
The sailor on his airy shrouds,
When wrecks and beacons strew the steep
And spectres walk along the deep.
Milder yet thy snowy breezes
  Pour on yonder tented shores,
Where the Rhine's broad billow freezes,
  Or the dark-brown Danube roars.
O winds of Winter ! list ye there
  To many a deep and dying groan ?
Or start, ye demons of the midnight air,
  At shrieks and thunders louder than your own ?
Alas ! e'en your unhallow'd breath
  May spare the victim fallen low ;
But Man will ask no truce to death,
  No bounds to human woe.

T. CAMPBELL.

257. YARROW UNVISITED
1803

From Stirling Castle we had seen
The mazy Forth unravell'd,
Had trod the banks of Clyde and Tay,
And with the Tweed had travell'd ;
And when we came to Clovenford,
Then said my " winsome Marrow,"
" Whate'er betide, we'll turn aside,
And see the Braes of Yarrow."

" Let Yarrow folk, frae Selkirk town,
  Who have been buying, selling,
Go back to Yarrow, 'tis their own,
Each maiden to her dwelling !

On Yarrow's banks let herons feed,
Hares couch, and rabbits burrow,
But we will downward with the Tweed,
Nor turn aside to Yarrow.

" There's Galla Water, Leader Haughs,
Both lying right before us ;
And Dryburgh, where with chiming Tweed
The lintwhites sing in chorus ;
There's pleasant Tiviotdale, a land
Made blythe with plough and harrow :
Why throw away a needful day
To go in search of Yarrow ?

" What's Yarrow but a river bare
That glides the dark hills under ?
There are a thousand such elsewhere
As worthy of your wonder."
—Strange words they seem'd of slight and scorn ;
My true-love sigh'd for sorrow,
And look'd me in the face, to think
I thus could speak of Yarrow !

" O green," said I, " are Yarrow's holms,
And sweet is Yarrow flowing !
Fair hangs the apple frae the rock,
But we will leave it growing.
O'er hilly path and open strath
We'll wander Scotland thorough ;
But, though so near, we will not turn
Into the dale of Yarrow.

" Let beeves and home-bred kine partake
The sweets of Burn-mill meadow ;
The swan on still Saint Mary's Lake
Float double, swan and shadow !
We will not see them ; will not go
To-day, nor yet to-morrow ;
Enough if in our hearts we know
There's such a place as Yarrow.

" Be Yarrow stream unseen, unknown ;
It must, or we shall rue it :
We have a vision of our own,
Ah ! why should we undo it ?

The treasured dreams of times long past,
We'll keep them, winsome Marrow !
For when we're there, although 'tis fair,
'Twill be another Yarrow !

" If care with freezing years should come
And wandering seem but folly,—
Should we be loth to stir from home,
And yet be melancholy ;
Should life be dull, and spirits low,
'Twill soothe us in our sorrow
That earth has something yet to show,
The bonny Holms of Yarrow ! "

W. WORDSWORTH.

258. YARROW VISITED
September, 1814

And is this—Yarrow ?—This the Stream
Of which my fancy cherish'd
So faithfully, a waking dream,
An image that hath perish'd ?
O that some minstrel's harp were near
To utter notes of gladness
And chase this silence from the air,
That fills my heart with sadness !

Yet why ?—a silvery current flows
With uncontroll'd meanderings ;
Nor have these eyes by greener hills
Been soothed, in all my wanderings.
And, through her depths, Saint Mary's Lake
Is visibly delighted ;
For not a feature of those hills
Is in the mirror slighted.

A blue sky bends o'er Yarrow Vale,
Save where that pearly whiteness
Is round the rising sun diffused,
A tender hazy brightness ;
Mild dawn of promise ! that excludes
All profitless dejection ;
Though not unwilling here to admit
A pensive recollection.

Where was it that the famous Flower
Of Yarrow Vale lay bleeding ?
His bed perchance was yon smooth mound
On which the herd is feeding :
And haply from this crystal pool,
Now peaceful as the morning,
The water-Wraith ascended thrice,
And gave his doleful warning.

Delicious is the Lay that sings
The haunts of happy lovers,
The path that leads them to the grove,
The leafy grove that covers :
And pity sanctifies the verse
That paints, by strength of sorrow,
The unconquerable strength of love ;
Bear witness, rueful Yarrow !

But thou that didst appear so fair
To fond imagination
Dost rival in the light of day
Her delicate creation :
Meek loveliness is round thee spread,
A softness still and holy :
The grace of forest charms decay'd,
And pastoral melancholy.

That region left, the vale unfolds
Rich groves of lofty stature,
With Yarrow winding through the pomp
Of cultivated Nature ;
And rising from those lofty groves
Behold a ruin hoary,
The shatter'd front of Newark's Towers,
Renown'd in Border story.

Fair scenes for childhood's opening bloom,
For sportive youth to stray in,
For manhood to enjoy his strength,
And age to wear away in !
Yon cottage seems a bower of bliss,
A covert for protection
Of studious ease and generous cares,
And every chaste affection !

How sweet on this autumnal day
The wild-wood fruits to gather,
And on my true-love's forehead plant
A crest of blooming heather!
And what if I enwreathed my own?
'Twere no offence to reason;
The sober hills thus deck their brows
To meet the wintry season.

I see—but not by sight alone
Loved Yarrow, have I won thee;
A ray of Fancy still survives—
Her sunshine plays upon thee!
Thy ever-youthful waters keep
A course of lively pleasure;
And gladsome notes my lips can breathe
Accordant to the measure.

The vapours linger round the heights,
They melt, and soon must vanish;
One hour is theirs, nor more is mine—
Sad thought! which I would banish,
But that I know, where'er I go,
Thy genuine image, Yarrow!
Will dwell with me, to heighten joy
And cheer my mind in sorrow.

W. WORDSWORTH.

259. THE INVITATION

Best and Brightest, come away,
Fairer far than this fair day,
Which, like thee, to those in sorrow
Comes to bid a sweet good-morrow
To the rough year just awake
In its cradle on the brake.
The brightest hour of unborn Spring
Through the winter wandering,
Found, it seems, the halcyon morn
To hoar February born;
Bending from Heaven, in azure mirth,
It kiss'd the forehead of the earth,
And smiled upon the silent sea,
And bade the frozen streams be free,

And waked to music all their fountains,
And breathed upon the frozen mountains,
And like a prophetess of May
Strew'd flowers upon the barren way,
Making the wintry world appear
Like one on whom thou smilest, Dear.

Away, away, from men and towns,
To the wild wood and the downs—
To the silent wilderness
Where the soul need not repress
Its music, lest it should not find
An echo in another's mind,
While the touch of Nature's art
Harmonises heart to heart.
Radiant Sister of the Day
Awake! arise! and come away!
To the wild woods and the plains,
To the pools were winter rains
Image all their roof of leaves,
Where the pine its garland weaves
Of sapless green, and ivy dun,
Round stems that never kiss the sun,
Where the lawns and pastures be
And the sandhills of the sea,
Where the melting hoar-frost wets
The daisy-star that never sets,
And wind-flowers and violets
Which yet join not scent to hue
Crown the pale year weak and new;
When the night is left behind
In the deep east, dim and blind,
And the blue noon is over us,
And the multitudinous
Billows murmur at our feet,
Where the earth and ocean meet,
And all things seem only one
In the universal Sun.

P. B. SHELLEY.

260. THE RECOLLECTION

Now the last day of many days
All beautiful and bright as thou,
The loveliest and the last, is dead,
Rise, Memory, and write its praise !
Up, do thy wonted work ! come, trace
The epitaph of glory fled,
For now the Earth has changed its face,
A frown is on the Heaven's brow.

We wander'd to the Pine Forest
   That skirts the Ocean's foam ;
The lightest wind was in its nest,
   The tempest in its home.
The whispering waves were half asleep,
   The clouds were gone to play,
And on the bosom of the deep
   The smile of Heaven lay ;
It seem'd as if the hour were one
   Sent from beyond the skies
Which scatter'd from above the sun
   A light of Paradise !

We paused amid the pines that stood
   The giants of the waste,
Tortured by storms to shapes as rude
   As serpents interlaced,—
And soothed by every azure breath
   That under heaven is blown
To harmonies and hues beneath,
   As tender as its own :
Now all the tree-tops lay asleep
   Like green waves on the sea,
As still as in the silent deep
   The ocean-woods may be.

How calm it was !—the silence there
   By such a chain was bound,
That even the busy woodpecker
   Made stiller by her sound
The inviolable quietness ;
   The breath of peace we drew

With its soft motion made not less
   The calm that round us grew.
There seem'd from the remotest seat
   Of the wide mountain waste
To the soft flower beneath our feet
   A magic circle traced,
A spirit interfused around,
   A thrilling silent life ;
To momentary peace it bound
   Our mortal nature's strife ;—
And still I felt the centre of
   The magic circle there
Was one fair Form that fill'd with love
   The lifeless atmosphere.

We paused beside the pools that lie
   Under the forest bough ;
Each seem'd as 'twere a little sky
   Gulf'd in a world below ;
A firmament of purple light
   Which in the dark earth lay,
More boundless than the depth of night
   And purer than the day—
In which the lovely forests grew
   As in the upper air,
More perfect both in shape and hue
   Than any spreading there.
There lay the glade and neighbouring lawn,
   And through the dark green wood
The white sun twinkling like the dawn
   Out of a speckled cloud.
Sweet views which in our world above
   Can never well be seen
Were imaged by the water's love
   Of that fair forest green :
And all was interfused beneath
   With an Elysian glow,
An atmosphere without a breath,
   A softer day below.
Like one beloved, the scene had lent
   To the dark water's breast
Its very leaf and lineament
   With more than truth exprest ;
Until an envious wind crept by,

Like an unwelcome thought
Which from the mind's too faithful eye
  Blots one dear image out.
—Though Thou art ever fair and kind,
  The forests ever green,
Less oft is peace in Shelley's mind
  Than calm in waters seen !

P. B. SHELLEY.

261. BY THE SEA

It is a beauteous evening, calm and free ;
The holy time is quiet as a nun
Breathless with adoration ; the broad sun
Is sinking down in its tranquillity ;

The gentleness of heaven is on the Sea :
Listen ! the mighty being is awake,
And doth with his eternal motion make
A sound like thunder—everlastingly.

Dear child ! dear girl ! that walkest with me here,
If thou appear untouch'd by solemn thought
Thy nature is not therefore less divine.

Thou liest in Abraham's bosom all the year,
And worshipp'st at the Temple's inner shrine,
God being with thee when we know it not.

W. WORDSWORTH.

262. TO THE EVENING STAR

Star that bringest home the bee,
  And sett'st the weary labourer free !
If any star shed peace, 'tis Thou
  That send'st it from above,
Appearing when Heaven's breath and brow
  Are sweet as hers we love.

Come to the luxuriant skies,
Whilst the landscape's odours rise,
Whilst far-off lowing herds are heard
  And songs when toil is done,
From cottages whose smoke unstirr'd
  Curls yellow in the sun.

Star of love's soft interviews,
Parted lovers on thee muse ;
Their remembrancer in Heaven
    Of thrilling vows thou art,
Too delicious to be riven
    By absence from the heart.

T. CAMPBELL.

263. DATUR HORA QUIETI

The sun upon the lake is low,
    The wild birds hush their song,
The hills have evening's deepest glow,
    Yet Leonard tarries long.
Now all whom varied toil and care
    From home and love divide,
In the calm sunset may repair
    Each to the loved one's side.

The noble dame on turret high,
    Who waits her gallant knight,
Looks to the western beam to spy
    The flash of armour bright.
The village maid, with hand on brow
    The level ray to shade,
Upon the footpath watches now
    For Colin's darkening plaid.

Now to their mates the wild swans row.
    By day they swam apart,
And to the thicket wanders slow
    The hind beside the hart.
The woodlark at his partner's side
    Twitters his closing song—
All meet whom day and care divide,
    But Leonard tarries long !

SIR W. SCOTT.

264. TO THE MOON

Art thou pale for weariness
Of climbing heaven, and gazing on the earth,
  Wandering companionless
Among the stars that have a different birth,—
And ever-changing, like a joyless eye
That finds no object worth its constancy?

P. B. SHELLEY.

265

A widow bird sate mourning for her Love
    Upon a wintry bough;
The frozen wind crept on above,
    The freezing stream below.

There was no leaf upon the forest bare,
    No flower upon the ground,
And little motion in the air
    Except the mill-wheel's sound.

P. B. SHELLEY.

266. TO SLEEP

A flock of sheep that leisurely pass by
One after one; the sound of rain, and bees
Murmuring; the fall of rivers, winds and seas,
Smooth fields, white sheets of water, and pure sky;—

I've thought of all by turns, and still I lie
Sleepless; and soon the small birds' melodies
Must hear, first utter'd from my orchard trees,
And the first cuckoo's melancholy cry.

Even thus last night, and two nights more I lay,
And could not win thee, Sleep! by any stealth:
So do not let me wear to-night away:

Without Thee what is all the morning's wealth?
Come, blessed barrier between day and day,
Dear mother of fresh thoughts and joyous health!

W. WORDSWORTH.

267. THE SOLDIER'S DREAM

Our bugles sang truce, for the night-cloud had lower'd,
  And the sentinel stars set their watch in the sky ;
And thousands had sunk on the ground overpower'd,
  The weary to sleep, and the wounded to die.

When reposing that night on my pallet of straw
  By the wolf-scaring faggot that guarded the slain,
At the dead of the night a sweet Vision I saw ;
  And thrice ere the morning I dreamt it again.

Methought from the battle-field's dreadful array
  Far, far I had roam'd on a desolate track :
'Twas Autumn,—and sunshine arose on the way
  To the home of my fathers, that welcomed me back.

I flew to the pleasant fields traversed so oft
  In life's morning march, when my bosom was young ;
I heard my own mountain-goats bleating aloft,
  And knew the sweet strain that the corn-reapers sung.

Then pledged me the wine-cup, and fondly I swore
  From my home and my weeping friends never to part ;
My little ones kiss'd me a thousand times o'er,
  And my wife sobb'd aloud in her fulness of heart.

" Stay—stay with us !—rest !—thou art weary and
      worn ! "—
  And fain was their war-broken soldier to stay ;—
But sorrow return'd with the dawning of morn,
  And the voice in my dreaming ear melted away.

                                    T. CAMPBELL.

268. A DREAM OF THE UNKNOWN

I dream'd that as I wander'd by the way
  Bare Winter suddenly was changed to Spring,
And gentle odours led my steps astray,
  Mix'd with a sound of waters murmuring
Along a shelving bank of turf, which lay
  Under a copse, and hardly dared to fling
Its green arms round the bosom of the stream,
But kiss'd it and then fled, as Thou mightest in dream.

There grew pied wind-flowers and violets,
  Daisies, those pearl'd Arcturi of the earth.
The constellated flower that never sets ;
  Faint oxlips ; tender blue-bells, at whose birth
The sod scarce heaved ; and that tall flower that wets
  Its mother's face with heaven-collected tears,
When the low wind, its playmate's voice, it hears.

And in the warm hedge grew lush eglantine,
  Green cow-bind and the moonlight-colour'd May,
And cherry-blossoms, and white cups, whose wine
  Was the bright dew yet drain'd not by the day ;
And wild roses, and ivy serpentine
  With its dark buds and leaves, wandering astray ;
And flowers azure, black, and streak'd with gold,
Fairer than any waken'd eyes behold.

And nearer to the rivers trembling edge
  There grew broad flag-flowers, purple prankt with white,
And starry river-buds among the sedge,
  And floating water-lilies, broad and bright,
Which lit the oak that overhung the hedge
  With moonlight beams of their own watery light ;
And bulrushes, and reeds of such deep green
As soothed the dazzled eye with sober sheen.

Methought that of these visionary flowers
  I made a nosegay, bound in such a way
That the same hues, which in their natural bowers
  Were mingled or oppressed, the like array
Kept these imprison'd children of the Hours
  Within my hand,—and then, elate and gay,
I hasten'd to the spot whence I had come
That I might there present it—O ! to Whom ?

                              P. B. SHELLEY.

269. THE INNER VISION

Most sweet it is with unuplifted eyes
To pace the ground, if path there be or none,
While a fair region round the Traveller lies
Which he forbears again to look upon ;

Pleased rather with some soft ideal scene
The work of Fancy, or some happy tone
Of meditation, slipping in between
The beauty coming and the beauty gone.

—If Thought and Love desert us, from that day
Let us break off all commerce with the Muse :
With Thought and Love companions of our way—

Whate'er the senses take or may refuse,—
The Mind's internal heaven shall shed her dews
Of inspiration on the humblest lay.

W. WORDSWORTH.

270. THE REALM OF FANCY

Ever let the Fancy roam !
Pleasure never is at home :
At a touch sweet Pleasure melteth,
Like to bubbles when rain pelteth ;
Then let wingèd Fancy wander
Through the thought still spread beyond her :
Open wide the mind's cage-door,
She'll dart forth, and cloudward soar.
O sweet Fancy ! let her loose ;
Summer's joys are spoilt by use,
And the enjoying of the Spring
Fades as does its blossoming :
Autumn's red-lipp'd fruitage too
Blushing through the mist and dew
Cloys with tasting : What do then ?
Sit thee by the ingle, when
The sear faggot blazes bright,
Spirit of a winter's night ;
When the soundless earth is muffled,
And the cakèd snow is shuffled
From the ploughboy's heavy shoon ;
When the Night doth meet the Noon
In dark conspiracy
To banish Even from her sky.
—Sit thee there, and send abroad
With a mind self-overawed
Fancy, high-commission'd :—send her !
She has vassals to attend her ;
She will bring, in spite of frost,
Beauties that the earth hath lost ;
She will bring thee, all together,
All delights of summer weather ;

All the buds and bells of May
From dewy sward or thorny spray;
All the heapèd Autumn's wealth,
With a still, mysterious stealth,
She will mix these pleasures up
Like three fit wines in a cup
And thou shalt quaff it:—thou shalt hear
Distant harvest-carols clear;
Rustle of the reapèd corn;
Sweet birds antheming the morn:
And in the same moment—hark!
'Tis the early April lark,
Or the rooks, with busy caw,
Foraging for sticks and straw.
Thou shalt, at one glance, behold
The daisy and the marigold;
White-plumed lilies, and the first
Hedge-grown primrose that hath burst;
Shaded hyacinth, alway
Sapphire queen of the mid-May;
And every leaf, and every flower
Pearlèd with the self-same shower.
Thou shalt see the field-mouse peep
Meagre from its cellèd sleep;
And the snake all winter-thin
Cast on sunny bank its skin;
Freckled nest eggs thou shalt see
Hatching in the hawthorn-tree,
When the hen-bird's wing doth rest
Quiet on her mossy nest;
Then the hurry and alarm
When the bee-hive casts its swarm;
Acorns ripe down-pattering
While the autumn breezes sing.
O sweet Fancy! let her loose;
Everything is spoilt by use:
Where's the cheek that doth not fade,
Too much gazed at? Where's the maid
Whose lip mature is ever new?
Where's the eye, however blue,
Doth not weary? Where's the face
One would meet in every place?
Where's the voice, however soft,
One would hear so very oft?

At a touch sweet Pleasure melteth
Like to bubbles when rain pelteth.
Let then wingèd Fancy find
Thee a mistress to thy mind :
Dulcet-eyed as Ceres' daughter,
Ere the God of Torment taught her
How to frown and how to chide :
With a waist and with a side
White as Hebe's, when her zone
Slipt its golden clasp, and down
Fell her kirtle to her feet,
While she held the goblet sweet,
And Jove grew languid.—Break the mesh
Of the Fancy's silken leash ;
Quickly break her prison-string,
And such joys as these she'll bring :
—Let the wingèd Fancy roam !
Pleasure never is at home.

J. KEATS.

271. HYMN TO THE SPIRIT OF NATURE

Life of Life ! Thy lips enkindle
 With their love the breath between them ;
And thy smiles before they dwindle
 Make the cold air fire ; then screen them
In those locks, where whoso gazes
Faints, entangled in their mazes

Child of light ! Thy limbs are burning
 Through the veil which seems to hide them,
As the radiant lines of morning
 Through thin clouds, ere they divide them ;
And this atmosphere divinest
Shrouds thee wheresoe'er thou shinest

Fair are others : none beholds Thee ;
 But thy voice sounds low and tender
Like the fairest, for it folds thee
 From the sight, that liquid splendour ;
And all feel, yet see thee never,—
As I feel now, lost for ever !

Lamp of Earth ! where'er thou movest
  Its dim shapes are clad with brightness,
And the souls of whom thou lovest
  Walk upon the winds with lightness
Till they fail, as I am failing,
Dizzy, lost, yet unbewailing !

P. B. SHELLEY.

272. WRITTEN IN EARLY SPRING

I heard a thousand blended notes
While in a grove I sat reclined,
In that sweet mood when pleasant thoughts
Bring sad thoughts to the mind.

To her fair works did Nature link
The human soul that through me ran ;
And much it grieved my heart to think
What Man has made of Man.

Through primrose tufts, in that sweet bower,
The periwinkle trail'd its wreaths ;
And 'tis my faith that every flower
Enjoys the air it breathes.

The birds around me hopp'd and play'd,
Their thoughts I cannot measure—
But the least motion which they made
It seem'd a thrill of pleasure.

The budding twigs spread out their fan
To catch the breezy air ;
And I must think, do all I can,
That there was pleasure there.

If this belief from heaven be sent,
If such be Nature's holy plan,
Have I not reason to lament
What Man has made of Man ?

W. WORDSWORTH.

273. RUTH : OR THE INFLUENCES
OF NATURE

When Ruth was left half desolate
Her father took another mate ;
And Ruth, not seven years old,
A slighted child, at her own will
Went wandering over dale and hill,
In thoughtless freedom bold.

And she had made a pipe of straw,
And music from that pipe could draw
Like sounds of winds and floods ;
Had built a bower upon the green,
As if she from her birth had been
An infant of the woods.

Beneath her father's roof, alone
She seem'd to live ; her thoughts her own ;
Herself her own delight :
Pleased with herself, nor sad nor gay,
She pass'd her time ; and in this way
Grew up to woman's height.

There came a youth from Georgia's shore—
A military casque he wore
With splendid feathers drest ;
He brought them from the Cherokees ;
The feathers nodded in the breeze
And made a gallant crest.

From Indian blood you deem him sprung :
But no ! he spake the English tongue
And bore a soldier's name ;
And, when America was free
From battle and from jeopardy,
He 'cross the ocean came.

With hues of genius on his cheek,
In finest tones the youth could speak :
—While he was yet a boy
The moon, the glory of the sun,
And streams that murmur as they run
Had been his dearest joy.

He was a lovely youth ! I guess
The panther in the wilderness
Was not so fair as he ;
And when he chose to sport and play,
No dolphin ever was so gay
Upon the tropic sea.

Among the Indians he had fought ;
And with him many tales he brought
Of pleasure and of fear ;
Such tales as, told to any maid
By such a youth, in the green shade,
Were perilous to hear.

He told of girls, a happy rout !
Who quit their fold with dance and shout,
Their pleasant Indian town,
To gather strawberries all day long ;
Returning with a choral song
When daylight is gone down.

He spake of plants that hourly change
Their blossoms, through a boundless range
Of intermingling hues ;
With budding, fading, faded flowers,
They stand the wonder of the bowers
From morn to evening dews.

He told of the Magnolia, spread
High as a cloud, high over head !
The cypress and her spire ;
—Of flowers that with one scarlet gleam
Cover a hundred leagues, and seem
To set the hills on fire.

The youth of green savannahs spake,
And many an endless, endless lake
With all its fairy crowds
Of islands that together lie
As quietly as spots of sky
Among the evening clouds.

And then he said, " How sweet it were
A fisher or a hunter there,
In sunshine or in shade
To wander with an easy mind
And build a household fire, and find
A home in every glade !

" What days and what bright years ! Ah me !
Our life were life indeed, with Thee
So pass'd in quiet bliss ;
And all the while," said he, " to know
That we were in a world of woe,
On such an earth as this ! "

And then he sometimes interwove
Fond thoughts about a father's love,
" For there," said he, " are spun
Around the heart such tender ties,
That our own children to our eyes
Are dearer than the sun.

" Sweet Ruth ! and could you go with me
My helpmate in the woods to be,
Our shed at night to rear ;
Or run, my own adopted bride,
A sylvan huntress at my side,
And drive the flying deer ! "

" Beloved Ruth ! "—No more he said.
The wakeful Ruth at midnight shed
A solitary tear :
She thought again—and did agree
With him to sail across the sea,
And drive the flying deer.

" And now, as fitting is and right,
We in the church our faith will plight,
A husband and a wife."
Even so they did ; and I may say
That to sweet Ruth that happy day
Was more than human life.

Through dream and vision did she sink,
Delighted all the while to think
That, on those lonesome floods
And green savannahs, she should share
His board with lawful joy, and bear
His name in the wild woods.

But, as you have before been told
This Stripling, sportive, gay, and bold,
And with his dancing crest
So beautiful, through savage lands

Had roam'd about, with vagrant bands
Of Indians in the West.

The wind, the tempest roaring high,
The tumult of a tropic sky
Might well be dangerous food
For him, a youth to whom was given
So much of earth—so much of heaven,
And such impetuous blood.

Whatever in those climes he found
Irregular in sight or sound
Did to his mind impart
A kindred impulse, seem'd allied
To his own powers, and justified
The workings of his heart.

Nor less, to feed voluptuous thought,
The beauteous forms of Nature wrought,—
Fair trees and gorgeous flowers ;
The breezes their own languor lent ;
The stars had feelings, which they sent
Into those favour'd bowers.

Yet, in his worst pursuits, I ween
That sometimes there did intervene
Pure hopes of high intent :
For passions link'd to forms so fair
And stately, needs must have their share
Of noble sentiment.

But ill he lived, much evil saw
With men to whom no better law
Nor better life was known ;
Deliberately and undeceived
Those wild men's vices he received,
And gave them back his own.

His genius and his moral frame
Were thus impair'd, and he became
The slave of low desires :
A man who without self-control
Would seek what the degraded soul
Unworthily admires.

And yet he with no feign'd delight
Had woo'd the maiden, day and night,
Had loved her, night and morn :
What could he less than love a maid
Whose heart with so much nature play'd—
So kind and so forlorn ?

Sometimes most earnestly he said,
" O Ruth ! I have been worse than dead ;
False thoughts, thoughts bold and vain
Encompass'd me on every side
When I, in confidence and pride,
Had cross'd the Atlantic main.

" Before me shone a glorious world
Fresh as a banner bright, unfurl'd
To music suddenly :
I look'd upon those hills and plains,
And seem'd as if let loose from chains
To live at liberty !

" No more of this—for now, by thee,
Dear Ruth ! more happily set free,
With nobler zeal I burn ;
My soul from darkness is released
Like the whole sky when to the east
The morning doth return."

Full soon that better mind was gone ;
No hope, no wish remain'd, not one,—
They stirr'd him now no more ;
New objects did new pleasure give,
And once again he wish'd to live
As lawless as before.

Meanwhile, as thus with him it fared,
They for the voyage were prepared,
And went to the sea-shore :
But, when they thither came, the youth
Deserted his poor bride, and Ruth
Could never find him more.

God help thee, Ruth !—Such pains she had
That she in half a year was mad
And in a prison housed ;

And there, exulting in her wrongs,
Among the music of her songs
She fearfully caroused.

Yet sometimes milder hours she knew,
Nor wanted sun, nor rain, nor dew,
Her pastimes of the May,
—They all were with her in her cell :
And a clear brook with cheerful knell
Did o'er the pebbles play.

When Ruth three seasons thus had lain.
There came a respite to her pain,
She from her prison fled ;
But of the vagrant none took thought ;
And where it liked her best she sought
Her shelter and her bread.

Among the fields she breathed again :
The master-current of her brain
Ran permanent and free ;
And, coming to the banks of Tone,
There did she rest ; and dwell alone
Under the greenwood tree.

The engines of her pain, the tools
That shaped her sorrow, rocks and pools,
And airs that gently stir
The vernal leaves, she loved them still,
Nor ever tax'd them with the ill
Which had been done to her.

A barn her Winter bed supplies ;
But, till the warmth of Summer skies
And Summer days is gone,
(And all do in this tale agree)
She sleeps beneath the greenwood tree,
And other home hath none.

An innocent life, yet far astray !
And Ruth will, long before her day,
Be broken down and old.
Sore aches she needs must have ! but less
Of mind, than body's wretchedness,
From damp, and rain, and cold.

If she is prest by want of food
She from her dwelling in the wood
Repairs to a road-side ;
And there she begs at one steep place,
Where up and down with easy pace
The horsemen-travellers ride.

That oaten pipe of hers is mute
Or thrown away : but with a flute
Her loneliness she cheers,
This flute, made of a hemlock stalk,
At evening in his homeward walk
The Quantock woodman hears.

I, too, have pass'd her on the hills
Setting her little water-mills
By spouts and fountains wild—
Such small machinery as she turn'd
Ere she had wept, ere she had mourn'd,
A young and happy child !

Farewell ! and when thy days are told,
Ill-fated Ruth ! in hallow'd mould
Thy corpse shall buried be ;
For thee a funeral bell shall ring,
And all the congregation sing
A Christian psalm for thee.   W. Wordsworth.

274. WRITTEN IN THE EUGANEAN HILLS, NORTH ITALY

Many a green isle needs must be
In the deep wide sea of misery,
Or the mariner, worn and wan,
Never thus could voyage on
Day and night, and night and day,
Drifting on his weary way,
With the solid darkness black
Closing round his vessel's track ;
Whilst above, the sunless sky
Big with clouds, hangs heavily,
And behind the tempest fleet
Hurries on with lightning feet,
Riving sail, and cord, and plank,
Till the ship has almost drank

Death from the o'er-brimming deep ;
And sinks down, down, like that sleep
When the dreamer seems to be
Weltering through eternity ;
And the dim low line before
Of a dark and distant shore
Still recedes, as ever still
Longing with divided will,
But no power to seek or shun,
He is ever drifted on
O'er the unreposing wave,
To the haven of the grave.

    Ah, many flowering islands lie
In the waters of wide agony :
To such a one this morn was led
My bark, by soft winds piloted.
—'Mid the mountains Euganean
I stood listening to the pæan
With which the legion'd rooks did hail
The Sun's uprise majestical :
Gathering round with wings all hoar,
Through the dewy mist they soar
Like gray shades, till the eastern heaven
Bursts, and then,—as clouds of even
Fleck'd with fire and azure, lie
In the unfathomable sky,—
So their plumes of purple grain
Starr'd with drops of golden rain
Gleam above the sunlight woods,
As in silent multitudes
On the morning's fitful gale
Through the broken mist they sail ;
And the vapours cloven and gleaming
Follow down the dark steep streaming,
Till all is bright, and clear, and still
Round the solitary hill.

    Beneath is spread like a green sea
The waveless plain of Lombardy,
Bounded by the vaporous air,
Islanded by cities fair ;
Underneath day's azure eyes,
Ocean's nursling, Venice lies,—

A peopled labyrinth of walls,
Amphitrite's destined halls,
Which her hoary sire now paves
With his blue and beaming waves.
Lo ! the sun upsprings behind,
Broad, red radiant, half-reclined
On the level quivering line
Of the waters crystalline ;
And before that chasm of light,
As within a furnace bright,
Column, tower, and dome, and spire,
Shine like obelisks of fire,
Pointing with inconstant motion
From the altar of dark ocean
To the sapphire-tinted skies ;
As the flames of sacrifice
From the marble shrines did rise
As to pierce the dome of gold
Where Apollo spoke of old.

Sun-girt City ! thou hast been
Ocean's child and then his queen ;
Now is come a darker day,
And thou soon must be his prey,
If the power that raised thee here
Hallow so thy watery bier.
A less drear ruin then than now
With thy conquest-branded brow
Stooping to the slave of slaves
From thy throne among the waves,
Wilt thou be,—when the sea-mew
Flies, as once before it flew,
O'er thine isles depopulate,
And all is in its ancient state,
Save where many a palace-gate
With green sea-flowers overgrown
Like a rock of ocean's own,
Topples o'er the abandon'd sea
As the tides change sullenly.
The fisher on his watery way
Wandering at the close of day,
Will spread his sail and seize his oar
Till he pass the gloomy shore,

Lest thy dead should, from their sleep
Bursting o'er the starlight deep,
Lead a rapid masque of death
O'er the waters of his path.

Noon descends around me now :
'Tis the noon of autumn's glow,
When a soft and purple mist
Like a vaporous amethyst,
Or an air-dissolvèd star
Mingling light and fragrance, far
From the curved horizon's bound
To the point of heaven's profound,
Fills the overflowing sky ;
And the plains that silent lie
Underneath ; the leaves unsodden
Where the infant frost has trodden
With his morning-wingèd feet
Whose bright print is gleaming yet ;
And the red and golden vines
Piercing with their trellised lines
The rough, dark-skirted wilderness ;
The dun and bladed grass no less,
Pointing from this hoary tower
In the windless air ; the flower
Glimmering at my feet ; the line
Of the olive-sandall'd Apennine
In the south dimly islanded ;
And the Alps, whose snows are spread
High between the clouds and sun ;
And of living things each one ;
And my spirit, which so long
Darken'd this swift stream of song,—
Interpenetrated lie
By the glory of the sky ;
Be it love, light, harmony,
Odour, or the soul of all
Which from Heaven like dew doth fall,
Or the mind which feeds this verse
Peopling the lone universe.

Noon descends, and after noon
Autumn's evening meets me soon.
Leading the infantine moon

And that one star, which to her
Almost seems to minister
Half the crimson light she brings
From the sunset's radiant springs :
And the soft dreams of the morn
(Which like wingèd winds had borne
To that silent isle, which lies
'Mid remember'd agonies,
The frail bark of this lone being),
Pass, to other sufferers fleeing,
And its ancient pilot, Pain,
Sits beside the helm again.

Other flowering isles must be
In the sea of life and agony :
Other spirits float and flee
O'er that gulf : ev'n now, perhaps,
On some rock the wild wave wraps,
With folding wings they waiting sit
For my bark, to pilot it
To some calm and blooming cover,
Where for me, and those I love,
May a windless bower be built,
Far from passion, pain, and guilt,
In a dell 'mid lawny hills
Which the wild sea-murmur fills,
And soft sunshine, and the sound
Of old forests echoing round,
And the light and smell divine
Of all flowers that breathe and shine
—We may live so happy there,
That the spirits of the air
Envying us, may even entice
To our healing paradise
The polluting multitude ;
But their rage would be subdued
By that clime divine and calm,
And the winds whose wings rain balm
On the uplifted soul, and leaves
Under which the bright sea heaves ;
While each breathless interval
In their whisperings musical
The inspired soul supplies
With its own deep melodies ;

And the Love which heals all strife
Circling, like the breath of life,
All things in that sweet abode
With its own mild brotherhood.
They, not it, would change ; and soon
Every sprite beneath the moon
Would repent its envy vain,
And the Earth grow young again !

P. B. SHELLEY.

275. ODE TO THE WEST WIND

O wild West Wind, thou breath of Autumn's being,
Thou, from whose unseen presence the leaves dead
Are driven, like ghosts from an enchanter fleeing,
Yellow, and black, and pale, and hectic red,
Pestilence-striken multitudes : O thou
Who chariotest to their dark wintry bed
The wingèd seeds, where they lie cold and low,
Each like a corpse within its grave, until
Thine azure sister of the spring shall blow
Her clarion o'er the dreaming earth, and fill
(Driving sweet buds like flocks to feed in air)
With living hues and odours plain and hill :
Wild Spirit, which art moving everywhere ;
Destroyer and Preserver ; Hear, O hear !

Thou on whose stream, 'mid the steep sky's commotion,
Loose clouds like earth's decaying leaves are shed
Shook from the tangled boughs of Heaven and Ocean,
Angels of rain and lightning ; there are spread
On the blue surface of thine airy surge,
Like the bright hair uplifted from the head
Of some fierce Mænad, ev'n from the dim verge
Of the horizon to the zenith's height—
The locks of the approaching storm. Thou dirge
Of the dying year, to which this closing night
Will be the dome of a vast sepulchre,
Vaulted with all thy congregated might
Of vapours, from whose solid atmosphere
Black rain, and fire, and hail, will burst : O hear !

Thou who didst waken from his summer-dreams
The blue Mediterranean, where he lay

Lull'd by the coil of his crystalline streams,
Beside a pumice isle in Baiae's bay,
And saw in sleep old palaces and towers
Quivering within the wave's intenser day,
All overgrown with azure moss and flowers
So sweet, the sense faints picturing them ! Thou
For whose path the Atlantic's level powers
Cleave themselves into chasms, while far below
The sea-blooms and the oozy woods which wear
The sapless foliage of the ocean, know
Thy voice, and suddenly grow gray with fear
And tremble and despoil themselves : O hear !

If I were a dead leaf thou mightest bear ;
If I were a swift cloud to fly with thee ;
A wave to pant beneath thy power, and share
The impulse of thy strength, only less free
Than Thou, O uncontrollable ! If even
I was as in my boyhood, and could be
The comrade of thy wanderings over heaven,
As then, when to outstrip the skyey speed
Scarce seem'd a vision, I would ne'er have striven
As thus with thee in prayer in my sore need.
O lift me as a wave, a leaf, a cloud !
I fall upon the thorns of life ! I bleed !
A heavy weight of hours has chain'd and bow'd
One too like thee : tameless, and swift, and proud.

Make me thy lyre, ev'n as the forest is :
What if my leaves are falling like its own !
The tumult of thy mighty harmonies
Will take from both a deep autumnal tone,
Sweet though in sadness. Be thou, Spirit fierce,
My spirit ! be thou me, impetuous one !
Drive my dead thoughts over the universe
Like wither'd leaves to quicken a new birth ;
And, by the incantation of this verse,
Scatter, as from an unextinguish'd hearth
Ashes and sparks, my words among mankind !
Be through my lips to unawaken'd earth
The trumpet of a prophecy ! O Wind,
If Winter comes, can Spring be far behind ?

P. B. SHELLEY.

276. NATURE AND THE POET

Suggested by a Picture of Peele Castle in a Storm painted by
Sir George Beaumont

I was thy neighbour once, thou rugged Pile !
Four summer weeks I dwelt in sight of thee :
I saw thee every day ; and all the while
Thy form was sleeping on a glassy sea.

So pure the sky, so quiet was the air !
So like, so very like, was day to day !
Whene'er I looked, thy image still was there ;
It trembled, but it never pass'd away,

How perfect was the calm ! It seem'd no sleep,
No mood, which season takes away, or brings :
I could have fancied that the mighty Deep
Was even the gentlest of all gentle things.

Ah ! then if mine had been the painter's hand
To express what then I saw : and add the gleam,
The light that never was on sea or land,
The consecration, and the Poet's dream,—

I would have planted thee, thou hoary pile,
Amid a world how different from this !
Beside a sea that could not cease to smile ;
On tranquil land, beneath a sky of bliss.

A picture had it been of lasting ease,
Elysian quiet, without toil or strife ;
No motion but the moving tide, a breeze,
Or merely silent Nature's breathing life.

Such, in the fond illusion of my heart,
Such picture would I at that time have made ;
And seen the soul of truth in every part,
A steadfast peace that might not be betray'd.

So once it would have been,—'tis so no more ;
I have submitted to a new control :
A power is gone, which nothing can restore ;
A deep distress hath humanized my soul.

Not for a moment could I now behold
A smiling sea, and be what I have been :
The feeling of my loss will ne'er be old ;
This, which I know, I speak with mind serene.

Then, Beaumont, Friend ! who would have been
    the Friend
If he had lived, of him whom I deplore,
This work of thine I blame not, but commend ;
This sea in anger, and that dismal shore.

O 'tis a passionate work !—yet wise and well,
Well chosen is the spirit that is here ;
That hulk which labours in the deadly swell,
This rueful sky, this pageantry of fear !

And this huge Castle, standing here sublime,
I love to see the look with which it braves,
——Cased in the unfeeling armour of old time——
The lightning, the fierce wind, and trampling waves.

Farewell, farewell the heart that lives alone,
Housed in a dream, at distance from the Kind !
Such happiness, wherever it be known,
Is to be pitied ; for 'tis surely blind.

But welcome fortitude, and patient cheer,
    And frequent sighs of what is to be borne !
Such sighs, or worse, as are before me here :——
    Not without hope we suffer and we mourn.

                          W. WORDSWORTH.

277. THE POET'S DREAM

On a Poet's lips I slept
Dreaming like a love-adept
In the sound his breathing kept ;
Nor seeks nor finds he mortal blisses,
But feeds on the aerial kisses
Of shapes that haunt Thought's wildernesses.
He will watch from dawn to gloom
The lake-reflected sun illume
The yellow bees in the ivy-bloom,
    Nor heed nor see what things they be—
But from these create he can
Forms more real than living Man,
    Nurslings of Immortality !

P. B. SHELLEY.

278

The World is too much with us ; late and soon,
Getting and spending, we lay waste our powers ;
Little we see in Nature that is ours ;
We have given our hearts away, a sordid boon !

This Sea that bares her bosom to the moon,
The winds that will be howling at all hours
And are up-gather'd now like sleeping flowers,
For this, for everything, we are out of tune ;

It moves us not.—Great God ! I'd rather be
A Pagan suckled in a creed outworn,—
So might I, standing on this pleasant lea,

Have glimpses that would make me less forlorn ;
Have sight of Proteus rising from the sea ;
Or hear old Triton blow his wreathéd horn.

W. WORDSWORTH.

279. WITHIN KING'S COLLEGE CHAPEL, CAMBRIDGE

Tax not the royal Saint with vain expense,
With ill-matched aims the Architect who plann'd
(Albeit labouring for a scanty band
Of white-robed scholars only) this immense

And glorious work of fine intelligence !
—Give all thou canst ; high heaven rejects the lore
Of nicely-calculated less or more :—
So deem'd the man who fashion'd for the sense

These lofty pillars, spread that branching roof
Self-poised, and scoop'd into ten thousand cells
Where light and shade repose, where music dwells

Lingering and wandering on as loth to die—
Like thoughts whose very sweetness yieldeth proof
That they were born for immortality.

W. WORDSWORTH.

280. YOUTH AND AGE

Verse, a breeze 'mid blossoms straying,
Where Hope clung feeding, like a bee—
Both were mine ! Life went a-maying
With Nature, Hope, and Poesy,
     When I was young !

When I was young ?—Ah, woeful when !
Ah ! for the change 'twixt Now and Then !
This breathing house not built with hands,
This body that does me grievous wrong,
O'er aery cliffs and glittering sands
How lightly then it flashed along :
Like those trim skiffs, unknown of yore,
On winding lakes and rivers wide,
That ask no aid of sail or oar,
That fear no spite of wind or tide !
Nought cared this body for wind or weather
When Youth and I lived in't together.

Flowers are lovely ; Love is flower-like ;
Friendship is a sheltering tree ;
O ! the joys, that came down shower-like,
Of Friendship, Love, and Liberty,
     Ere I was old !

Ere I was old ? Ah woful Ere,
Which tells me, Youth's no longer here !
O Youth ! for years so many and sweet

'Tis known that Thou and I were one,
I'll think it but a fond conceit—
It cannot be, that Thou art gone !
Thy vesper-bell hath not yet toll'd :—
And thou wert aye a masker bold !
What strange disguise hast now put on
To make believe that thou art gone ?
I see these locks in silvery slips,
This drooping gait, this alter'd size :
But Springtide blossoms on thy lips,
And tears take sunshine from thine eyes !
Life is but Thought : so think I will
That Youth and I are housemates still.

Dew-drops are the gems of morning,
But the tears of mournful eve !
Where no hope is, life's a warning
That only serves to make us grieve
        When we are old :
—That only serves to make us grieve
With oft and tedious taking-leave,
Like some poor nigh-related guest
That may not rudely be dismist,
Yet hath out-stay'd his welcome while,
And tells the jest without a smile.

S. T. COLERIDGE.

281. THE TWO APRIL MORNINGS

We walk'd along, while bright and red
Uprose the morning sun ;
And Matthew stopp'd, he look'd, and said
" The will of God be done ! "

A village schoolmaster was he,
With hair of glittering gray ;
As blithe a man as you could see
On a spring holiday.

And on that morning, through the grass
And by the steaming rills
We travell'd merrily, to pass
A day among the hills.

" Our work," said I, " was well begun ;
Then, from thy breast what thought,
Beneath so beautiful a sun,
So sad a sigh has brought ? "

A second time did Matthew stop ;
And fixing still his eye
Upon the eastern mountain-top,
To me he made reply :

" Yon cloud with that long purple cleft
Brings fresh into my mind
A day like this, which I have left
Full thirty years behind.

" And just above yon slope of corn
Such colours, and no other,
Were in the sky that April morn
Of this the very brother.

" With rod and line I sued the sport
Which that sweet season gave,
And coming to the church, stopp'd short
Beside my daughter's grave.

" Nine summers had she scarcely seen,
The pride of all the vale ;
And then she sang :—she would have been
A very nightingale.

" Six feet in earth my Emma lay ;
And yet I loved her more—
For so it seem'd,—than till that day
I e'er had loved before.

" And turning from her grave, I met
Beside the churchyard yew
A blooming Girl, whose hair was wet
With points of morning dew.

" A basket on her head she bare ;
Her brow was smooth and white :
To see a child so very fair,
It was a pure delight !

" No fountain from its rocky cave
E'er tripp'd with foot so free ;
She seem'd as happy as a wave
That dances on the sea.

" There came from me a sigh of pain,
Which I could ill confine ;
I look'd at her, and look'd again :
And did not wish her mine ! "

—Matthew is in his grave, yet now
Methinks I see him stand
As at that moment, with a bough
Of wilding in his hand.
                    W. WORDSWORTH.

282. THE FOUNTAIN

A Conversation

We talk'd with open heart, and tongue
Affectionate and true,
A pair of friends, though I was young,
And Matthew seventy-two.

We lay beneath a spreading oak,
Beside a mossy seat ;
And from the turf a fountain broke
And gurgled at our feet.

" Now, Matthew ! " said I " let us match
This water's pleasant tune
With some old border song, or catch
That suits a summer's noon.

" Or of the church-clock and the chimes
Sing here beneath the shade
That half-mad thing of witty rhymes
Which you last April made ! "

In silence Matthew lay, and eyed
The spring beneath the tree ;
And thus the dear old man replied,
The gray-hair'd man of glee :

" No check, no stay, this Streamlet fears,
How merrily it goes !
'Twill murmur on a thousand years
And flow as now it flows.

" And here, on this delightful day
I cannot choose but think
How oft, a vigorous man, I lay
Beside this fountain's brink.

" My eyes are dim with childish tears,
My heart is idly stirr'd,
For the same sound is in my ears
Which in those days I heard.

" Thus fares is still in our decay :
And yet the wiser mind
Mourns less for what Age takes away,
Than what it leaves behind.

" The blackbird amid leafy trees—
The lark above the hill
Let loose their carols when they please,
Are quiet when they will.

" With Nature never do they wage
A foolish strife ; they see
A happy youth, and their old age
Is beautiful and free :

" But we are press'd by heavy laws
And often, glad no more,
We wear a face of joy, because
We have been glad of yore.

" If there be one who need bemoan
His kindred laid in earth,
The household hearts that were his own,—
It is the man of mirth.

" My days, my friend, are almost gone,
My life has been approved,
And many love me ; but by none
Am I enough beloved."

" Now both himself and me he wrongs,
The man who thus complains !
I live and sing my idle songs
Upon these happy plains :

" And Matthew, for thy children dead
I'll be a son to thee ! "
At this he grasp'd my hand and said,
" Alas ! that cannot be."

We rose up from the fountain-side ;
And down the smooth descent
Of the green sheep-track did we glide
And through the wood we went ;

And ere we came to Leonard's Rock
He sang those witty rhymes
About the crazy old church-clock,
And the bewilder'd chimes.

W. WORDSWORTH.

283. THE RIVER OF LIFE

The more we live, more brief appear
  Our life's succeeding stages :
A day to childhood seems a year,
  And years like passing ages.

The gladsome current of our youth
  Ere passion yet disorders,
Steals lingering like a river smooth
  Along its grassy borders.

But as the careworn cheek grows wan,
  And sorrow's shafts fly thicker,
Ye stars, that measure life to man,
  Why seem your courses quicker ?

When joys have lost their bloom and breath
  And life itself is vapid,
Why, as we reach the Falls of Death,
  Feel we its tide more rapid ?

It may be strange—yet who would change
 Time's course to slower speeding,
When one by one our friends have gone
 And left our bosoms bleeding ?

Heaven gives our years of fading strength
 Indemnifying fleetness ;
And those of youth, a seeming length,
 Proportion'd to their sweetness.

T. CAMPBELL.

284. THE HUMAN SEASONS

Four Seasons fill the measure of the year ;
There are four seasons in the mind of Man :
He has his lusty Spring, when fancy clear
Takes in all beauty with an easy span :

He has his Summer, when luxuriously
Spring's honey'd cud of youthful thought he loves
To ruminate, and by such dreaming high
Is nearest unto heaven : quiet coves

His soul has in its Autumn, when his wings
He furleth close ; contented so to look
On mists in idleness—to let fair things
Pass by unheeded as a threshold brook :—

He has his Winter too of pale misfeature,
Or else he would forego his mortal nature.

J. KEATS.

285. A LAMENT

O World ! O Life ! O Time !
On whose last steps I climb,
 Trembling at that where I had stood before ;
When will return the glory of your prime ?
 No more—O never more !

Out of the day and night
A joy has taken flight :
    Fresh spring, and summer, and winter hoar
Move my faint heart with grief, but with delight
    No more——O never more !

P. B. SHELLEY.

286

My heart leaps up when I behold
    A rainbow in the sky :
So was it when my life began,
So is it now I am a man,
So be it when I shall grow old
    Or let me die !
The Child is father of the Man :
And I could wish my days to be
Bound each to each by natural piety.

W. WORDSWORTH

287. ODE ON INTIMATIONS OF IMMORTALITY FROM RECOLLECTIONS OF EARLY CHILDHOOD

There was a time when meadow, grove, and stream,
The earth, and every common sight
        To me did seem
        Apparell'd in celestial light,
The glory and the freshness of a dream.
It is not now as it has been of yore ;——
        Turn wheresoe'er I may,
            By night or day,
The things which I have seen I now can see no more !

        The rainbow comes and goes,
        And lovely is the rose ;
        The moon doth with delight
Look round her when the heavens are bare ;
        Waters on a starry night
        Are beautiful and fair ;
    The sunshine is a glorious birth ;
    But yet I know, where'er I go,
That there hath pass'd away a glory from the earth.

G.T.

Now, while the birds thus sing a joyous song,
    And while the young lambs bound
      As to the tabor's sound,
To me alone there came a thought of grief :
A timely utterance gave that thought relief,
    And I again am strong.
The cataracts blow their trumpets from the steep,—
No more shall grief of mine the season wrong :
I hear the echoes through the mountains throng,
The winds come to me from the fields of sleep,
      And all the earth is gay ;
        Land and sea
    Give themselves up to jollity,
      And with the heart of May
    Dost every beast keep holiday ;—
        Thou child of joy
Shout around me, let me hear thy shouts, thou happy
      Shepherd boy !

Ye blessèd creatures, I have heard the call
    Ye to each other make ; I see
The heavens laugh with you in your jubilee ;
    My heart is at your festival,
    My head hath its coronal,
The fulness of your bliss, I feel—I feel it all.
      O evil day ! if I were sullen
      While Earth herself is adorning
        This sweet May morning ;
      And the children are pulling
        On every side
      In a thousand valleys far and wide
    Fresh flowers ; while the sun shines warm,
And the babe leaps up on his mother's arm :—
      I hear, I hear, with joy I hear !
    —But there's a tree, of many, one,
A single field which I have look'd upon,
Both of them speak of something that is gone :
      The pansy at my feet
      Doth the same tale repeat :
Whither is fled the visionary gleam ?
Where is it now, the glory and the dream ?

Our birth is but a sleep and a forgetting ;
The Soul that rises with us, our life's Star,

Hath had elsewhere its setting
  And cometh from afar ;
Not in entire forgetfulness
And not in utter nakedness
But trailing clouds of glory do we come
  From God, who is our home :
Heaven lies about us in our infancy !
Shades of the prison-house begin to close
  Upon the growing boy,
But he beholds the light, and whence it flows,
  He sees it in his joy,
The youth, who daily farther from the east
 Must travel, still is Nature's priest,
  And by the vision splendid
  Is on his way attended ;
At length the man perceives it die away,
And fade into the light of common day.

Earth fills her lap with pleasures of her own ;
Yearnings she hath in her own natural kind,
And, even with something of a mother's mind
  And no unworthy aim,
 The homely nurse doth all she can
To make her foster-child, her inmate, Man,
  Forget the glories he hath known
And that imperial palace whence he came.

Behold the Child among his new-born blisses,
A six years' darling of a pigmy size !
See, where 'mid work of his own hand he lies,
Fretted by sallies of his mother's kisses,
With light upon him from his father's eyes !
See, at his feet, some little plan or chart,
Some fragment from his dream of human life,
Shaped by himself with newly-learned art ;
  A wedding or a festival,
  A mourning or a funeral ;
  And this hath now his heart,
  And unto this he frames his song :
  Then will he fit his tongue
To dialogues of business, love, or strife ;
  But it will not be long
  Ere this be thrown aside,

And with new joy and pride
The little actor cons another part ;
Filling from time to time his " humorous stage "
With all the Persons, dawn to palsied Age,
That life brings with her in her equipage ;
　　As if his whole vocation
　　Were endless imitation.

Thou, whose exterior semblance doth belie
　　Thy soul's immensity ;
Thou best philosopher, who yet dost keep
Thy heritage, thou eye among the blind,
That, deaf and silent, read'st the eternal deep,
Haunted for ever by the eternal Mind,—
　　Mighty Prophet ! Seer blest !
　　On whom those truths do rest
Which we are toiling all our lives to find ;
Thou, over whom thy immortality
Broods like the day, a master o'er a slave,
A presence which is not to be put by ;
Thou little child, yet glorious in the might
Of heaven-born freedom on thy being's height,
Why with such earnest pains dost thou provoke
The years to bring the inevitable yoke,
Thus blindly with thy blessedness at strife ?
Full soon thy soul shall have her earthly freight,
And custom lie upon thee with a weight
Heavy as frost, and deep almost as life !

　　O joy ! that in our embers
　　Is something that doth live,
　　That Nature yet remembers
　　What was so fugitive !
The thought of our past years in me doth breed
Perpetual benediction : not indeed
For that which is most worthy to be blest,
Delight and liberty, the simple creed
Of childhood, whether busy or at rest,
With new-fledged hope still fluttering in his breast :
　　—Not for these I raise
　　The song of thanks and praise ;
But for those obstinate questionings
Of sense and outward things,
Fallings from us, vanishings,
Blank misgivings of a creature

Moving about in worlds not realised,
High instincts, before which our mortal nature
Did tremble like a guilty thing surprised :
    But for those first affections,
    Those shadowy recollections,
      Which, be they what they may,
Are yet the fountain-light of all our day,
Are yet a master-light of all our seeing ;
      Uphold us—cherish—and have power to make
Our noisy years seem moments in the being
Of the eternal silence : truths that wake,
      To perish never ;
Which neither listlessness, nor mad endeavour
      Nor man nor boy
Nor all that is at enmity with joy,
Can utterly abolish or destroy !
    Hence, in a season of calm weather
      Though inland far we be,
Our souls have sight of that immortal sea
      Which brought us hither ;
      Can in a moment travel thither—
And see the children sport upon the shore,
And hear the mighty waters rolling evermore.

Then, sing ye birds, sing, sing a joyous song !
      And let the young lambs bound
      As to the tabor's sound !
We, in thought, will join your throng
    Ye that pipe and ye that play,
    Ye that through your hearts to-day
    Feel the gladness of the May !
What though the radiance which was once so bright
Be now for ever taken from my sight,
    Though nothing can bring back the hour
Of splendour in the grass, of glory in the flower ;
      We will grieve not, rather find
      Strength in what remains behind,
      In the primal sympathy
      Which having been must ever be,
      In the soothing thoughts that spring
      Out of human suffering,
      In the faith that looks through death,
In years that bring the philosophic mind.

And O, ye Fountains, Meadows, Hills, and Groves,
Forbode not any severing of our loves !
Yet in my heart of hearts I feel your might ;
I only have relinquish'd one delight
To live beneath your more habitual sway ;
I love the brooks which down their channels fret
Even more than when I tripp'd lightly as they ;
The innocent brightness of a new-born day
        Is lovely yet ;
The clouds that gather round the setting sun
Do take a sober colouring from an eye
That hath kept watch o'er man's mortality ;
Another race hath been, and other palms are won.
Thanks to the human heart by which we live,
Thanks to its tenderness, its joys, and fears,
To me the meanest flower that blows can give
Thoughts that do often lie too deep for tears.

                   WILLIAM WORDSWORTH.

288

Music, when soft voices die,
Vibrates in the memory—
Odours, when sweet violets sicken,
Live within the sense they quicken.

Rose leaves, when the rose is dead,
Are heap'd for the beloved's bed ;
And so thy thoughts, when Thou art gone,
Love itself shall slumber on.

                   P. B. SHELLEY.

289. THE SCHOLAR-GIPSY

Go, for they call you, Shepherd, from the hill ;
  Go, Shepherd, and untie the wattled cotes :
    No longer leave thy wistful flock unfed,
  Nor let thy bawling fellows rack their throats,
    Nor the cropp'd grasses shoot another head.
      But when the fields are still,
  And the tired men and dogs all gone to rest,
    And only the white sheep are sometimes seen
    Cross and recross the strips of moon-blanch'd green ;
Come, Shepherd, and again begin the quest.

Here, where the reaper was at work of late,
  In this high field's dark corner, where he leaves
    His coat, his basket, and his earthen cruse,
  And in the sun all morning binds the sheaves,
    Then here, at noon, comes back his stores to use ;
      Here will I sit and wait,
  While to my ear from uplands far away
    The bleating of the folded flocks is borne,
    With distant cries of reapers in the corn—
All the live murmur of a summer's day.

Screen'd is this nook o'er the high, half-reap'd field,
  And here till sundown, Shepherd, will I be.
    Through the thick corn the scarlet poppies peep,
  And round green roots and yellowing stalks I see
    Pale blue convolvulus in tendrils creep :
      And air-swept lindens yield
  Their scent, and rustle down their perfumed showers
    Of bloom on the bent grass where I am laid,
    And bower me from the August sun with shade ;
And the eye travels down to Oxford's towers :

And near me on the grass lies Glanvil's book—
  Come, let me read the oft-read tale again :
    The story of that Oxford scholar poor,
  Of pregnant parts and quick inventive brain,

Who, tired of knocking at Preferment's door,
 One summer eve forsook
His friends, and went to learn the Gipsy lore,
 And roam'd the world with that wild brotherhood,
 And came, as most men deem'd, to little good,
But came to Oxford and his friends no more.

But once, years after, in the country lanes,
 Two scholars, whom at college erst he knew,
 Met him, and of his way of life inquired.
Whereat he answer'd that the Gipsy crew,
 His mates, had arts to rule as they desired
 The workings of men's brains :
And they can bind them to what thoughts they will :
 " And I," he said, " the secret of their art,
 When fully learn'd, will to the world impart :
But it needs heaven-sent moments for this skill ! "

This said, he left them, and return'd no more,
 But rumours hung about the country-side
 That the lost Scholar long was seen to stray,
Seen by rare glimpses, pensive and tongue-tied,
 In hat of antique shape, and cloak of grey,
 The same the Gipsies wore.
Shepherd had met him on the Hurst in spring ;
 At some lone alehouse in the Berkshire moors,
 On the warm ingle-bench, the smock-frock'd boors
Had found him seated at their entering,

But, 'mid their drink and clatter, he would fly :
 And I myself seem half to know thy looks,
 And put the shepherds, Wanderer, on thy trace ;
And boys who in lone wheatfields scare the rooks
 I ask if thou hast pass'd their quiet place ;
 Or in my boat I lie
Moor'd to the cool bank in the summer heats,
 'Mid wide grass meadows which the sunshine fills,
 And watch the warm green-muffled Cumner hills,
And wonder if thou haunt'st their shy retreats.

For most, I know, thou lov'st retired ground.
 Thee, at the ferry, Oxford riders blithe,
 Returning home on summer nights, have met
Crossing the stripling Thames at Bablock-hithe,

Trailing in the cool stream thy fingers wet,
   As the slow punt swings round :
And leaning backwards in a pensive dream,
   And fostering in thy lap a heap of flowers
   Pluck'd in shy fields and distant Wychwood bowers,
And thine eyes resting on the moonlit stream :

And then they land, and thou art seen no more.
   Maidens who come from the distant hamlets come
      To dance around the Fyfield elm in May,
   Oft through the darkening fields have seen thee roam,
      Or cross a stile into the public way.
         Oft thou hast given them store
      Of flowers—the frail-leaf'd white anemone—
   Dark bluebells drench'd with dews of summer eves,
   And purple orchises with spotted leaves—
But none has words she can report of thee.

And, above Godstow Bridge, when hay-time's here
   In June, and many a scythe in sunshine flames,
      Men who through those wide fields of breezy grass
   Where black-wing'd swallows haunt the glittering
            Thames,
      To bathe in the abandon'd lasher pass,
         Have often pass'd thee near
   Sitting upon the river bank o'ergrown :
      Mark'd thine outlandish garb, thy figure spare,
      Thy dark vague eyes, and soft abstracted air ;
But, when they came from bathing, thou wert gone.

At some lone homestead in the Cumner hills,
   Where at her open door the housewife darns,
      Thou hast been seen, or hanging on a gate
   To watch the threshers in the mossy barns.
      Children, who early range these slopes and late
         For cresses from the rills,
   Have known thee watching, all an April day,
      The springing pastures and the feeding kine ;
      And mark'd thee, when the stars come out and shine,
Through the long dewy grass move slow away.

In autumn, on the skirts of Bagley Wood,
   Where most the gipsies by the turf-edged way
      Pitch their smoked tents, and every bush you see
   With scarlet patches tagg'd and shreds of grey,

Above the forest-ground call'd Thessaly—
  The blackbird picking food
Sees thee, nor stops his meal, nor fears at all ;
  So often has he known thee past him stray
  Rapt, twirling in thy hand a wither'd spray,
And waiting for the spark from Heaven to fall.

And once, in winter, on the causeway chill
  Where home through flooded fields foot-travellers go,
    Have I not pass'd thee on the wooden bridge
  Wrapt in thy cloak and battling with the snow,
    Thy face towards Hinksey and its wintry ridge ?
      And thou hast climb'd the hill
  And gain'd the white brow of the Cumner range ;
    Turn'd once to watch, while thick the snowflakes fall,
    The line of festal light in Christ Church hall—
Then sought thy straw in some sequester'd grange.

But what—I dream ! Two hundred years are flown
  Since first thy story ran through Oxford halls,
    And the grave Glanvil did the tale inscribe
  That thou wert wander'd from the studious walls
    To learn strange arts, and join a Gipsy tribe :
      And thou from earth art gone
  Long since, and in some quiet churchyard laid ;
    Some country nook, where o'er thy unknown grave
    Tall grasses and white flowering nettles wave—
Under a dark red-fruited yew-tree's shade.

—No, no, thou hast not felt the lapse of hours.
  For what wears out the life of mortal men ?
    'Tis that from change to change their being rolls :
  'Tis that repeated shocks, again, again,
    Exhaust the energy of strongest souls,
      And numb the elastic powers.
  Till having us'd our nerves with bliss and teen,
    And tired upon a thousand schemes our wit,
    To the just-pausing Genius we remit
Our worn-out life, and are—what we have been.

Thou hast not lived, why should'st thou perish, so ?
  Thou hadst *one* aim, *one* business, *one* desire :
    Else wert thou long since number'd with the dead—
Else hadst thou spent, like other men, thy fire.

The generations of thy peers are fled,
    And we ourselves shall go ;
But thou possessest an immortal lot,
    And we imagine thee exempt from age
    And living as thou liv'st on Glanvil's page,
Because thou hadst—what we, alas, have not !

For early didst thou leave the world, with powers
    Fresh, undiverted to the world without,
      Firm to their mark, not spent on other things ;
    Free from the sick fatigue, the languid doubt,
      Which much to have tried, in much been baffled,
          brings.
      O Life unlike to ours !
Who fluctuate idly without term or scope,
    Of whom each strives, nor knows for what he strives,
    And each half lives a hundred different lives ;
Who wait like thee, but not, like thee, in hope.

Thou waitest for the spark from Heaven : and we,
    Vague half-believers of our casual creeds,
      Who never deeply felt, nor clearly will'd,
    Whose insight never has borne fruit in deeds,
      Whose weak resolves never have been fulfill'd ;
      For whom each year we see
Breeds new beginnings, disappointments new ;
    Who hesitate and falter life away,
    And lose to-morrow the ground won to-day—
Ah, do not we, Wanderer, await it too ?

Yes, we await it, but it still delays,
    And then we suffer ; and amongst us One,
      Who most has suffer'd, takes dejectedly
    His seat upon the intellectual throne ;
      And all his store of sad experience he
      Lays bare of wretched days ;
Tell us his misery's birth and growth and signs,
    And how the dying spark of hope was fed,
    And how the breast was soothed, and how the head,
And all his hourly varied anodynes.

This for our wisest : and we others pine,
    And wish the long unhappy dream would end,
      And waive all claim to bliss, and try to bear,
With close-lipp'd Patience for our only friend,

Sad Patience, too near neighbour to Despair :
　　But none has hope like thine.
Thou through the fields and through the woods dost
　　　　stray,
　　Roaming the country-side, a truant boy,
　　Nursing thy project in unclouded joy,
And every doubt long blown by time away.

O born in days when wits were fresh and clear,
　　And life ran gaily as the sparkling Thames ;
　　Before this strange disease of modern life,
With its sick hurry, its divided aims,
　　Its heads o'ertaxed, its palsied hearts, was rife—
　　　　Fly hence, our contact fear !
Still fly, plunge deeper in the bowering wood !
　　Averse, as Dido did with gesture stern
　　From her false friend's approach in Hades turn,
Wave us away, and keep thy solitude.

Still nursing the unconquerable hope,
　　Still clutching the inviolable shade,
　　With a free onward impulse brushing through,
By night, the silver'd branches of the glade—
　　Far on the forest-skirts, where none pursue,
　　　　On some mild pastoral slope
Emerge, and resting on the moonlit pales,
　　Freshen thy flowers, as in former years,
　　With dew, or listen with enchanted ears,
From the dark dingles, to the nightingales.

But fly our paths, our feverish contact fly !
　　For strong the infection of our mental strife,
　　Which, though it gives no bliss, yet spoils for rest ;
And we should win thee from thy own fair life,
　　Like us, distracted, and like us unblest.
　　　　Soon, soon thy cheer would die,
Thy hopes grow timorous, and unfix'd thy powers,
　　And thy clear aims be cross and shifting made :
　　And then thy glad perennial youth would fade,
Fade, and grow old at last, and die like ours.

Then fly our greetings, fly our speech and smiles !
　　—As some grave Tyrian trader, from the sea,
　　Descried at sunrise an emerging prow
Lifting the cool-hair'd creepers stealthily,

The fringes of a southward-facing brow
    Among the Aegean isles ;
And saw the merry Grecian coaster come,
    Freighted with amber grapes, and Chian wine,
    Green bursting figs, and tunnies steep'd in brine :
And knew the intruders on his ancient home,

The young light-hearted Masters of the waves ;
    And snatch'd his rudder, and shook out more sail,
    And day and night held on indignantly
O'er the blue Midland waters with the gale,
    Betwixt the Syrtes and soft Sicily,
    To where the Atlantic raves
Outside the Western Straits, and unbent sails
There, where down cloudy cliffs, through sheets of foam,
    Shy traffickers, the dark Iberians come ;
And on the beach undid his corded bales.

                        MATTHEW ARNOLD.

290. DOVER BEACH

The sea is calm to-night,
The tide is full, the moon lies fair
Upon the Straits ;—on the French coast, the light
Gleams, and is gone ; the cliffs of England stand,
Glimmering and vast, out in the tranquil bay.
Come to the window, sweet is the night air !
Only from the long line of spray
Where the ebb meets the moon-blanch'd sand,
Listen ! you hear the grating roar
Of pebbles which the waves suck back, and fling,
At their return, up the high strand,
Begin, and cease, and then again begin,
With tremulous cadence slow, and bring
The eternal note of sadness in.

Sophocles long ago
Heard it on the Aegean, and it brought
Into his mind the turbid ebb and flow
Of human misery ; we
Find also in the sound a thought,
Hearing it by this distant northern sea.
The sea of faith

Was once, too, at the full, and round earth's shore
Lay like the folds of a bright girdle furl'd ;
But now I only hear
Its melancholy, long, withdrawing roar,
Retreating to the breath
Of the night-wind down the vast edges drear
And naked shingles of the world.

Ah, love, let us be true
To one another ! for the world, which seems
To lie before us like a land of dreams,
So various, so beautiful, so new,
Hath really neither joy, nor love, nor light,
Nor certitude, nor peace, nor help for pain ;
And we are here as on a darkling plain
Swept with confused alarms of struggle and flight,
Where ignorant armies clash by night.

MATTHEW ARNOLD.

291. REQUIESCAT

Strew on her roses, roses,
  And never a spray of yew.
In quiet she reposes :
  Ah ! would that I did too.

Her mirth the world required :
  She bath'd it in smiles of glee.
But her heart was tired, tired,
  And now they let her be.

Her life was turning, turning,
  In mazes of heat and sound.
But for peace her soul was yearning,
  And now peace laps her round.

Her cabin'd, ample Spirit,
  It flutter'd and fail'd for breath.
To-night it doth inherit
  The vasty Hall of Death.

MATTHEW ARNOLD.

292. SHAKESPEARE

Others abide our question. Thou art free.
We ask and ask : Thou smilest and art still,
Out-topping knowledge. For the loftiest hill
That to the stars uncrowns his majesty,
Planting his stedfast footsteps in the sea,
Making the Heaven of Heavens his dwelling-place,
Spares but the cloudy border of his base
To the foil'd searching of mortality :
And thou, who didst the stars and sunbeams know,
Self-school'd, self-scann'd, self-honour'd, self-secure,
Didst walk on Earth unguess'd at. Better so !
All pains the immortal spirit must endure,
All weakness that impairs, all griefs that bow,
Find their sole voice in that victorious brow.

MATTHEW ARNOLD.

293. DREAM-PEDLARY

If there were dreams to sell,
   What would you buy ?
Some cost a passing bell ;
Some a light sigh,
That shakes from Life's fresh crown
Only a rose-leaf down.
If there were dreams to sell,
Merry and sad to tell,
And the crier rang the bell,
   What would you buy ?

A cottage lone and still,
   With bowers nigh,
Shadowy, my woes to still,
   Until I die.
Such pearl from Life's fresh crown
Fain would I shake me down,
Were dreams to have at will,
This would best heal my ill,
   This would I buy.

THOMAS LOVELL BEDDOES.

294. FOR THE FALLEN

With proud thanksgiving, a mother for her children,
  England mourns for her dead across the sea.
Flesh of her flesh they were, spirit of her spirit,
  Fallen in the cause of the free.

Solemn the drums thrill: Death august and royal
  Sings sorrow up into immortal spheres.
There is music in the midst of desolation
  And a glory that shines upon our tears.

They went with songs to the battle, they were young,
  Straight of limb, true of eye, steady and aglow.
They were staunch to the end against odds uncounted,
  They fell with their faces to the foe.

They shall not grow old, as we that are left grow old:
  Age shall not weary them, nor the years condemn.
At the going down of the sun and in the morning
  We will remember them.

They mingle not with their laughing comrades again;
  They sit no more at familiar tables at home;
They have no lot in our labour of the day-time:
  They sleep beyond England's foam.

But where our desires are and our hopes profound,
  Felt as a well-spring that is hidden from sight,
To the innermost heart of their own land they are known
  As the stars are known to the Night.

As the stars that shall be bright when we are dust,
  Moving in marches upon the heavenly plain,
As the stars that are starry in the time of our darkness,
  To the end, to the end, they remain.

LAURENCE BINYON.

295. A PASSER-BY

Whither, O splendid ship, thy white sails crowding,
  Leaning across the bosom of the urgent West,
That fearest nor sea rising, nor sky clouding,
  Whither away, fair rover, and what thy quest?

Ah ! soon, when Winter has all our vales opprest,
When skies are cold and misty, and hail is hurling,
   Wilt thou glide on the blue Pacific, or rest
In a summer haven asleep, thy white sails furling.

I there before thee, in the country that well thou knowest,
   Already arrived am inhaling the odorous air :
I watch thee enter unerringly where thou goest,
   And anchor queen of the strange shipping there,
   Thy sails for awnings spread, thy masts bare :
Nor is aught from the foaming reef to the snow-capp'd grandest
   Peak, that is over the feathery palms, more fair
Than thou, so upright, so stately, and still thou standest.

And yet, O splendid ship, unhail'd and nameless,
   I know not if, aiming a fancy, I rightly divine
That thou hast a purpose joyful, a courage blameless,
   Thy port assured in a happier land than mine.
   But for all I have given thee, beauty enough is thine,
As thou, aslant with trim tackle and shrouding,
   From the proud nostril curve of a prow's line
In the offing scatterest foam, thy white sails crowding.

ROBERT BRIDGES.

296. MY DELIGHT AND THY DELIGHT

My delight and thy delight
Walking, like two angels white,
In the gardens of the night :

My desire and thy desire
Twining to a tongue of fire,
Leaping live, and laughing higher :

Thro' the everlasting strife
In the mystery of life.

Love, from whom the world begun,
Hath the secret of the sun.

Love can tell, and love alone,
Whence the million stars were strewn,
Why each atom knows its own
How, in spite of woe and death,
Gay is life, and sweet is breath :

This he taught us, this we knew,
Happy in his science true,
Hand in hand as we stood
'Neath the shadows of the wood,
Heart to heart as we lay
In the dawning of the day.

ROBERT BRIDGES.

297. LAST LINES

No coward soul is mine,
No trembler in the world's storm-troubled sphere :
   I see Heaven's glories shine,
And faith shines equal, arming me from fear.

O God within my breast,
Almighty, ever-present Deity !
   Life—that in me has rest,
As I—undying Life—have power in Thee !

Vain are the thousand creeds
That move men's hearts : unalterably vain ;
   Worthless as wither'd weeds,
Or idlest froth amid the boundless main,

To waken doubt in one
Holding so fast by Thine infinity ;
   So surely anchor'd on
The stedfast rock of immortality.

With wide-embracing love
Thy Spirit animates eternal years,
   Pervades and broods above,
Changes, sustains, dissolves, creates, and rears.

Though earth and man were gone,
And suns and universes ceased to be,
   And Thou wert left alone,
Every existence would exist in Thee.

There is not room for Death,
Nor atom that his might could render void :
   Thou—Thou art Being and Breath,
And what Thou art may never be destroyed.

EMILY BRONTË.

298. THE SOLDIER

If I should die, think only this of me :
   That there's some corner of a foreign field
That is for ever England. There shall be
   In that rich earth a richer dust concealed ;
A dust whom England bore, shaped, made aware,
   Gave, once, her flowers to love, her ways to roam,
A body of England's, breathing English air,
   Washed by the rivers, blest by suns of home.

And think, this heart, all evil shed away,
   A pulse in the eternal mind, no less
Gives somewhere back the thoughts by England given ;
Her sights and sounds ; dreams happy as her day,
   And laughter, learnt of friends ; and gentleness,
In hearts at peace, under an English heaven.
RUPERT BROOKE.

299. A MUSICAL INSTRUMENT

What was he doing, the great god Pan,
   Down in the reeds by the river ?
Spreading ruin and scattering ban,
Splashing and paddling with hoofs of a goat,
And breaking the golden lilies afloat
   With the dragon-fly on the river.

He tore out a reed, the great god Pan,
   From the deep cool bed of the river ;
The limpid water turbidly ran,
And the broken lilies a-dying lay,
And the dragon-fly had fled away,
Ere he brought it out of the river.

High on the shore sat the great god Pan,
   While turbidly flowed the river ;
And hack'd and hew'd as a great god can
With his hard bleak steel at the patient reed,
Till there was not a sign of the leaf indeed
   To prove it fresh from the river.

He cut it short, did the great god Pan
  (How tall it stood in the river !),
Then drew the pith, like the heart of a man,
Steadily from the outside ring,
And notch'd the poor dry empty thing
  In holes, as he sat by the river.

" This is the way," laugh'd the great god Pan
  (Laugh'd while he sat by the river),
" The only way, since gods began
To make sweet music, they could succeed."
Then dropping his mouth to a hole in the reed,
  He blew in power by the river.

Sweet, sweet, sweet, O Pan !
  Piercing sweet by the river !
Blinding sweet, O great god Pan !
The sun on the hill forgot to die,
And the lilies revived, and the dragon-fly
  Came back to dream on the river.

Yet half a beast is the great god Pan,
  To laugh as he sits by the river,
Making a poet out of a man :
The true gods sigh for the cost and pain—
For the reed which grows nevermore again
  As a reed with the reeds of the river.
                                        E. B. BROWNING.

300

How do I love thee ? Let me count the ways.
I love thee to the depth and breadth and height
My soul can reach, when feeling out of sight
For the ends of Being and ideal Grace.
I love thee to the level of every day's
Most quiet need, by sun and candlelight.
I love thee freely, as men strive for Right ;
I love thee purely, as they turn from Praise,
I love thee with the passion put to use
In my old griefs, and with my childhood's faith.
I love thee with a love I seemed to lose
With my lost saints,—I love thee with the breath,
Smiles, tears, of all my life !—and, if God choose,
I shall but love thee better after death.
                                        E. B. BROWNING.

301

I thought once how Theocritus had sung
Of the sweet years, the dear and wish'd-for years,
  Who each one in a gracious hand appears
To bear a gift for mortals old or young :
And, as I mused it in his antique tongue,
  I saw in gradual vision through my tears
  The sweet, sad years, the melancholy years—
Those of my own life, who by turns had flung
A shadow across me. Straightway I was 'ware,
  So weeping, how a mystic Shape did move
Behind me, and drew me backward by the hair ;
  And a voice said in mastery, while I strove,
" Guess now who holds thee ? "—" Death," I said. But
    there
  The silver answer rang—" Not Death, but Love."
                               E. B. BROWNING.

302

If thou must love me, let it be for naught
  Except for love's sake only. Do not say,
  " I love her for her smile—her look—her way
Of speaking gently,—for a trick of thought
That falls in well with mine, and certes brought
  A sense of pleasant ease on such a day "—
  For these things in themselves, Belovèd, may
Be changed, or change for thee—and love, so wrought,
May be unwrought so. Neither love me for
  Thine own dear pity's wiping my cheeks dry :
A creature might forget to weep, who bore
  Thy comfort long, and lose thy love thereby !
But love me for love's sake, that evermore
  Thou mayst love on, through love's eternity.
                               E. B. BROWNING.

303. EPILOGUE TO ASOLANDO

At the midnight in the silence of the sleep-time,
  When you set your fancies free,
Will they pass to where—by death, fools think, imprisoned—
Low he lies who once so loved you, whom you loved so,
      —Pity me ?

Oh to love so, be so loved, yet so mistaken !
   What had I on earth to do
With the slothful, with the mawkish, the unmanly ?
Like the aimless, helpless, hopeless, did I drivel
     —Being—who ?

One who never turned his back but marched breast forward,
   Never doubted clouds would break,
Never dreamed, though right were worsted, wrong would
    triumph,
Held we fall to rise, are baffled to fight better,
    Sleep to wake.

No, at noonday in the bustle of man's work-time
   Greet the unseen with a cheer !
Bid him forward, breast and back as either should be,
" Strive and thrive ! " cry " Speed,—fight on, fare ever
    There as here ! "

ROBERT BROWNING.

304. A WOMAN'S LAST WORD

Let's contend no more, Love,
   Strive nor weep ;
All be as before, Love,
   —Only sleep !

What so wild as words are ?
   I and thou
In debate, as birds are,
   Hawk on bough !

See the creature stalking
   While we speak !
Hush and hide the talking,
   Cheek on cheek !

What so false as truth is,
   False to thee ?
Where the serpent's tooth is,
   Shun the tree—

Where the apple reddens
   Never pry—
Lest we lose our Edens,
   Eve and I !

Be a god and hold me
   With a charm !
Be a man and fold me
   With thine arm !

Teach me, only teach, Love !
   As I ought
I will speak thy speech, Love,
   Think thy thought—

Meet, if thou require it,
   Both demands,
Laying flesh and spirit
   In thy hands.

That shall be to-morrow
   Not to-night :
I must bury sorrow
   Out of sight :

—Must a little weep, Love,
   (Foolish me !)
And so fall asleep, Love,
   Loved by thee.
               ROBERT BROWNING.

305. EVELYN HOPE

Beautiful Evelyn Hope is dead.
   Sit and watch by her side an hour.
That is her book-shelf, this her bed ;
   She plucked that piece of geranium flower,
Beginning to die too, in the glass ;
   Little has yet been changed, I think :
The shutters are shut, no light may pass
   Save two long rays thro' the hinge's chink.
Sixteen years old when she died.
   Perhaps she had scarcely heard my name ;
It was not her time to love ; beside,
   Her life had many a hope and aim,
Duties enough and little cares,
   And now was quite, now astir,
Till God's hand beckoned unawares—
   And the sweet white brow is all of her.

Is it too late then, Evelyn Hope?
   What, your soul was pure and true,
The good stars met in your horoscope,
   Made you a spirit, fire and dew—
And, just because I was thrice as old
   And our paths in the world diverged so wide,
Each was nought to each, must I be told?
   We were fellow mortals, nought beside?

No, indeed, for God above
   Is great to grant, as mighty to make,
And creates the love to reward the love:
   I claim you still, for my own love's sake.
Delayed it may be for more lives yet,
   Through worlds I shall traverse, not a few:
Much is to learn, much to forget
   Ere the time be come for taking you.

But the time will come—at last it will,
   When, Evelyn Hope, what meant (I shall say)
In the lower earth, in the years long still,
   That body and soul so pure and gay?
Why your hair was amber, I shall divine,
   And your mouth of your own geranium's red—
And what you would do with me, in fine,
   In the new life come in the old one's stead.

I have lived (I shall say) so much since then,
   Given up myself so many times,
Gained me the gains of various men,
   Ransacked the ages, spoiled the climes;
Yet one thing, one, in my soul's full scope,
   Either I missed or itself missed me:
And I want and find you, Evelyn Hope.
   What is the issue? let us see.

I loved you, Evelyn, all the while,
   My heart seemed full as it could hold?
There was place and to spare for the frank young smile,
   And the red young mouth, and the hair's young gold.
So, hush—I will give you this leaf to keep:
   See, I shut it inside the sweet cold hand!
There, that is our secret: go to sleep.
   You will wake, and remember, and understand.

ROBERT BROWNING.

306. THE LAST RIDE TOGETHER

I

I said—Then, dearest, since 'tis so,
Since now at length my fate I know,
Since nothing all my love avails,
Since all my life seemed meant for, fails,
　Since this was written and needs must be—
My whole heart rises up to bless
Your name in pride and thankfulness !
Take back the hope you gave,—I claim
Only a memory of the same,
—And this beside, if you will not blame,
　Your leave for one more last ride with me.

II

My mistress bent that brow of hers,
Those deep dark eyes where pride demurs
When pity would be softening through,
Fixed me a breathing-while or two
　With life or death in the balance—Right !
The blood replenished me again :
My last thought was at least not vain.
I and my mistress, side by side
Shall be together, breathe and ride,
So one day more am I deified.
　Who knows but the world may end to-night :

III

Hush ! if you saw some western cloud
All billowy-bosomed, over-bowed
By many benedictions—sun's
And moon's and evening-star's at once—
　And so, you, looking and loving best,
Conscious grew, your passion drew
Cloud, sunset, moonrise, star-shine too
Down on you, near and yet more near,
Till flesh must fade for heaven was here !—
Thus leant she and lingered—joy and fear !
　Thus lay she a moment on my breast.

IV

Then we began to ride. My soul
Smoothed itself out, a long-cramped scroll

Freshening and fluttering in the wind.
Past hopes already lay behind.
    What need to strive with a life awry?
Had I said that, had I done this,
So might I gain, so might I miss.
Might she have loved me? just as well
She might have hated,—who can tell?
Where had I been now if the worst befell?
    And here we are riding, she and I.

V

Fail I alone, in words and deeds?
Why, all men strive, and who succeeds?
We rode; it seemed my spirit flew,
Saw other regions, cities new,
    As the world rushed by on either side.
I thought, All labour yet no less
Bear up beneath their unsuccess.
Look at the end of work, contrast
The petty Done, the Undone vast,
This present of theirs with the hopeful past!
    I hoped she would love me. Here we ride.

VI

What hand and brain went ever paired?
What heart alike conceived and dared?
What act proved all its thought had been?
    What will but felt the fleshly screen?
    We ride and I see her bosom heave.
There's many a crown for who can reach.
Ten lines, a statesman's life in each!
The flag stuck on a heap of bones,
A soldier's doing! what atones?
They scratch his name on the Abbey-stones.
    My riding is better, by their leave.

VII

What does it all mean, poet? well,
Your brain's beat into rhythm—you tell
What we felt only; you expressed.
You hold things beautiful the best,
    And pace them in rhyme so, side by side.
'Tis something, nay 'tis much—but then,
Have you yourself what's best for men?

Are you—poor, sick, old ere your time—
Nearer one whit your own sublime
Than we who never have turned a rhyme?
    Sing, riding's a joy! For me, I ride.

VIII

And you, great sculptor—so you gave
A score of years to art, her slave,
And that's your Venus—whence we turn
To yonder girl that fords the burn!
    You acquiesce and shall I repine?
What, man of music, you, grown gray
With notes and nothing else to say,
Is this your sole praise from a friend,
"Greatly his opera's strains intend,
But in music we know how fashions end!"
    I gave my youth—but we ride, in fine.

IX

Who knows what's fit for us? Had fate
Proposed bliss here should sublimate
My being; had I signed the bond—
Still one must lead some life beyond,
    —Have a bliss to die with, dim-described.
This foot once planted on the goal,
This glory-garland round my soul,
Could I descry such? Try and test!
I sink back shuddering from the quest—
Earth being so good, would Heaven seem best?
    Now, Heaven and she are beyond this ride.

X

And yet—she has not spoke so long!
What if Heaven be that, fair and strong
At life's best, with our eyes upturned
Whither life's flower is first discerned,
    We, fixed so, ever should so abide?
What if we still ride on, we two,
With life for ever old yet new,
Changed not in kind but in degree,
The instant made eternity,—
And Heaven just prove that I and she
    Ride, ride together, for ever ride?

                                ROBERT BROWNING

307. PORPHYRIA'S LOVER

The rain set early in to-night,
   The sullen wind was soon awake,
It tore the elm-tops down for spite,
   And did its worst to vex the lake :
   I listened with heart fit to break.
When glided in Porphyria ; straight
   She shut the cold out and the storm.
And kneeled and made the cheerless grate
   Blaze up, and all the cottage warm ;
   Which done, she rose, and from her form
Withdrew the dripping cloak and shawl,
   And laid her soiled gloves by, untied
Her hat and let the damp hair fall,
   And, last, she sat down by my side
   And called me. When no voice replied,
She put my arm about her waist,
   And made her smooth white shoulder bare,
And all her yellow hair displaced,
   And, stooping made my cheek lie there,
   And spread, o'er all, her yellow hair,
Murmuring how she loved me—she
   Too weak, for all her heart's endeavour,
To set its struggling passion free
   From pride, and vainer ties dissever,
   And give herself to me for ever.
But passion sometimes would prevail,
   Nor could to-night's gay feast restrain
A sudden thought of one so pale
   For love of her, and all in vain :
   So, she was come through wind and rain.
Be sure I looked up at her eyes
   Happy and proud ; at last I knew
Porphyria worshipped me ; surprise
   Made my heart swell, and still it grew
   While I debated what to do.
That moment she was mine, mine, fair,
   Perfectly pure and good : I found
A thing to do, and all her hair
   In one long yellow string I wound
   Three times her little throat around,
And strangled her. No pain felt she ;
   I am quite sure she felt no pain.

As a shut bud that holds the bee,
  I warily oped her lids : again
  Laughed the blue eyes without a stain.
And I untightened next the tress
  About her neck ; her cheek once more
Blushed bright beneath my burning kiss :
  I propped her head up as before,
  Only, this time my shoulder bore
Her head, which droops upon it still :
  The smiling rosy little head,
So glad it has its utmost will,
  That all it scorned at once is fled,
  And I, its love, am gained instead !
Porphyria's love : she guessed not how
  Her darling one wish would be heard.
And thus we sit together now,
  And all night long we have not stirred,
  And yet God has not said a word !

                  ROBERT BROWNING.

308. ABT VOGLER

*(After he has been extemporising upon the musical instrument
of his invention)*

I

Would that the structure brave, the manifold music I build,
  Bidding my organ obey, calling its keys to their work,
Claiming each slave of the sound, at a touch, as when
  Solomon willed
Armies of angels that soar, legions of demons that lurk,
Man, brute, reptile, fly,—alien of end and of aim,
  Adverse, each from the other heaven-high, hell-deep
    removed,—
Should rush into sight at once as he named the ineffable
  Name,
  And pile him a palace straight, to pleasure the princess
    he loved !

II

Would it might tarry like his, the beautiful building of
  mine,
  This which my keys in a crowd pressed and importuned
    to raise !

Ah, one and all, how they helped, would dispart now and
    now combine,
    Zealous to hasten the work, heighten their master his
        praise !
And one would bury his brow with a blind plunge down
    to hell,
    Burrow awhile and build, broad on the roots of things,
Then up again swim into sight, having based me my
    palace well,
    Founded it, fearless of flame, flat on the nether springs.

III

And another would mount and march, like the excellent
    minion he was,
    Ay, another and yet another, one crowd but with many
        a crest,
Raising my rampired walls of gold as transparent as glass,
    Eager to do and die, yield each his place to the rest ;
For higher still and higher (as a runner tips with fire,
    When a great illumination surprises a festal night—
Outlining round and round Rome's dome from space to
    spire)
    Up, the pinnacled glory reached, and the pride of my
        soul was in sight.

IV

In sight ? Not half ! for it seemed, it was certain, to
    match man's birth,
    Nature in turn conceived, obeying an impulse as I ;
And the emulous heaven yearned down, made effort to
    reach the earth,
    As the earth had done her best, in my passion, to scale
    the sky :
Novel splendours burst forth, grew familiar and dwelt with
    mine,
    Not a point nor peak but found and fixed its wandering
    star ;
Meteor-moons, balls of blaze : and they did not pale nor
    pine,
    For earth had attained to heaven, there was no more
    near nor far.

V

Nay more ; for there wanted not who walked in the glare
    and glow,
  Presences plain in the place ; or, fresh from the Protop-
    last,
Furnished for ages to come, when a kindlier wind should
    blow,
  Lured now to begin and live, in a house to their liking
    at last ;
Or else the wonderful Dead who have passed through the
    body and gone,
  But were back once more to breathe in an old world
    worth their new :
What never had been was now ; what was, as it shall be
    anon ;
  And what is,—shall I say—matched both ? for I was
    made perfect too.

VI

All through my keys that gave their sounds to a wish of my
    soul,
  All through my soul that praised as its wish flowed
    visibly forth,
All through music and me ! For think, had I painted the
    whole,
  Why, there it had stood, to see, nor the process so
    wonder-worth :
Had I written the same, made verse—still, effect proceeds
    from cause,
  Ye know why the forms are fair, ye hear how the tale is
    told ;
It is all triumphant art, but art in obedience to laws,
  Painter and poet are proud in the artist-list enrolled :—

VII

But here is the finger of God, a flash of the will that can,
  Existent behind all laws, that made them, and, lo, they are !
And I know not if, save in this, such gift be allowed to man,
  That out of three sounds he frame, not a fourth sound,
    but a star.
Consider it well : each tone of our scale in itself is nought ;
  It is everywhere in the world—loud, soft, and all is said :
Give it to me to use ! I mix it with two in my thought ;
  And, there ! Ye have heard and seen : consider and
    bow the head !

VIII

Well, it is gone at last, the palace of music I reared ;
  Gone ! and the good tears start, the praises that come
    too slow ;
For one is assured at first, one scarce can say that he
  feared,
  That he even gave it a thought, the gone thing was to go.
Never to be again ! But many more of the kind
  As good, nay, better perchance : is this your comfort to
    me ?
To me, who must be saved because I cling with my mind
  To the same, same self, same love, same God : ay, what
    was shall be.

IX

Therefore to whom turn I but to Thee, the ineffable
  Name ?
  Builder and maker, Thou, of houses not made with
    hands !
What, have fear of change from Thee who art ever the
  same ?
  Doubt that Thy power can fill the heart that Thy power
    expands ?
There shall never be one lost good ! What was, shall live
  as before ;
  The evil is null, is nought, is silence implying sound ;
What was good, shall be good, with, for evil, so much good
  more ;
  On the earth the broken arcs ; in the heaven, a perfect
    round.

X

All we have willed or hoped or dreamed of good, shall
  exist ;
  Not its semblance, but itself ; no beauty, nor good, nor
    power
Whose voice has gone forth, but each survives for the
  melodist
  When eternity affirms the conception of an hour.
The high that proved too high, the heroic for earth too
  hard,
  The passion that left the ground to lose itself in the sky,
Are music sent up to God by the lover and the bard ;
  Enough that he heard it once : we shall hear it by and
    by.

XI

And what is our failure here but a triumph's evidence
    For the fullness of the days? Have we withered or
        agonised?
Why else was the pause prolonged but that singing might
    issue thence?
Why rushed the discords in, but that harmony should
    be prized?
Sorrow is hard to bear, and doubt is slow to clear,
    Each sufferer says his say, his scheme of the weal and
        woe:
But God has a few of us whom He whispers in the ear;
    The rest may reason and welcome: 'tis we musicians
        know.

XII

Well, it is earth with me; silence resumes her reign:
    I will be patient and proud, and soberly acquiesce.
Give me the keys. I feel for the common chord again,
    Sliding by semitones, till I sink to the minor,—yes,
And I blunt it into a ninth, and I stand on alien ground,
    Surveying a while the heights I rolled from into the
        deep;
Which, hark, I have dared and done, for my resting-place
    is found,
    The C Major of this life: so, now I will try to sleep.
                        ROBERT BROWNING.

309.

    The year's at the spring,
    And day's at the morn;
    Morning's at seven;
    The hill-side's dew-pearled:
    The lark's on the wing;
    The snail's on the thorn;
    God's in his heaven—
    All's right with the world!
                  ROBERT BROWNING.

310. HOME-THOUGHTS, FROM THE SEA

Nobly, nobly Cape Saint Vincent to the north-west died
    away ;
Sunset ran, one glorious blood-red, reeking into Cadiz
    Bay ;
Bluish 'mid the burning water, full in face Trafalgar lay ;
In the dimmest north-east distance, dawned Gibraltar
    grand and gray ;
" Here and here did England help me,—how can I help
    England ? "—say,
Whoso turns as I, this evening, turn to God to praise and
    pray,
While Jove's planet rises yonder, silent over Africa.

                                ROBERT BROWNING.

311. HOME-THOUGHTS, FROM ABROAD

I

Oh, to be in England
Now that April's there,
And whoever wakes in England
Sees, some morning, unaware,
That the lowest boughs and the brush-wood sheaf
Round the elm-tree bole are in tiny leaf,
While the chaffinch sings on the orchard bough
In England—now !

II

And after April, when May follows,
And the whitethroat builds, and all the swallows—
Hark ! where my blossomed pear-tree in the hedge
Leans to the field and scatters on the clover
Blossoms and dewdrops—at the bent-spray's edge—
That's the wise thrush ; he sings each song twice over,
Lest you should think he never could recapture
The first fine careless rapture !
And though the fields look rough with hoary dew,
All will be gay when noontide wakes anew
The buttercups, the little children's dower,
—Far brighter than this gaudy melon-flower !

                                ROBERT BROWNING.

313. THE OLD WOMAN

As a white candle
In a holy place,
So is the beauty
Of an aged face.

As the spent radiance
Of the winter sun,
So is a woman
With her travail done.

Her brood gone from her,
And her thoughts as still
As the waters
Under a ruined mill.

JOSEPH CAMPBELL.

314. THE DONKEY

When fishes flew and forests walked,
    And figs grew upon thorn,
Some moments when the moon was blood,
    Then surely I was born;

With monstrous head and sickening cry
    And ears like errant wings,
The devil's walking parody
    On all four-footed things.

The tattered outlaw of the earth,
    Of ancient crooked will;
Starve, scourge, deride me; I am dumb,
    I keep my secret still.

Fools! For I also had my hour;
    One far fierce hour and sweet:
There was a shout about my ears,
    And palms before my feet.

G. K. CHESTERTON.

315. A CRADLE SONG

O, men from the fields!
Come gently within.
Tread softly, softly,
O! men coming in.

Mavourneen is going
From me and from you,
Where Mary will fold him
With mantle of blue !

From reek of the smoke
And cold of the floor,
And the peering of things
Across the half-door.

O, men from the fields !
Soft, softly come thro' !
Mary puts round him
Her mantle of blue.

PADRAIC COLUM.

316. NO CHILD

I heard in the night the pigeons
   Stirring within their nest :
The wild pigeon's stir was tender,
   Like a child's hand at the breast.

I cried, " O, stir no more !
   (My breast was touched of tears),
O pigeons, make no stir—
   A childless woman hears."

PADRAIC COLUM.

317. HERACLITUS

They told me, Heraclitus, they told me you were dead,
They brought me bitter news to hear and bitter tears to
   shed.
I wept, as I remembered how often you and I
Had tired the sun with talking and sent him down the sky.

And now that thou art lying, my dear old Carian guest,
A handful of gray ashes, long long ago at rest,
Still are thy pleasant voices, thy nightingales, awake ;
For Death, he taketh all away, but them he cannot take.

WILLIAM CORY.

318. "—BUT A SHORT TIME TO LIVE"

Our little hour,—how swift it flies
  When poppies flare and lilies smile ;
How soon the fleeting minute dies,
  Leaving us but a little while
To dream our dream, to sing our song,
  To pick the fruit, to pluck the flower,
The Gods—They do not give us long,—
  One little hour.

One little hour,—how short it is
  When Love with dew-eyed loveliness
Raises her lips for ours to kiss
  And dies within our first caress.
Youth flickers out like wind-blown flame,
  Sweets of to-day to-morrow sour,
For Time and Death relentless claim
  Our little hour.

Our little hour,—how short a time
  To wage our wars, to fan our hates,
To take our fill of armoured crime,
  To troop our banners, storm the gates.
Blood on the sword, our eyes blood-red,
  Blind in our puny reign of power,
Do we forget how soon is sped
  Our little hour ?

Our little hour,—how soon it dies :
  How short a time to tell our beads,
To chant our feeble Litanies,
  To think sweet thoughts, to do good deeds.
The altar lights grow pale and dim,
  The bells hang silent in the tower—
So passes with the dying hymn
  Our little hour.

LESLIE COULSON.

319. THE ROBIN'S CROSS

A little cross
To tell my loss ;
A little bed
To rest my head ;

A little tear is all I crave
Upon my very little grave.

I strew thy bed
Who loved thy lays;
The tear I shed,
The cross I raise,
With nothing more upon it than
" Here lies the little friend of man."

GEORGE DARLEY.

320. THE EXAMPLE

Here's an example from
A butterfly;
That on a rough hard rock
Happy can lie;
Friendless and all alone
On this unsweetened stone.

Now let my bed be hard
No care take I;
I'll make my joy like this
Small butterfly;
Whose happy heart has power
To make a stone a flower.

W. H. DAVIES.

321. LEISURE

What is this life if, full of care,
We have no time to stand and stare.

No time to stand beneath the boughs
And stare as long as sheep or cows

No time to see, when woods we pass,
Where squirrels hide their nuts in grass.

No time to see, in broad daylight,
Steams full of stars, like skies at night.

No time to turn at Beauty's glance,
And watch her feet, how they can dance.

No time to wait till her mouth can
Enrich that smile her eyes began.

A poor life this if, full of care,
We have no time to stand and stare.

W. H. Davies.

322. THE MOON

Thy beauty haunts me heart and soul,
   O thou fair Moon, so close and bright ;
Thy beauty makes me like the child
   That cries aloud to own thy light :
The little child that lifts each arm
To press thee to her bosom warm.

Though there are birds that sing this night
   With thy white beams across their throats,
Let my deep silence speak for me
   More than for them their sweetest notes :
Who worships thee till music fails
Is greater than thy nightingales.

W. H. Davies.

323. THE SCRIBE

What lovely things
Thy hand hath made,
The smooth-plumed bird
In its emerald shade,
The seed of the grass,
The speck of stone
Which the wayfaring ant
Stirs, and hastes on
Though I should sit
By some tarn in Thy hills,
Using its ink
As the spirit wills
To write of Earth's wonders,
Its live willed things,
Flit would the ages
On soundless wings

Ere unto Z
My pen drew nigh,
Leviathan told,
And the honey-fly ;
And still would remain
My wit to try—
My worn reeds broken,
The dark tarn dry,
All words forgotten—
Thou, Lord, and I.

WALTER DE LA MARE.

324. AN EPITAPH

Here lies a most beautiful lady,
Light of step and heart was she ;
I think she was the most beautiful lady
That ever was in the West Country.
But beauty vanishes ; beauty passes ;
However rare—rare it be ;
And when I crumble, who will remember
The lady of the West Country ?

WALTER DE LA MARE.

325. SONG

Girls, when I am gone away,
    On this bosom strew
Only flowers meek and pale,
    And the yew.

Lay these hands down by my side,
    Let my face be bare ;
Bind a kerchief round the face,
    Smooth my hair.

Let my bier be borne at dawn,
    Summer grows so sweet,
Deep into the forest green
    Where boughs meet.

Then pass away, and let me lie
    One long, warm, sweet day
There alone with face upturn'd,
    One sweet day.

> While the morning light grows broad,
> While noon sleepeth sound,
> While the evening falls and faints,
> While the world goes round.
>
> EDWARD DOWDEN.

326. FARE WELL

WHEN I lie where shades of darkness
Shall no more assail mine eyes,
Nor the rain make lamentation
    When the wind sighs;
How will fare the world whose wonder
Was the very proof of me?
Memory fades, must the remembered
    Perishing be?

Oh, when this my dust surrenders
Hand, foot, lip, to dust again,
May these loved and loving faces
    Please other men!
May the rusting harvest hedgerow
Still the Traveller's Joy entwine,
And as happy children gather
    Posies once mine.

Look thy last on all things lovely,
Every hour. Let no night
Seal thy sense in deathly slumber
    Till to delight
Thou have paid thy utmost blessing;
Since that all things thou wouldst praise
Beauty took from those who loved them
    In other days.

WALTER DE LA MARE.

327. "NON SUM QUALIS ERAM BONAE SUB REGNO CYNARAE"

Last night, ah, yesternight, betwixt her lips and mine
There fell thy shadow, Cynara! thy breath was shed
Upon my soul between the kisses and the wine;
And I was desolate and sick of an old passion,
    Yea, I was desolate and bowed my head:
I have been faithful to thee, Cynara! in my fashion.

All night upon mine heart I felt her warm heart beat,
Night-long within mine arms in love and sleep she lay
Surely the kisses of her bought red mouth were sweet
But I was desolate and sick of an old passion,
    When I awoke and found the dawn was gray :
I have been faithful to thee, Cynara ! in my fashion.

I have forgot much, Cynara ! gone with the wind,
Flung roses, roses, riotously with the throng,
Dancing, to put thy pale, lost lilies out of mind ;
But I was desolate and sick of an old passion,
    Yea, all the time, because the dance was long :
I have been faithful to thee, Cynara ! in my fashion.

I cried for madder music and for stronger wine,
But when the feast is finished and the lamps expire,
Then falls thy shadow, Cynara ! the night is thine :
And I am desolate and sick of an old passion,
    Yea, hungry for the lips of my desire :
I have been faithful to thee, Cynara ! in my fashion.

                                    ERNEST DOWSON.

328. STANZAS FROM THE RUBÁIYÁT OF OMAR KHAYYÁM OF NAISHÁPÚR

Come, fill the Cup, and in the Fire of Spring
The Winter Garment of Repentance fling :
    The Bird of Time has but a little way
To fly—and Lo ! the Bird is on the Wing.

And look—a thousand Blossoms with the Day
Woke—and a thousand scatter'd into Clay :
    And this first Summer Month that brings the Rose
Shall take Jamshyd and Kaikobád away.

But come with old Khayyám, and leave the Lot
Of Kaikobád and Kaikhosrú forgot :
    Let Restum lay about him as he will,
Or Hátim Tai cry Supper—heed them not.

With me along some Strip of Herbage strown
That just divides the Desert from the sown,
    Where name of Slave and Sultán scarce is known,
And pity Sultán Máhmúd on his Throne.

Here with a Loaf of Bread beneath the Bough,
A Flask of Wine, a Book of Verse—and Thou
   Besides me singing in the Wilderness—
And Wilderness is Paradise enow.

" How sweet is mortal Sovranty ! "—think some :
Others—" How blest the Paradise to come ! "
   Ah, take the Cash in hand and wave the Rest ;
Oh, the brave Music of a *distant* Drum !

Look to the Rose that blows about us—" Lo,
Laughing," she says, " into the World I blow :
   At once the silken Tassel of my Purse
Tear, and its Treasure on the Garden throw."

The Worldly Hope men set their Hearts upon
Turns Ashes—or it prospers ; and anon,
   Like Snow upon the Desert's dusty Face
Lighting a little Hour or two—is gone.

    .   .   .   .   .

I sometimes think that never blows so red
The Rose as where some buried Cæsar bled ;
   That every Hyacinth the Garden wears
Dropt in its Lap from some once lovely Head.

And this delightful Herb whose tender Green
Fledges the River's Lip on which we lean—
   Ah, lean upon it lightly ! for who knows
From what once lovely Lip it springs unseen !

Ah, my Beloved, fill the Cup that clears
To-DAY of past Regrets and future Fears—
   To-morrow ?—Why, To-morrow I may be
Myself with Yesterday's Sev'n Thousand Years.

Lo ! some we loved, the loveliest and best
That Time and Fate of all their Vintage prest,
   Have drunk their Cup a Round or two before,
And one by one crept silently to Rest.

Oh, come with old Khayyám, and leave the Wise
To talk ; one thing is certain, that Life flies ;
   One thing is certain, and the Rest is Lies ;
The Flower that once has blown for ever dies.

Myself when young did eagerly frequent
Doctor and Saint, and heard great Argument
   About it and about : but evermore
Came out by the same Door as in I went.

With them the Seed of Wisdom did I sow,
And with my own hand labour'd it to grow :
   And this was all the Harvest that I reap'd—
" I came like Water, and like Wind I go."

Into this Universe, and *why* not knowing,
Nor *whence*, like Water willy-nilly flowing :
   And out of it, as Wind along the Waste,
I know not *whither*, willy-nilly blowing.

KUZA-NAMA

Ah, with the Grape my fading Life provide,
And wash my Body whence the Life has died,
   And in a Windingsheet of Vine-leaf wrapt,
So bury me by some sweet Garden-side.

That ev'n my buried Ashes such a Snare
Of Perfume shall fling up into the Air,
   As not a True Believer passing by
But shall be overtaken unaware.

Indeed the Idols I have loved so long
Have done my Credit in Men's Eye much wrong :
   Have drown'd my Honour in a shallow Cup,
And sold my Reputation for a Song.

Indeed, indeed, Repentance oft before
I swore—but was I sober when I swore ?
   And then and then came Spring, and Rose-in-hand
My thread-bare Penitence apieces tore.

And much as Wine has play'd the Infidel,
And robb'd me of my Robe of Honour—well,
   I often wonder what the Vintners buy
One half so precious as the Goods they sell.

Alas, that Spring should vanish with the Rose !
That Youth's sweet-scented Manuscript should close !
   The Nightingale that in the Branches sang,
Ah, whence, and whither flown again, who knows !

Ah Love ! could thou and I with Fate conspire
To grasp this sorry Scheme of Things entire,
   Would not we shatter it to bits—and then
Re-mould it nearer to the Heart's Desire !

Ah, Moon of my Delight who know'st no wane,
The Moon of Heav'n is rising once again :
   How oft hereafter rising shall she look
Through this same Garden after me—in vain !

And when Thyself with shining Foot shall pass
Among the Guests Star-scatter'd on the Grass,
   And in thy joyous Errand reach the Spot
Where I made one—turn down an empty Glass !

Tamám Shud.

Edward Fitzgerald.

329. YASMIN

A Ghazel

How splendid in the morning glows the lily : with what
   grace he throws
His supplication to the rose : do roses nod the head,
   Yasmin ?

But when the silver dove descends I find the little flower
   of friends
Whose very name that sweetly ends I say when I have said
   Yasmin.

The morning light is clear and cold : I dare not in that
   light behold
A whiter light, a deeper gold, a glory too far shed, Yasmin.

But when the deep red eye of day is level with the lone
   highway,
And some to Meccah turn to pray, and I towards thy bed,
   Yasmin ;

Or when the wind beneath the moon is drifting like a soul
   aswoon,
And harping planets talk love's tune with milky wings
   outspread, Yasmin,

Shower down thy love, O burning bright ! For one night or
    the other night
Will come the Gardener in white, and gathered flowers are
    dead, Yasmin.

JAMES ELROY FLECKER.

330. THE GOLDEN JOURNEY TO SAMARKAND
EPILOGUE

At the Gate of the Sun, Bagdad, in olden time

The Merchants (*together*)

Away, for we are ready to a man !
    Our camels sniff the evening and are glad.
Lead on, O Master of the Caravan :
    Lead on the Merchant-Princes of Bagdad.

The Chief Draper

Have we not Indian carpets dark as wine,
    Turbans and sashes, gowns and bows and veils,
And broideries of intricate design,
    And printed hangings in enormous bales ?

The Chief Grocer

We have rose-candy, we have spikenard,
    Mastic and terebinth and oil and spice,
And such sweet jams meticulously jarred
    As God's own Prophet eats in Paradise.

The Principal Jews

And we have manuscripts in peacock styles
    By Ali of Damascus ; we have swords
Engraved with storks and apes and crocodiles,
    And heavy beaten necklaces, for Lords.

The Master of the Caravan

But you are nothing but a lot of Jews.

The Principal Jews

Sir, even dogs have daylight, and we pay.

The Master of the Caravan

But who are ye in rags and rotten shoes,
    You dirty-bearded, blocking up the way ?

The Pilgrims

We are the pilgrims, master ; we shall go
  Always a little further : it may be
Beyond that last blue mountain barred with snow,
  Across that angry or that glimmering sea,
White on a throne or guarded in a cave
  There lives a prophet who can understand
Why men were born : but surely we are brave,
  Who make the Golden Journey to Samarkand.

The Chief Merchant

We gnaw the nail of hurry. Master, away !

One of the Women

  O turn your eyes to where your children stand.
Is not Bagdad the beautiful ? O stay !

The Merchants (*in chorus*)

We take the Golden Road to Samarkand.

An Old Man

Have you not girls and garlands in your homes,
  Eunuchs and Syrian boys at your command ?
Seek not excess : God hateth him who roams !

The Merchants (*in chorus*)

We make the Golden Journey to Samarkand.

A Pilgrim with a Beautiful Voice

Sweet to ride forth at evening from the wells
  When shadows pass gigantic on the sand,
And softly through the silence beat the bells
  Along the Golden Road to Samarkand.

A Merchant

We travel not for trafficking alone :
  By hotter winds our fiery hearts are fanned :
For lust of knowing what should not be known
  We make the Golden Journey to Samarkand.

The Master of the Caravan

Open the gate, O watchman of the night !

The Watchman

  Ho, travellers, I open. For what land
Leave you the dim-moon city of delight ?

The Merchants (*with a shout*)
We make the Golden Journey to Samarkand.
(*The Caravan passes through the gate*)

The Watchman (*consoling the women*)
What would ye, ladies? It was ever thus.
Men are unwise and curiously planned.

A Woman
They have their dreams, and do not think of us.

Voices of the Caravan (*in the distance, singing*)
We make the Golden Journey to Samarkand.

JAMES ELROY FLECKER.

331. THE COUNTRY FAITH

Here in the country's heart
Where the grass is green
Life is the same sweet life
As it e'er hath been.

Trust in a God still lives,
And the bell at morn
Floats with a thought of God
O'er the rising corn.

God comes down in the rain,
And the crop grows tall—
This is the country faith,
And the best of all!

NORMAN GALE.

332. INTO BATTLE

The naked earth is warm with Spring,
    And with green grass and bursting trees
Leans to the sun's gaze glorying,
    And quivers in the sunny breeze;
And Life is Colour and Warmth and Light,
    And a striving evermore for these;
And he is dead who will not fight;
    And who dies fighting has increase.

The fighting man shall from the sun
  Take warmth, and life from the glowing earth;
Speed with the light-foot winds to run,
  And with the trees to newer birth;
And find, when fighting shall be done,
  Great rest, and fulness after dearth.

All the bright company of Heaven
  Hold him in their high comradeship,
The Dog-Star, and the Sisters Seven,
  Orion's Belt and sworded hip.

The woodland trees that stand together,
  They stand to him each one a friend;
They gently speak in the windy weather;
  They guide to valley and ridge's end.

The kestrel hovering by day,
  And the little owls that call by night,
Bid him be swift and keen as they,
  As keen of ear, as swift of sight.

The blackbird sings to him, " Brother, brother,
  If this be the last song you shall sing
Sing well, for you may not sing another;
  Brother, sing."

In dreary, doubtful, waiting hours,
  Before the brazen frenzy starts,
The horses show him nobler powers;
  O patient eyes, courageous hearts!

And when the burning moment breaks,
  And all things else are out of mind,
And only Joy of Battle takes
  Him by the throat, and makes him blind,

Through joy and blindness he shall know,
  Not caring much to know, that still
Nor lead nor steel shall reach him, so
  That it be not the Destined Will.

The thundering line of battle stands,
  And in the air, Death moans and sings;
But Day shall clasp him with strong hands,
  And Night shall fold him in soft wings.

                              JULIAN GRENFELL.

Flanders, April, 1915.

333. TO A BLACK GREYHOUND

Shining black in the shining light
　　Inky black in the golden sun,
Graceful as the swallow's flight,
　　Light as swallow, winged one,
Swift as driven hurricane—
　　Double-sinewed stretch and spring,
Muffled thud of flying feet,
　　See the black dog galloping,
　　Hear his wild foot-beat.

See him lie when the day is dead,
　　Black curves curled on the boarded floor.
Sleepy eyes, my sleepy head—
　　Eyes that were aflame before.
Gentle now, they burn no more ;
　　Gentle now and softly warm,
With the fire that made them bright
　　Hidden—as when after storm
　　Softly falls the night.

God of Speed, who makes the fire—
　　God of Peace, who lulls the same—
God who gives the fierce desire,
　　Lust for blood as fierce as flame—
God who stands in Pity's name—
　　Many may ye be or less,
Ye who rule the earth and sun ;
　　Gods of strength and gentleness,
　　Ye are ever one.

JULIAN GRENFELL.

334. BY THE STATUE OF KING CHARLES AT CHARING CROSS

Sombre and rich, the skies ;
Great glooms, and starry plains.
Gently the night wind sighs ;
Else a vast silence reigns.

The splendid silence clings
Around me : and around
The saddest of all kings
Crowned, and again discrowned.

Comely and calm, he rides
Hard by his own Whitehall :
Only the night wind glides :
No crowds, nor rebels, brawl.

Gone, too, his Court : and yet,
The stars his courtiers are :
Stars in their stations set ;
And every wandering star.

Alone he rides, alone,
The fair and fatal king :
Dark night is all his own,
That strange and solemn thing.

Which are more full of fate :
The stars ; or those sad eyes ?
Which are more still and great :
Those brows ; or the dark skies ?

Although his whole heart yearn
In passionate tragedy :
Never was face so stern
With sweet austerity.

Vanquished in life, his death
By beauty made amends :
The passing of his breath
Won his defeated ends.

Brief life, and hapless ? Nay !
Through death, life grew sublime.
Speak after sentence ? Yea :
And to the end of time.

Armoured he rides, his head
Bare to the stars of doom :
He triumphs now, the dead,
Beholding London's gloom.

Our wearier spirit faints,
Vexed in the world's employ :
His soul was of the saints ;
And art to him was joy.

King, tried in fires of woe !
Men hunger for thy grace :

And through the night I go,
Loving thy mournful face.

Yet, when the city sleeps ;
When all the cries are still :
The stars and heavenly deeps
Work out a perfect will.

LIONEL JOHNSON.

335. TREES

I think that I shall never see
A poem lovely as a tree.

A tree whose hungry mouth is prest
Against the sweet earth's flowing breast ;

A tree that looks at God all day,
And lifts her leafy arms to pray ;

A tree that may in summer wear
A nest of robins in her hair ;

Upon whose bosom snow has lain ;
Who intimately lives with rain.

Poems are made by fools like me,
But only God can make a tree.

JOYCE KILMER.

336. YOUNG AND OLD

When all the world is young, lad,
    And all the trees are green ;
And every goose a swan, lad,
    And every lass a queen ;
Then hey for boot and horse, lad,
    And round the world away ;
Young blood must have its course, lad,
    And every dog his day.

When all the world is old, lad,
    And all the trees are brown ;
And all the sport is stale, lad,
    And all the wheels run down :

Creep home, and take your place there,
    The spent and maimed among:
God grant you find one face there
    You loved when all was young.
                        CHARLES KINGSLEY.

337. THE SANDS OF DEE

" O Mary, go and call the cattle home,
    And call the cattle home,
    And call the cattle home
        Across the sands of Dee; "
The western wind was wild and dank with foam,
    And all alone went she.

The western tide crept up along the sand,
    And o'er and o'er the sand,
    And round and round the sand,
        As far as eye could see.
The rolling mist came down, and hid the land:
    And never home came she.

" Oh! is it weed, or fish, or floating hair—
    A tress of golden hair,
    A drownèd maiden's hair,
        Above the nets at sea? "
Was never salmon yet that shone so fair
    Among the stakes on Dee.

They row'd her in across the rolling foam,
    The cruel crawling foam,
    The cruel hungry foam,
        To her grave beside the sea.
But still the boatmen hear her call the cattle home
    Across the sands of Dee.
                        CHARLES KINGSLEY.

338. RECESSIONAL
June 22, 1897

God of our fathers, known of old—
    Lord of our far-flung battle-line—

Beneath whose awful Hand we hold
  Dominion over palm and pine—
Lord God of Hosts, be with us yet,
Lest we forget, lest we forget !

The tumult and the shouting dies—
  The captains and the kings depart—
Still stands Thine ancient sacrifice,
  An humble and a contrite heart.
Lord God of Hosts, be with us yet,
Lest we forget, lest we forget !

Far-call'd our navies melt away—
  On dune and headland sinks the fire—
Lo, all our pomp of yesterday
  Is one with Nineveh and Tyre !
Judge of the Nations, spare us yet,
Lest we forget, lest we forget !

If, drunk with sight of power, we loose
  Wild tongues that have not Thee in awe—
Such boasting as the Gentiles use
  Or lesser breeds without the Law—
Lord God of Hosts, be with us yet,
Lest we forget, lest we forget !

For heathen heart that puts her trust
  In reeking tube and iron shard—
All valiant dust that builds on dust,
  And guarding calls not Thee to guard—
For frantic boast and foolish word,
Thy Mercy on Thy People, Lord !
                    RUDYARD KIPLING.

339. ON HIS SEVENTY-FIFTH BIRTHDAY

I strove with none, for none was worth my strife,
  Nature I loved, and next to Nature, Art ;
I warmed both hands before the fire of life,
  It sinks, and I am ready to depart.
                    WALTER SAVAGE LANDOR.

340. DEATH STANDS ABOVE ME

Death stands above me, whispering low
  I know not what into my ear :
Of his strange language all I know
  Is, there is not a word of fear.
                    WALTER SAVAGE LANDOR.

341. THE ODYSSEY

As one that for a weary space has lain
  Lulled by the song of Circe and her Wine
  In gardens near the pale of Proserpine,
Where that Ægean Isle forgets the main,
And only the low lutes of love complain,
  And only shadows of wan lovers pine ;
  As such an one were glad to know the brine
Salt on his lips, and the large air again.
So gladly, from the songs of modern speech
  Men turn, and see the stars, and feel the free
Shrill wind beyond the close of heavy flowers
And through the music of the languid hours,
  They hear like ocean on a Western beach
  The surge and thunder of the Odyssey.
                    ANDREW LANG.

342. WEARINESS

O little feet ! that such long years
Must wander on through hopes and fears,
  Must ache and bleed beneath your load ;
I, nearer to the wayside inn
Where toil shall cease and rest begin,
  Am weary, thinking of your road !

O little hands ! that, weak or strong,
Have still to serve or rule so long,
  Have still so long to give or ask ;
I, who so much with book and pen
Have toiled among my fellow-men,
  Am weary, thinking of your task.

O little hearts ! that throb and beat
With such impatient, feverish heat,
   Such limitless and strong desires ;
Mine, that so long has glowed and burned,
With passion into ashes turned,
   Now covers and conceals its fires.

O little souls ! as pure and white
And crystalline as rays of light
   Direct from heaven, their source divine ;
Refracted through the mist of years,
How red my setting sun appears,
   How lurid looks this soul of mine !

H. W. LONGFELLOW.

343. SNOW-FLAKES

Out of the bosom of the air,
   Out of the cloud-folds of her garments shaken,
Over the woodlands brown and bare,
   Over the harvest-fields forsaken,
      Silent, and soft, and slow
      Descends the snow.

Even as our cloudy fancies take
   Suddenly shape in some divine expression,
Even as the troubled heart doth make
   In the white countenance confession,
      The troubled sky reveals
      The grief it feels.

This is the poem of the air,
   Slowly in silent syllables recorded ;
This is the secret of despair,
   Long in its cloudy bosom hoarded,
      Now whispered and revealed
      To wood and field.

H. W. LONGFELLOW

344

" Onaway ! Awake, beloved !
Thou the wild-flower of the forest !
Thou the wild-bird of the prairie !
Thou with eyes so soft and fawn-like !
" If thou only lookest at me,
I am happy, I am happy,
As the lilies of the prairie,
When they feel the dew upon them !
" Sweet thy breath is as the fragrance
Of the wild-flowers in the morning,
As their fragrance is at evening,
In the Moon when leaves are falling.
" Does not all the blood within me
As the springs to meet the sunshine,
Leap to meet thee, leap to meet thee,
In the Moon when nights are brightest ?
" Onaway ! my heart sings to thee,
Sings with joy when thou art near me,
As the sighing, singing branches
In the pleasant Moon of Strawberries !
" When thou art not pleased, beloved,
Then my heart is sad and darkened,
As the shining river darkens
When the clouds drop shadows on it !
" When thou smilest, my beloved,
Then my troubled heart is brightened,
As in sunshine gleam the ripples
That the cold wind makes in rivers.
" Smiles the earth, and smile the waters,
Smile the cloudless skies above us,
But I lose the way of smiling
When thou art no longer near me !
" I myself, myself ! behold me !
Blood of my beating heart, behold me !
O awake, awake, beloved !
Onaway ! awake, beloved ! "

H. W. LONGFELLOW.

345. SHIPS THAT PASS IN THE NIGHT

Ships that pass in the night, and speak each other in
    passing,
Only a signal shown and a distant voice in the darkness :
So on the ocean of life, we pass and speak one another,
Only a look and a voice, then darkness again and a silence.
                    H. W. LONGFELLOW.

346. CHILDREN

Come to me, O ye children !
    For I hear you at your play,
And the questions that perplexed me
    Have vanished quite away.

Ye open the eastern windows,
    That look towards the sun,
Where thoughts are singing swallows,
    And the brooks of morning run.

In your hearts are the birds and the sunshine,
    In your thoughts the brooklet's flow,
But in mine is the wind of Autumn,
    And the first fall of the snow.

Ah ! what would the world be to us,
    If the children were no more ?
We should dread the desert behind us
    Worse than the dark before.

What the leaves are to the forest,
    With light and air for food,
Ere their sweet and tender juices
    Have been hardened into wood,—

That to the world are children ;
    Through them it feels the glow
Of a brighter and sunnier climate
    Than reaches the trunks below.

Come to me, O ye children !
    And whisper in my ear
What the birds and the winds are singing
    In your sunny atmosphere.

For what are all our contrivings,
   And the wisdom of our books,
When compared with your caresses,
   And the gladness of your looks ?

Ye are better than all the ballads
   That ever were sung or said ;
For ye are living poems,
   And all the rest are dead.
                        H. W. LONGFELLOW.

347. SEA-FEVER

I must down to the seas again, to the lonely sea and the sky,
And all I ask is a tall ship and a star to steer her by,
And the wheel's kick and the wind's song and the white
   sail's shaking,
And a gray mist on the sea's face and a gray dawn breaking.

I must down to the seas again, for the call of the running
   tide
Is a wild call and a clear call that may not be denied ;
And all I ask is a windy day with the white clouds flying,
And the flung spray and the blown spume, and the seagulls
   crying.

I must down to the seas again, to the vagrant gipsy life,
To the gull's way and the whale's way where the wind's
   like a whetted knife ;
And all I ask is a merry yarn from a laughing fellow-rover
And quiet sleep and a sweet dream when the long trick's
   over.

                        JOHN MASEFIELD.

348. BEAUTY

I have seen dawn and sunset on moors and windy hills
Coming in solemn beauty like slow old tunes of Spain :
I have seen the lady April bringing the daffodils,
Bringing the springing grass and the soft warm April rain.

I have heard the song of the blossoms and the old chant of
   the sea,
And seen strange lands from under the arched white sails
   of ships ;

But the loveliest things of beauty God ever has showed to
   me,
Are her voice, and her hair, and eyes, and the dear red
   curve of her lips.

JOHN MASEFIELD.

349. FROM "LOVE IN THE VALLEY"

Under yonder beech-tree single on the green-sward,
   Couched with her arms behind her golden head,
Knees and tresses folded to slip and ripple idly,
   Lies my young love sleeping in the shade.
Had I the heart to slide an arm beneath her,
   Press her parting lips as her waist I gather slow,
Waking in amazement she could not but embrace me :
   Then would she hold me and never let me go ?

Shy as the squirrel and wayward as the swallow,
   Swift as the swallow along the river's light
Circleting the surface to meet his mirror'd winglets,
   Fleeter she seems in her stay than in her flight.
Shy as the squirrel that leaps among the pine-tops,
   Wayward as the swallow overhead at set of sun,
She whom I love is hard to catch and conquer,
   Hard, but O the glory of the winning were she won !

When her mother tends her before the laughing mirror,
   Tying up her laces, looping up her hair,
Often she thinks, were this wild thing wedded,
   More love should I have, and much less care.
When her mother tends her before the lighted mirror,
   Loosening her laces, combing down her curls,
Often she thinks, were this wild thing wedded,
   I should miss but one for many boys and girls.

Heartless she is as the shadow in the meadows
   Flying to the hills on a blue and breezy noon.
No, she is athirst and drinking up her wonder :
   Earth to her is young as the slip of the new moon.
Deals she an unkindness, 'tis but her rapid measure,
   Even as in a dance ; and her smile can heal no less :
Like the swinging May-cloud that pelts the flowers with
   hailstones
   Off a sunny border, she was made to bruise and bless.

GEORGE MEREDITH.

350. RENOUNCEMENT

I must not think of thee ; and, tired yet strong,
  I shun the thought that lurks in all delight—
  The thought of thee—and in the blue Heaven's height,
And in the sweetest passage of a song.
O just beyond the fairest thoughts that throng
  This breast, the thought of thee waits, hidden yet bright ;
  But it must never, never come in sight ;
I must stop short of thee the whole day long.
But when sleep comes to close each difficult day,
  When night gives pause to the long watch I keep,
    And all my bonds I needs must loose apart,
Must doff my will as raiment laid away,—
  With the first dream that comes with the first sleep
    I run, I run, I am gathered to thy heart.

ALICE MEYNELL.

351. THE SHEPHERDESS

She walks—the lady of my delight—
  A shepherdess of sheep.
Her flocks are thoughts. She keeps them white ;
  She guards them from the steep ;
She feeds them on the fragrant height,
  And folds them in for sleep.

She roams maternal hills and bright,
  Dark valleys safe and deep.
Into that tender breast at night
  The chastest stars may peep.
She walks—the lady of my delight—
  A shepherdess of sheep.

She holds her little thoughts in sight,
  Though gay they run and leap.
She is so circumspect and right ;
  She has her soul to keep.
She walks—the lady of my delight—
  A shepherdess of sheep.

ALICE MEYNELL.

352. A LETTER FROM A GIRL TO HER OWN OLD AGE

Listen, and when thy hand this paper presses,
O time-worn woman, think of her who blesses
What thy thin fingers touch, with her caresses.

O mother, for the weight of years that break thee !
O daughter, for slow time must yet awake thee,
And from the changes of my heart must make thee !

O fainting traveller, morn is gray in heaven.
Dost thou remember how the clouds were driven ?
And are they calm about the fall of even ?

Pause near the ending of thy long migration,
For this one sudden hour of desolation
Appeals to one hour of thy meditation.

Suffer, O silent one, that I remind thee
Of the great hills that stormed the sky behind thee,
Of the wild winds of power that have resigned thee.

Know that the mournful plain where thou must wander
Is but a gray and silent world, but ponder
The misty mountains of the morning yonder.

Listen :—the mountain winds with rain were fretting,
And sudden gleams the mountain-tops besetting.
I cannot let thee fade to death, forgetting.

What part of this wild heart of mine I know not
Will follow with thee where the great winds blow not,
And where the young flowers of the mountain grow not,

Yet let my letter with thy lost thoughts in it
Tell what the way was when thou didst begin it,
And win with thee the goal when thou shalt win it.

Oh, in some hour of thine thy thoughts shall guide thee.
Suddenly, though time, darkness, silence, hide thee,
This wind from thy lost country flits beside thee,—

Telling thee : all thy memories moved the maiden,
With thy regrets was morning over-shaden,
With sorrow, thou hast left, her life was laden.

But whither shall my thoughts turn to pursue thee ?
Life changes, and the years and days renew thee.
Oh, Nature brings my straying heart unto thee.

Her winds will join us, with their constant kisses
Upon the evening as the morning tresses,
Her summers breathe the same unchanging blisses.

And we, so altered in our shifting phases,
Track one another 'mid the many mazes
By the eternal child-breath of the daisies.

I have not writ this letter of divining
To make a glory of thy silent pining,
A triumph of thy mute and strange declining.

Only one youth, and the bright life was shrouded.
Only one morning, and the day was clouded.
And one old age with all regrets is crowded.

O hush, O hush ! Thy tears my words are steeping.
O hush, hush, hush ! So full, the fount of weeping ?
Poor eyes, so quickly moved, so near to sleeping ?

Pardon the girl ; such strange desires beset her.
Poor woman, lay aside the mournful letter
That breaks thy heart ; the one who wrote, forget her ;

The one who now thy faded features guesses,
With filial fingers thy gray hair caresses,
With morning tears thy mournful twilight blesses.

                                    ALICE MEYNELL.

353. THE EVE OF CRECY

Gold on her head, and gold on her feet,
  And gold where the hems of her kirtle meet,
And a golden girdle round my sweet ;—
    Ah ! qu'elle est belle La Marguerite.

Margaret's maids are fair to see,
Freshly dress'd and pleasantly ;
Margaret's hair falls down to her knee ;—
    Ah ! qu'elle est belle La Marguerite.

If I were rich I would kiss her feet,
I would kiss the place where the gold hems meet,
And the golden girdle round my sweet—
    Ah! qu'elle est belle La Marguerite.

Ah me! I have never touch'd her hand;
When the arriere-ban goes through the land,
Six basnets under my pennon stand,—
    Ah! qu'elle est belle La Marguerite.

And many an one grins under his hood:
" Sir Lambert de Bois, with all his men good,
Has neither food nor firewood; "—
    Ah! qu'elle est belle La Marguerite.

If I were rich I would kiss her feet,
And the golden girdle of my sweet,
And thereabouts where the gold hems meet;—
    Ah! qu'elle est belle La Marguerite.

Yet even now it is good to think,
While my few poor varlets grumble and drink
In my desolate hall, where the fires sink,—
    Ah! qu'elle est belle La Marguerite.

Of Margaret sitting glorious there,
In glory of gold and glory of hair,
And glory of glorious face most fair;—
    Ah! qu'elle est belle La Marguerite.

Likewise to-night I make good cheer,
Because this battle draweth near:
For what have I to lose or fear?—
    Ah! qu'elle est belle La Marguerite.

For, look you, my horse is good to prance
A right fair measure in this war-dance,
Before the eyes of Philip of France;—
    Ah! qu'elle est belle La Marguerite.

And sometime it may hap, perdie,
While my new towers stand up three and three,
And my hall gets painted fair to see—
    Ah! qu'elle est belle La Marguerite.

That folks may say : " Times change, by the rood,
For Lambert, banneret of the wood,
Has heaps of food and firewood ;—
   Ah ! qu'elle est belle La Marguerite.

" And wonderful eyes, too, under the hood
Of a damsel of right noble blood : "
St. Ives, for Lambert of the wood !—
   Ah ! qu'elle est belle La Marguerite.
WILLIAM MORRIS.

354

  " I know a little garden close
Set thick with lily and red rose,
Where I would wander if I might
From dewy dawn to dewy night,
And have one with me wandering.
  " And though within it no birds sing,
And though no pillar'd house is there,
And though the apple boughs are bare
Of fruit and blossom, would to God,
Her feet upon the green grass trod,
And I beheld them as before.
  " There comes a murmur from the shore,
And in the place two fair streams are,
Drawn from the purple hills afar,
Drawn down unto the restless sea ;
The hills whose flowers ne'er fed the bee,
The shore no ship has ever seen,
Still beaten by the billows green,
Whose murmur comes unceasingly
Unto the place for which I cry.
  " For which I cry both day and night,
For which I let slip all delight,
That maketh me both deaf and blind,
Careless to win, unskilled to find,
And quick to lose what all men seek.
  " Yet tottering as I am, and weak,
Still have I left a little breath
To seek within the jaws of death
An entrance to that happy place,
To seek the unforgotten face

Once seen, once kissed, once reft from me
  Anigh the murmuring of the sea."
            WILLIAM MORRIS.
            (*Life and Death of Jason.*)

355. TWO RED ROSES ACROSS THE MOON

There was a lady lived in a hall,
Large in the eyes, and slim and tall ;
And ever she sung from noon to noon,
Two red roses across the moon.

There was a knight came riding by
In early spring, when the roads were dry ;
And he heard that lady sing at the noon,
Two red roses across the moon.

Yet none the more he stopp'd at all,
But he rode a-gallop past the hall ;
And left that lady singing at noon,
Two red roses across the moon.

Because, forsooth, the battle was set,
And the scarlet and blue had got to be met,
He rode on the spur till the next warm noon :—
Two red roses across the moon.

But the battle was scatter'd from hill to hill,
From the windmill to the watermill ;
And he said to himself, as it near'd the moon,
Two red roses across the moon.

You scarce could see for the scarlet and blue,
A golden helm or a golden shoe ;
So he cried, as the fight grew thick at the noon,
Two red roses across the moon !

Verily then the gold bore through
The huddled spears of the scarlet and blue ;
And they cried, as they cut them down at the noon,
Two red roses across the moon !

I trow he stopp'd when he rode again
By the hall, though draggled sore with the rain ;
And his lips were pinch'd to kiss at the noon
Two red roses across the moon.

Under the may she stoop'd to the crown,
All was gold, there was nothing of brown ;
And the horns blew up in the hall at noon,
Two red roses across the moon.

WILLIAM MORRIS.

356. SUMMER DAWN

Pray but one prayer for me 'twixt thy closed lips,
 Think but one thought of me up in the stars.
The summer night waneth, the morning light slips,
 Faint and gray 'twixt the leaves of the aspen, betwixt
  the cloud-bars,
That are patiently waiting there for the dawn :
 Patient and colourless, though Heaven's gold
Waits to float through them along with the sun.
Far out in the meadows, above the young corn,
 The heavy elms wait, and restless and cold
The uneasy wind rises ; the roses are dun ;
Through the long twilight they pray for the dawn,
Round the lone house in the midst of the corn.
 Speak but one word to me over the corn,
 Over the tender, bow'd locks of the corn.

WILLIAM MORRIS.

357. YATTENDON

Among the woods and tillage
 That fringe the topmost downs,
All lonely lies the village,
 Far off from seas and towns.
Yet when her own folk slumbered
 I heard within her street
Murmur of men unnumbered
 And march of myriad feet.

For all she lies so lonely,
 Far off from towns and seas,
The village holds not only
 The roofs beneath her trees :

While Life is sweet and tragic
    And Death is veiled and dumb,
Hither, by singer's magic,
    The pilgrim world must come.
                        HENRY NEWBOLT.

358. I DO NOT LOVE THEE

I do not love thee !—no ! I do not love thee !
And yet when thou art absent I am sad ;
    And envy even the bright blue sky above thee,
Whose quiet stars may see thee and be glad.

I do not love thee !—yet, I know not why,
What'er thou dost seems still well done, to me :
    And often in my solitude I sigh
That those I do love are not more like thee !

I do not love thee !—yet, when thou art gone,
I hate the sound (though those who speak be dear)
    Which breaks the lingering echo of the tone
Thy voice of music leaves upon my ear.

I do not love thee !—yet thy speaking eyes,
With their deep, bright, and most expressive blue,
    Between me and the midnight heaven arise,
Oftener than any eyes I ever knew.

I know I do not love thee ! yet, alas !
Others will scarcely trust my candid heart ;
    And oft I catch them smiling as thou pass,
Because they see me gazing where thou art.
                    CAROLINE ELIZABETH SARAH NORTON.

359. THE MARRIED LOVER

Why, having won her, do I woo ?
    Because her spirit's vestal grace
Provokes me always to pursue,
    But, spirit-like, eludes embrace ;
Because her womanhood is such
    That, as on court-days subjects kiss

The Queen's hand, yet so near a touch
　　Affirms no mean familiarness,
Nay, rather marks more fair the height
　　Which can with safety so neglect
To dread, as lower ladies might,
　　That grace could meet with disrespect.
Thus she with happy favour feeds
　　Allegiance from a love so high
That thence no false conceit proceeds
　　Of difference bridged, or state put by ;
Because, although in act and word
　　As lowly as a wife can be,
Her manners, when they call me lord,
　　Remind me 'tis by courtesy ;
Not with her least consent of will,
　　Which would my proud affection hurt,
But by the noble style that still
　　Imputes an unattain'd desert ;
Because her gay and lofty brows,
　　When all is won which hope can ask,
Reflect a light of hopeless snows
　　That bright in virgin ether bask ;
Because, though free of the outer court
　　I am, this Temple keeps its shrine
Sacred to Heaven ; because, in short,
　　She's not and never can be mine.

COVENTRY PATMORE.

360. UNTHRIFT

Ah, wasteful woman, she who may
　　On her sweet self set her own price,
Knowing man cannot choose but pay,
　　How has she cheapen'd paradise ;
How given for nought her priceless gift,
　　How spoil'd the bread and spill'd the wine,
Which, spent with due respective thrift,
　　Had made brutes men, and men divine.

COVENTRY PATMORE.

361. THE TOYS

My little son, who look'd from thoughtful eyes
And moved and spoke in quiet grown-up wise,
Having my law the seventh time disobey'd,
I struck him, and dismiss'd
With hard words and unkiss'd—
His mother, who was patient, being dead—
Then, fearing lest his grief should hinder sleep,
I visited his bed,
But found him slumbering deep,
With darken'd eyelids, and their lashes yet
From his late sobbing wet.
And I, with moan,
Kissing away his tears, left others of my own ;
For, on a table drawn beside his head,
He had put, within his reach,
A box of counters, and a red-vein'd stone,
A piece of grass abraded by the peach,
And six or seven shells,
A bottle with bluebells,
And two French copper coins, ranged there with careful
    art,
To comfort his sad heart.
So when that night I pray'd
To God, I wept, and said :
Ah, when at last we lie with tranced breath,
Not vexing Thee in death,
And thou rememberest of what toys
We made our joys,
How weakly understood,
Thy great commanded good,
Then, fatherly not less
Than I whom Thou hast moulded from the clay,
Thou'lt leave Thy wrath, and say,
" I will be sorry for their childishness."
COVENTRY PATMORE.

362. TO HELEN

Helen, thy beauty is to me
  Like those Nicæan barks of yore,
That gently, o'er a perfumed sea,
  The weary, wayworn wanderer bore
  To his own native shore.

On desperate seas long wont to roam,
　　Thy hyacinth hair, thy classic face,
Thy Naiad airs, have brought me home
　　　To the glory that was Greece,
　　And the grandeur that was Rome.

Lo ! in yon brilliant window-niche
　　How statue-like I see thee stand,
The agate lamp within thy hand,
　　Ah ! Psyche, from the regions which
　　Are holy land !

Edgar Allan Poe.

363. TO ONE IN PARADISE

Thou wast all that to me, love,
　　For which my soul did pine :
A green isle in the sea, love,
　　A fountain and a shrine
All wreathed with fairy fruits and flowers,
　　And all the flowers were mine.

Ah, dream too bright to last !
　　Ah, starry Hope, that didst arise
But to be overcast !
　　A voice from out the Future cries,
" On ! on ! "—but o'er the Past
　　(Dim gulf !) my spirit hovering lies
Mute, motionless, aghast.

For, alas ! alas ! with me
　　The light of Life is o'er !
No more—no more—no more—
(Such language holds the solemn sea
　　To the sands upon the shore)
Shall bloom the thunder-blasted tree,
　　Or the stricken eagle soar.

And all my days are trances,
　　And all my nightly dreams
Are where thy gray eye glances,
　　And where thy footsteps gleams—
In what ethereal dances,
　　By what eternal streams.

Edgar Allan Poe.

364. SONNET

Remember me when I am gone away,
　　Gone far away into the silent land;
　　When you can no more hold me by the hand,
Nor I half turn to go yet turning stay.
Remember me when no more day by day
　　You tell me of our future that you planned;
　　Only remember me; you understand
It will be late to counsel then or pray.
Yet if you should forget me for a while
　　And afterwards remember, do not grieve:
　　For if the darkness and corruption leave
　　A vestige of the thoughts that once I had,
Better by far you should forget and smile
　　Than that you should remember and be sad.

CHRISTINA ROSSETTI.

365. SONG

Oh roses for the flush of youth,
　　And laurel for the perfect prime;
But pluck an ivy branch for me
　　Grown old before my time.

Oh violets for the grave of youth,
　　And bay for these dead in their prime;
Give me the withered leaves I chose
　　Before in the old time.

CHRISTINA ROSSETTI.

366. SONG

When I am dead, my dearest,
　　Sing no sad songs for me;
Plant thou no roses at my head,
　　Nor shady cypress tree:
Be the green grass above me
　　With showers and dewdrops wet;
And if thou wilt, remember,
　　And if thou wilt, forget.

I shall not see the shadows,
   I shall not feel the rain;
I shall not hear the nightingale
   Sing on, as if in pain:
And dreaming through the twilight
   That doth not rise nor set,
Haply I may remember,
   And haply may forget.

                 CHRISTINA ROSSETTI.

367. UP-HILL

Does the road wind up-hill all the way?
   Yes, to the very end.
Will the day's journey take the whole long day?
   From morn to night, my friend.

But is there for the night a resting-place?
   A roof for when the slow dark hours begin.
May not the darkness hide it from my face?
   You cannot miss that inn.

Shall I meet other wayfarers at night?
   Those who have gone before.
Then must I knock, or call when just in sight?
   They will not keep you standing at that door.

Shall I find comfort, travel-sore and weak?
   Of labour you shall find the sum.
Will there be beds for me and all who seek?
   Yea, beds for all who come.

                 CHRISTINA ROSSETTI.

368. THE BLESSÈD DAMOZEL

The blessèd Damozel lean'd out
   From the gold bar of Heaven:
Her blue grave eyes were deeper much
   Than a deep water, even.
She had three lilies in her hand,
   And the stars in her hair were seven.

Her robe, ungirt from clasp to hem,
　　No wrought flowers did adorn,
But a white rose of Mary's gift
　　On the neck meetly worn ;
And her hair, lying down her back,
　　Was yellow like ripe corn.

Herseem'd she scarce had been a day
　　One of God's choristers ;
The wonder was not yet quite gone
　　From that still look of hers ;
Albeit, to them she left, her day
　　Had counted as ten years.

(To *one* it is ten years of years :
　　. . . Yet now, here in this place,
Surely she lean'd o'er me,—her hair
　　Fell all about my face. . . .
Nothing : the Autumn-fall of leaves.
　　The whole year sets apace.)

It was the terrace of God's house
　　That she was standing on,—
By God built over the sheer depth
　　In which is Space begun ;
So high, that looking downward thence,
　　She scarce could see the sun.

It lies from Heaven across the flood
　　Of ether, as a bridge
Beneath, the tides of day and night
　　With flame and darkness ridge
The void, as low as where this earth
　　Spins like a fretful midge.

But in those tracts, with her, it was
　　The peace of utter light
And silence. For no breeze may stir
　　Along the steady flight
Of seraphim ; no echo there,
　　Beyond all depth or height.

Heard hardly, some of her new friends,
　　Playing at holy games,

Spake, gentle-mouth'd, among themselves,
   Their virginal chaste names ;
And the souls, mounting up to God,
   Went by her like thin flames.

And still she bow'd herself, and stoop'd
   Into the vast waste calm ;
Till her bosom's pressure must have made
   The bar she lean'd on warm,
And the lilies lay as if asleep
   Along her bended arm.

From the fixt lull of Heaven, she saw
Time, like a pulse, shake fierce
Through all the worlds. Her gaze still strove,
   In that steep gulf, to pierce
The swarm ; and then she spoke, as when
   The stars sang in their spheres.

" I wish that he were come to me,
   For he will come," she said.
" Have I not pray'd in solemn Heaven ?
   On earth, has he not pray'd ?
Are not two prayers a perfect strength ?
   And shall I feel afraid ?

" When round his head the aureole clings,
   And he is clothed in white,
I'll take his hand, and go with him
   To the deep wells of light,
And we will step down as to a stream
   And bathe there in God's sight.

" We two will stand beside that shrine,
   Occult, withheld, untrod,
Whose lamps tremble continually
   With prayer sent up to God ;
And where each need, reveal'd, expects
   Its patient period.

" We two will lie i' the shadow of
   That living mystic tree
Within whose secret growth the Dove
   Sometimes is felt to be,

While every leaf that His plumes touch
   Saith His name audibly.

"And I myself will teach to him,—
   I myself, lying so,—
The songs I sing here; which his mouth
   Shall pause in, hush'd and slow,
Finding some knowledge at each pause,
   And some new thing to know."

(Alas! to *her* wise simple mind
   These things were all but known
Before: they trembled on her sense,—
   Her voice had caught their tone.
Alas for lonely Heaven! Alas
   For life wrung out alone!

Alas, and though the end were reach'd? . .
   Was *thy* part understood
Or borne in trust? And for her sake
   Shall this too be found good?—
May the close lips that knew not prayer
   Praise ever, though they would?)

"We two," she said, "will seek the groves
   Where the lady Mary is,
With her five handmaidens, whose names
   Are five sweet symphonies:—
Cecily, Gertrude, Magdalen,
   Margaret and Rosalys.

"Circle-wise sit they, with bound locks
   And bosoms coverèd;
Into the fine cloth, white like flame,
   Weaving the golden thread,
To fashion the birth-robes for them
   Who are just born, being dead.

"He shall fear, haply, and be dumb.
   Then I will lay my cheek
To his, and tell about our love,
   Not once abash'd or weak:
And the dear Mother will approve
   My pride, and let me speak.

" Herself shall bring us, hand in hand,
　　To Him round whom all souls
Kneel—the unnumber'd solemn heads
　　Bow'd with their aureoles :
And Angels, meeting us, shall sing
　　To their citherns and citoles.

" There will I ask of Christ the Lord
　　Thus much for him and me :—
To have more blessing than on earth
　　In nowise ; but to be
As then we were,—being as then
　　At peace. Yea, verily.

" Yea, verily ; when he is come
　　We will do thus and thus :
Till this my vigil seem quite strange
　　And almost fabulous ;
We two will live at once, one life ;
　　And peace shall be with us."

She gazed, and listen'd, and then said,
　　Less sad of speech than mild,—
" All this is when he comes." She ceased :
　　The light thrill'd past her fill'd
With Angels, in strong level lapse.
　　Her eyes pray'd, and she smiled.

(I saw her smile.) But soon their flight
　　Was vague 'mid the poised spheres.
And then she cast her arms along
　　The golden barriers,
And laid her face between her hands,
　　And wept. (I heard her tears.)

　　　　　　　　　　　　D. G. ROSSETTI.

369. "I HAVE A RENDEZVOUS WITH DEATH"

I have a rendezvous with Death
At some disputed barricade,
When Spring comes back with rustling shade
And apple-blossoms fill the air—
I have a rendezvous with Death
When Spring brings back blue days and fair.

It may be he shall take my hand
And lead me into his dark land
And close my eyes and quench my breath—
It may be I shall pass him still.
I have a rendezvous with Death
On some scarred slope of battered hill,
When Spring comes round again this year
And the first meadow-flowers appear.

God knows 'twere better to be deep
Pillowed in silk and scented down,
Where Love throbs out in blissful sleep,
Pulse nigh to pulse, and breath to breath,
Where hushed awakenings are dear . . .
But I've a rendezvous with Death
At midnight in some flaming town,
When Spring trips north again this year,
And I to my pledged word am true,
I shall not fail that rendezvous.

ALAN SEEGER.

370. TO S. R. CROCKETT
(In Reply to a Dedication)

Blows the wind to-day, and the sun and the rain are flying,
    Blows the wind on the moors to-day and now,
Where about the graves of the martyrs the whaups are
    crying,
    My heart remembers how !

Gray recumbent tombs of the dead in desert places,
    Standing stones on the vacant wine-red moor,
Hills of sheep, and the homes of the silent vanquished races,
    And winds, austere and pure :

Be it granted me to behold you again in dying,
    Hills of home ! and to hear again the call ;
Hear about the graves of the martyrs the peewees crying,
    And hear no more at all.

ROBERT LOUIS STEVENSON.

371

Bright is the ring of words
 When the right man rings them,
Fair the fall of songs
 When the singer sings them.
Still they are carolled and said—
 On wings they are carried—
After the singer is dead
 And the maker buried.

Low as the singer lies
 In the field of heather,
Songs of his fashion bring
 The swains together.
And when the west is red
 With the sunset embers,
The lover lingers and sings
 And the maid remembers.
     ROBERT LOUIS STEVENSON.

372 ROMANCE

I will make you brooches and toys for your delight
Of bird-song at morning and star-shine at night.
I will make a palace fit for you and me
Of green days in forest and blue days at sea.

I will make my kitchen, and you shall keep your room,
Where white flows the river and bright blows the broom,
And you shall wash your linen and keep your body white
In rainfall at morning and dewfall at night.

And this shall be for music when no one else is near,
The fine song for singing, the rare song to hear !
That only I remember, that only you admire,
Of the broad road that stretches and the roadside fire.
     ROBERT LOUIS STEVENSON.

373. MY WIFE

Trusty, dusky, vivid, true,
With eyes of gold and bramble-dew,
 Steel-true and blade-straight,
  The great artificer
   Made my mate.

Honour, anger, valour, fire;
A love that life could never tire,
 Death quench or evil stir,
  The mighty master
   Gave to her.

Teacher, tender, comrade, wife,
A fellow-farer true through life,
 Heart-whole and soul-free,
  The august father
   Gave to me.
       ROBERT LOUIS STEVENSON.

374. REQUIEM

Under the wide and starry sky,
Dig the grave and let me lie.
Glad did I live and gladly die,
 And I laid me down with a will.

This be the verse you grave for me:
Here he lies where he longed to be,
Home is the sailor, home from sea,
 And the hunter home from the hill.
       ROBERT LOUIS STEVENSON.

375. ITYLUS

Swallow, my sister, O sister swallow,
 How can thine heart be full of the spring?
A thousand summers are over and dead.
 What hast thou found in the spring to follow?
 What hast thou found in thine heart to sing?
 What wilt thou do when the summer is shed?

O swallow, sister, O fair swift swallow,
  Why wilt thou fly after spring to the south,
    The soft south whither thine heart is set ?
Shall not the grief of the old time follow ?
  Shall not the song thereof cleave to thy mouth ?
    Hast thou forgotten ere I forget ?

Sister, my sister, O fleet sweet swallow,
  Thy way is long to the sun and the south ;
    But I, fulfilled of my heart's desire,
Shedding my song upon height, upon hollow,
  From tawny body and sweet small mouth
    Feed the heart of the night with fire.

I the nightingale all spring through,
  O swallow, sister, O changing swallow,
    All spring through till the spring be done,
Clothed with the light of the night on the dew,
  Sing, while the hours and the wild birds follow,
    Take flight and follow and find the sun.

Sister, my sister, O soft light swallow,
  Though all things feast in the spring's guest-chamber,
    How hast thou heart to be glad thereof yet ?
For where thou fliest I shall not follow,
  Till life forget and death remember,
    Till thou remember and I forget.

Swallow, my sister, O singing swallow,
  I know not how thou hast heart to sing.
    Hast thou the heart ? is it all past over ?
Thy lord the summer is good to follow,
  And fair the feet of thy lover the spring :
    But what wilt thou say to the spring thy lover ?

O swallow, sister, O fleeting swallow,
  My heart in me is a molten ember
    And over my head the waves have met.
But thou wouldst tarry or I would follow,
  Could I forget or thou remember,
    Couldst thou remember and I forget.

O sweet stray sister, O shifting swallow,
  The heart's division divideth us.

Thy heart is light as a leaf of a tree;
But mine goes forth among sea-gulfs hollow
    To the place of the slaying of Itylus,
        The feast of Daulis, the Thracian sea.

O swallow, sister, O rapid swallow,
    I pray thee sing not a little space.
        Are not the roofs and the lintels wet?
The woven web that was plain to follow,
    The small slain body, the flowerlike face,
        Can I remember if thou forget?

O sister, sister, thy first-begotten!
    The hands that cling and the feet that follow,
        The voice of the child's blood crying yet
Who hath remembered me? who hath forgotten?
    Thou hast forgotten, O summer swallow,
        But the world shall end when I forget.

A. C. SWINBURNE.

376

I will go back to the great sweet mother,
    Mother and lover of men, the sea.
I will go down to her, I and none other,
    Close with her, kiss her and mix her with me;
Cling to her, strive with her, hold her fast:
O fair white mother, in days long past
Born without sister, born without brother,
    Set free my soul as thy soul is free.

O fair green-girdled mother of mine,
    Sea, that art clothed with the sun and the rain,
Thy sweet hard kisses are strong like wine,
    Thy large embraces are keen like pain.
Save me and hide me with all thy waves,
Find me one grave of thy thousand graves,
Those pure cold populous graves of thine
    Wrought without hand in a world without stain.

I shall sleep, and move with the moving ships,
    Change as the winds change, veer in the tide;
My lips will feast on the foam of thy lips,
    I shall rise with thy rising, with thee subside;

Sleep, and not know if she be, if she were,
Filled full with life to the eyes and hair,
As a rose is fulfilled to the roselead tips
   With splendid summer and perfume and pride.

This woven raiment of nights and days,
   Were it once cast off and unwound from me,
Naked and glad would I walk in thy ways,
   Alive and aware of thy ways and thee ;
Clear of the whole world, hidden at home,
Clothed with the green and crowned with the foam ;
A pulse of the life of thy straits and bays,
   A vein in the heart of the streams of the sea.

Fair mother, fed with the lives of men,
   Thou art subtle and cruel of heart, men say.
Thou hast taken, and shalt not render again ;
   Thou art full of thy dead, and cold as they.
But death is the worst that comes of thee ;
Thou art fed with our dead, O mother, O sea,
But when hast thou fed on our hearts ? or when,
   Having given us love, hast thou taken away ?
                                    A. C. SWINBURNE.

377. CHORUS

When the hounds of spring are on winter's traces,
   The mother of months in meadow or plain
Fills the shadows and windy places
   With lisp of leaves and ripple of rain ;
And the brown bright nightingale amorous
Is half assuaged for Itylus,
For the Thracian ships and the foreign faces.
   The tongueless vigil, and all the pain.

Come with bows bent and with emptying of quivers,
   Maiden most perfect, lady of light,
With a noise of winds and many rivers,
   With a clamour of waters, and with might ;
Bind on thy sandals, O thou most fleet,
Over the splendour and speed of thy feet ;
For the faint east quickens, the wan west shivers,
   Round the feet of the day and the feet of the night.

Where shall we find her, how shall we sing to her,
    Fold our hands round her knees, and cling?
O that man's heart were as fire and could spring to her,
    Fire, or the strength of the streams that spring!
For the stars and the winds are unto her
As raiment, as songs of the harp-player;
For the risen stars and the fallen cling to her,
    And the southwest-wind and the west-wind sing.

For winter's rains and ruins are over,
    And all the season of snows and sins;
The days dividing lover and lover,
    The light that loses, the night that wins;
And time remember'd is grief forgotten,
And frosts are slain and flowers begotten,
And in green underwood and cover
    Blossom by blossom the spring begins.

The full streams feed on flower of rushes,
    Ripe grasses trammel a travelling foot,
The faint fresh flame of the young year flushes
    From leaf to flower and flower to fruit;
And fruit and leaf are as gold and fire,
And the oat is heard above the lyre,
And the hoofed heel of a satyr crushes
    The chestnut-husk at the chestnut-root.

And Pan by noon and Bacchus by night,
    Fleeter of foot than the fleet-foot kid,
Follows with dancing and fills with delight
    The Mænad and the Bassarid;
And soft as lips that laugh and hide
The laughing leaves of the trees divide,
And screen from seeing and leave in sight
    The god pursuing, the maiden hid.

The ivy falls with the Bacchanal's hair
    Over her eyebrows hiding her eyes;
The wild vine slipping down leaves bare
    Her bright breast shortening into sighs;
The wild vine slips with the weight of its leaves,
But the berried ivy catches and cleaves
To the limbs that glitter, the feet that scare
    The wolf that follows, the fawn that flies.

                                        A. C. SWINBURNE.

378. A FORSAKEN GARDEN

In a coign of the cliff between lowland and highland,
  At the sea-down's edge between windward and lee,
Walled round with rocks as an inland island,
  The ghost of a garden fronts the sea.
A girdle of brushwood and thorn encloses
  The steep square slope of the blossomless bed
Where the weeds that grew green from the graves of its roses
    Now lie dead.

The fields fall southward, abrupt and broken,
  To the low last edge of the long lone land.
If a step should sound or a word be spoken,
  Would a ghost not rise at the strange guest's hand ?
So long have the gray bare walks lain guestless,
  Through branches and briars if a man make way,
He shall find no life but the sea-wind's, restless
    Night and day.

The dense hard passage is blind and stifled
  That crawls by a track none turn to climb
To the strait waste place that the years have rifled
  Of all but the thorns that are touched not of time.
The thorns he spares when the rose is taken ;
  The rocks are left when he wastes the plain.
The wind that wanders, the weeds wind-shaken,
    These remain.

Not a flower to be pressed of the foot that falls not ;
  As the heart of a dead man the seed-plots are dry ;
From the thicket of thorns whence the nightingale calls not,
  Could she call, there were never a rose to reply.
Over the meadows that blossom and wither
  Rings but the note of a sea-bird's song ;
Only the sun and the rain come hither
    All year long.

The sun burns sere and the rain dishevels
  One gaunt bleak blossom of scentless breath.
Only the wind here hovers and revels
  In a round where life seems barren as death.
Here there was laughing of old, there was weeping,
  Haply, of lovers none ever will know,
Whose eyes went seaward a hundred sleeping
    Years ago.

Heart handfast in heart as they stood, " Look thither."
   Did he whisper ? " look forth from the flowers to the sea ;
For the foam-flowers endure when the rose-blossoms
     wither,
   And men that love lightly may die—but we ? "
And the same wind sang and the same waves whitened,
   And or ever the garden's last petals were shed,
In the lips that had whispered, the eyes that had lightened,
     Love was dead.

Or they loved their life through, and then went whither ?
   And were one to the end—but what end who knows ?
Love deep as the sea as a rose must wither,
   As the rose-red seaweed that mocks the rose.
Shall the dead take thought for the dead to love them ?
   What love was ever as deep as a grave ?
They are loveless now as the grass above them
     Or the wave.

All are at one now, roses and lovers,
   Not known of the cliffs and the fields and the sea.
Not a breath of the time that has been hovers
   In the air now soft with a summer to be.
Not a breath shall there sweeten the seasons hereafter
   Of the flowers or the lovers that laugh now or weep,
When as they that are free now of weeping and laughter
     We shall sleep.

Here death may deal not again for ever ;
   Here change may come not till all change end.
From the graves they have made they shall rise up never,
   Who have left nought living to ravage and rend.
Earth, stones, and thorns of the wild ground growing,
   While the sun and the rain live, these shall be ;
Till a last wind's breath upon all these blowing
     Roll the sea.

Till the slow sea rise and the sheer cliff crumble,
   Till terrace and meadow the deep gulfs drink,
Till the strength of the waves of the high tides humble
   The fields that lessen, the rocks that shrink,
Here now in his triumph where all things falter,
   Stretched out on the spoils that his own hand spread,
As a god self-slain on his own strange altar,
     Death lies dead.

                   A. C. SWINBURNE.

379. CHORUS

Before the beginning of years
  There came to the making of man
Time, with a gift of tears ;
  Grief, with a glass that ran ;
Pleasure, with pain for leaven ;
  Summer, with flowers that fell ;
Remembrance fallen from heaven,
  And madness risen from hell ;
Strength without hands to smite ;
  Love that endures for a breath ;
Night, the shadow of light,
  And life, the shadow of death.

And the high gods took in hand
  Fire, and the falling of tears,
And a measure of sliding sand
  From under the feet of the years ;
And froth and drift of the sea ;
  And dust of the labouring earth ;
And bodies of things to be
  In the houses of death and of birth ;
And wrought with weeping and laughter,
  And fashioned with loathing and love,
With life before and after,
  And death beneath and above,
For a day and a night and a morrow,
  That his strength might endure for a span,
With travail and heavy sorrow,
  The holy spirit of man.

From the winds of the north and the south
  They gathered as unto strife ;
They breathed upon his mouth,
  They filled his body with life ;
Eyesight and speech they wrought
  For the veils of the soul therein,
A time for labour and thought,
  A time to serve and to sin ;
They gave him light in his ways,
  And love, and a space for delight,
And beauty, and length of days,
  And night, and sleep in the night.

His speech is a burning fire ;
    With his lips he travaileth ;
In his heart is a blind desire,
    In his eyes foreknowledge of death ;
He weaves, and is clothed with derision ;
    Sows, and he shall not reap ;
His life is a watch or a vision
    Between a sleep and a sleep.
                A. C. SWINBURNE.

380. THE CRYING OF WATER

O water, voice of my heart, crying in the sand,
All night long crying with a mournful cry,
As I lie and listen, and cannot understand
The voice of my heart in my side or the voice of the sea,
O water, crying for rest, is it I, is it I ?
All night long the water is crying to me.

Unresting water, there shall never be rest
Till the last moon drop and the last tide fail,
And the fire of the end begin to burn in the west ;
And the heart shall be weary and wonder and cry like the
    sea,
All life long crying without avail,
As the water all night long is crying to me.
                ARTHUR SYMONS.

381. ST. AGNES' EVE

Deep on the convent roof the snows
    Are sparkling to the moon :
My breath to heaven like vapour goes :
    May my soul follow soon !
The shadows of the convent towers
    Slant down the snowy sward,
Still creeping with the creeping hours
    That lead me to the Lord :
Make Thou my spirit pure and clear
    As are the frosty skies,
Or this first snowdrop of the year
    That in my bosom lies.

As these white robes are soiled and dark,
  To yonder shining ground ;
As this pale taper's earthly spark,
  To yonder argent round ;
So shows my soul before the Lamb,
  My spirit before Thee ;
So in mine earthly house I am,
  To that I hope to be.
Break up the heavens, O Lord ! and far,
  Through all yon starlight keen,
Draw me, thy bride, a glittering star,
  In raiment white and clean.

He lifts me to the golden doors ;
  The flashes come and go ;
All heaven bursts her starry floors,
  And strows her lights below,
And deepens on and up : the gates
  Roll back, and far within
For me the Heavenly Bridegroom waits,
  To make me pure of sin.
The sabbaths of Eternity,
  One sabbath deep and wide—
A light upon the shining sea—
  The Bridegroom with his bride !

LORD TENNYSON.

382. COME NOT WHEN I AM DEAD

Come not, when I am dead,
  To drop thy foolish tears upon my grave,
To trample round my fallen head,
  And vex the unhappy dust thou wouldst not save.
There let the wind sweep and the plover cry ;
    But thou, go by.

Child, if it were thine error or thy crime
  I care no longer, being all unblest :
Wed whom thou wilt, but I am sick of Time,
  And I desire to rest.
Pass on, weak heart, and leave me where I lie :
    Go by, go by.

LORD TENNYSON.

383. MOVE EASTWARD, HAPPY EARTH

Move eastward, happy earth, and leave
   Yon orange sunset waning slow :
From fringes of the faded eve,
   O happy planet, eastward go ;
Till over thy dark shoulder glow
   Thy silver sister world, and rise
   To glass herself in dewy eyes
That watch me from the glen below.
Ah, bear me with thee, smoothly borne
   Dip forward under starry light,
And move me to my marriage morn,
   And round again to happy night.
                   LORD TENNYSON.

384. BREAK, BREAK, BREAK

Break, break, break,
   On thy cold gray stones, O Sea !
And I would that my tongue could utter
   The thoughts that arise in me.

Oh well for the fisherman's boy,
That he shouts with his sister at play !
Oh well for the sailor lad,
   That he sings in his boat on the bay !

And the stately ships go on
   To their haven under the hill ;
But oh for the touch of a vanish'd hand,
   And the sound of a voice that is still !

Break, break, break,
   At the foot of thy crags, O Sea !
But the tender grace of a day that is dead
   Will never come back to me.
                   LORD TENNYSON.

385

Tears, idle tears, I know not what they mean,
Tears from the depth of some divine despair
Rise in the heart and gather to the eyes,
In looking on the happy Autumn fields,
And thinking of the days that are no more.

Fresh as the first beam glittering on a sail,
That brings our friends up from the underworld,
Sad as the last which reddens over one
That sinks with all we love below the verge ;
So sad, so fresh, the days that are no more.

Ah, sad and strange as in dark summer dawns
The earliest pipe of half awaken'd birds
To dying ears, when unto undying eyes
The casement slowly grows a glimmering square ;
So sad, so strange, the days that are no more.

Dear as remember'd kisses after death,
And sweet as those by hopeless fancy feign'd
On lips that are for others ; deep as love,
Deep as first love, and wild with all regret ;
O Death in Life, the days that are no more.

LORD TENNYSON.

386

Home they brought her warrior dead :
    She nor swoon'd nor utter'd cry :
All her maidens watching, said,
    " She must weep, or she will die."

Then they praised him, soft and low,
    Call'd him worthy to be loved,
Truest friend and noblest foe :
    Yet she neither spoke nor moved.

Stole a maiden from her place,
    Lightly to the warrior stept,
Took the face-cloth from the face ;
    Yet she neither moved nor wept.

Rose a nurse of ninety years,
    Set his child upon her knee ;
Like summer tempest came her tears—
    " Sweet, my child, I live for thee."
                LORD TENNYSON.

387

Ask me no more : the moon may draw the sea;
    The cloud may stoop from Heaven and take the shape
    With fold to fold, of mountain or of cape ;
But, O too fond, when have I answer'd thee ?
    Ask me no more.

Ask me no more : what answer should I give ?
    I love not hollow cheek or faded eye :
    Yet, O my friend, I will not have thee die !
Ask me no more, lest I should bid thee live ;
    Ask me no more.

Ask me no more : thy fate and mine are seal'd :
    I strove against the stream, and all in vain :
    Let the great river take me to the main :
No more, dear love, for at a touch I yield ;
    Ask me no more.
                LORD TENNYSON.

388

Now sleeps the crimson petal, now the white ;
Nor waves the cypress in the palace walk ;
Nor winks the gold fin in the porphyry font :
The fire-fly wakens : waken thou with me.

Now droops the milkwhite peacock like a ghost,
And like a ghost she glimmers on to me.

Now lies the Earth all Danaë to the stars,
And all thy heart lies open unto me.

Now slides the silent meteor on, and leaves
A shining furrow, as thy thoughts in me.

Now folds the lily all her sweetness up,
And slips into the bosom of the lake :
So fold thyself, my dearest, thou, and slip
Into my bosom and be lost in me.

LORD TENNYSON

389

In Love, if Love be Love, if Love be ours,
Faith and unfaith can ne'er be equal powers,
Unfaith in aught is want of faith in all.

It is the little rift within the lute,
That by-and-by will make the music mute,
And ever widening slowly silence all ;

The little rift within the lover's lute,
Or little pitted speck in gardener'd fruit,
That rotting inward slowly moulders all.

It is not worth the keeping : let it go :
But shall it ? answer, darling, answer, no.
And trust me not at all or all in all.

LORD TENNYSON.

390. ROMANCE

When I was but thirteen or so
   I went into a golden land,
Chimborazo, Cotopaxi
   Took me by the hand.

My father died, my brother too
   They passed like fleeting dreams,
I stood where Popocatapetl
   In the sunlight gleams.

I dimly heard the master's voice
   And boys far off at play,
Chimborazo, Cotopaxi
   Had stolen me away

I walked in a great golden dream
    To and fro from school—
Shining Popocatapetl
    The dusty streets did rule.

I walked home with a gold dark boy,
    And never a word I'd say,
Chimborazo, Cotopaxi
    Had taken my speech away;

I gazed entranced upon his face
    Fairer than any flower—
O shining Popocatapetl
    It was thy magic hour:

The houses, people, traffic seemed
    Thin fading dreams by day.
Chimborazo, Cotopaxi
    They had stolen my soul away!
                    W. J. TURNER.

391. THE MAKING OF BIRDS

God made Him birds in a pleasant humour;
    Tired of planets and suns was He.
He said: "I will add a glory to summer,
    Gifts for my creatures banished from Me!"

He had a thought and it set Him smiling
    Of the shape of a bird and its glancing head,
Its dainty air and its grace beguiling:
    "I will make feathers," the Lord God said.

He made the robin; He made the swallow;
    His deft hands moulding the shape to His mood,
The thrush and the lark and the finch to follow,
    And laughed to see that His work was good.

He Who has given men gift of laughter,
    Made in His image; He fashioned fit
The blink of the owl and the stork thereafter,
    The little wren and the long-tailed tit.

He spent in the making His wit and fancies ;
   The wing-feathers He fashioned them strong ;
Deft and dear as daisies and pansies,
   He crowned His work with the gift of song.

" Dearlings," He said, " make songs for my praises ! "
   He tossed them loose to the sun and wind,
Airily sweet as pansies and daisies ;
   He taught them to build a nest to their mind.

The dear Lord God of His glories weary—
   Christ our Lord had the heart of a boy—
Made Him birds in a moment merry,
   Bade them soar and sing for His joy.
                     KATHARINE TYNAN.

392. SONG

April, April,
Laugh thy girlish laughter ;
Then, the moment after,
Weep thy girlish tears !
April, that mine ears
Like a lover greetest,
If I tell thee, sweetest,
All my hopes and fears,
April, April,
Laugh thy golden laughter,
But, the moment after,
Weep thy golden tears !
                 WILLIAM WATSON.

393. THE HEART OF THE WOMAN

O what to me the little room
That was brimmed up with prayer and rest ;
He bade me out into the gloom,
And my breast lies upon his breast.

O what to me my mother's care,
The house where I was safe and warm ;
The shadowy blossom of my hair
Will hide us from the bitter storm.

O hiding hair and dewy eyes,
I am no more with life and death,
My heart upon his warm heart lies,
My breath is mixed into the breath.

W. B. YEATS.

394. A CRADLE SONG

Coth yani me von gilli beg,
'N heur ve thu more a creena.

The angels are stooping
Above your bed ;
They weary of trooping
With the whimpering dead.

God's laughing in heaven
To see you so good ;
The Shining Seven
Are gay with His mood.

I kiss you and kiss you,
My pigeon, my own ;
Ah, how I shall miss you
When you have grown.

W. B. YEATS.

395. WHEN YOU ARE OLD

When you are old and gray and full of sleep,
And nodding by the fire, take down this book,
And slowly read, and dream of the soft look
Your eyes had once, and of their shadows deep ;

How many loved your moments of glad grace,
And loved your beauty with love false or true ;
But one man loved the pilgrim soul in you,
And loved the sorrows of your changing face.

And bending down beside the glowing bars
Murmur, a little sadly, how love fled
And paced upon the mountains overhead
And hid his face amid a crowd of stars.

W. B. YEATS.

396. DOWN BY THE SALLEY GARDENS

Down by the salley gardens my love and I did meet ;
She passed the salley gardens with little snow-white feet.
She bid me take love easy, as the leaves grow on the tree ;
But I, being young and foolish, with her would not agree.

In a field by the river my love and I did stand,
And on my leaning shoulder she laid her snow-white hand.
She bid me take life easy, as the grass grows on the weirs ;
But I was young and foolish, and now am full of tears.

W. B. YEATS.

PALGRAVE'S NOTES

12   2 *Rouse Memnon's mother* : Awaken the Dawn from
the dark earth and the clouds where she is resting. Aurora in the old mythology is mother of
Memnon (the East), and wife of Tithonus (the
appearances of Earth and Sky during the last
hours of Night). She leaves him every morning
in renewed youth, to prepare the way for Phoebus
(the Sun), whilst Tithonus remains in perpetual
old age and grayness.

13   — l. 4 *by Peneus' streams* : Phoebus loved the
Nymph Daphne whom he met by the river
Peneus in the vale of Tempe. This legend expressed the attachment of the Laurel (Daphne)
to the Sun, under whose heat the tree both fades
and flourishes. It has been thought worth while
to explain these allusions, because they illustrate
the character of the Grecian Mythology, which
arose in the Personification of natural phenomena,
and was totally free from those debasing and
ludicrous ideas with which, through Roman and
later misunderstanding or perversion, it has been
associated.

—   — l. 8 *Amphion's lyre* : He was said to have built
the walls of Thebes to the sound of his music.

—   — l. 16 *Night like a drunkard reels* : Compare Romeo
and Juliet, Act II. Scene 3: " The gray-eyed morn
smiles," etc.—It should be added that three lines,
which appear hopelessly misprinted, have been
omitted in this Poem.

14   4 *Time's chest* : in which he is figuratively supposed
to lay up past treasures. So in Troilus, Act III.
Scene 3, " Time hath a wallet at his back," etc.

—   5 A fine example of the high-wrought and conventional Elizabethan Pastoralism, which it would
be ludicrous to criticise on the ground of the un-
shepherdlike or unreal character of some images
suggested. Stanza 6 was probably inserted by
Izaac Walton.

16   9   This Poem, with 25 and 94, is taken from
          Davidson's "Rhapsody," first published in 1602.
          One stanza has been here omitted, in accordance
          with the principle noticed in the Preface. Similar
          omissions occur in 45, 87, 100, 128, 160, 165, 227,
          235. The more serious abbreviation by which it
          has been attempted to bring Crashaw's "Wishes"
          and Shelley's "Euganean Hills" within the limits
          of lyrical unity, is commended with much diffidence
          to the judgment of readers acquainted with the
          original pieces.

          Presence in line 12 is here conjecturally printed
          for *present*. A very few similar corrections of
          (it is presumed) misprints have been made :—as
          thy for *my*, 22, 9 : *men* for *me*, 41, 3 : *viol* for *idol*,
          252, 43 : and *one* for *our*, 90 : *locks* for *looks*, 271,
          5 : *dome* for *doom*, 275, 25 :—with two or three
          more less important.

19   15 This charming little poem, truly "old and plain,
          and dallying with the innocence of love" like
          that spoken of in Twelfth Night, is taken with
          5, 17, 20, 34, and 40, from the most characteristic
          collections of Elizabeth's reign, "England's Heli-
          con," first published in 1600.

20   16 Readers who have visited Italy will be reminded
          of more than one picture by this gorgeous Vision
          of Beauty, equally sublime and pure in its
          Paradisaical naturalness. Lodge wrote it on a
          voyage to "the Islands of Terceras and the
          Canaries;" and he seems to have caught, in
          those southern seas, no small portion of the
          qualities which marked the almost contemporary
          Art of Venice,—the glory and the glow of
          Veronese, or Titian, or Tintoret, when he most
          resembles Titian, and all but surpasses him.

          The clear (l. 1) is the crystalline or outermost
          heaven of the old cosmography. For *resembling*
          (l. 7) other copies give *refining* : the correct read-
          ing is perhaps *revealing*. For *a fair there's fairer
          none* : If you desire a Beauty, there is none more
          beautiful than Rosaline.

22   18 *that fair thou owest* : that beauty thou ownest.

24   23 *the star Whose worth's unknown, although his
          height be taken* : apparently, Whose stellar

influence is uncalculated, although his angular altitude from the plane of the astrolabe or artificial horizon used by astrologers has been determined.

26   27 *keel* : skim.

27   29 *expense* : waste.

—   30 *Nativity once in the main of light* : when a star has risen and entered on the full stream of light ;—another of the astrological phrases no longer familiar. *Crooked* eclipses : as coming athwart the Sun's apparent course.

Wordsworth, thinking probably of the "Venus" and the "Lucrece," said finely of Shakespeare : "Shakespeare *could* not have written an Epic ; he would have died of plethora of thought." This prodigality of nature is exemplified equally in his Sonnets. The copious selection here given (which from the wealth of the material, required greater consideration than any other portion of the Editor's task) contains many that will not be fully felt and understood without some earnestness of thought on the reader's part. But he is not likely to regret the labour.

28   31 *upon misprision growing*: either, granted in error, or, on the growth of contempt.

—   32 With the tone of this Sonnet compare Hamlet's "Give me that man That is not passion's slave," etc. Shakespeare's writings show the deepest sensitiveness to passion :—hence the attraction he felt in the contrasting effects of apathy.

29   33 *grame* : sorrow. It was long before English Poetry returned to the charming simplicity of this and a few other poems by Wyat.

30   34 Pandion in the ancient fable was father to Philomela.

31   38 *ramage* : confused noise.

32   39 *censures* : judges.

—   40 By its style this beautiful example of old simplicity and feeling may be referred to the early years of Elizabeth. *Late* forgot : lately.

33   41 *haggards* : the least tameable hawks.

34   44 *cypres* or cyprus,—used by the old writers for *crape* : whether from the French *crespe* or from the Island whence it was imported. Its accidental

similarity in spelling to *cypress* has, here and in
Milton's Penseroso, probably confused readers.

35   46   "I never saw anything like this funeral dirge,"
36   47   says Charles Lamb, "except the ditty
which reminds Ferdinand of his drowned father in the
Tempest. As that is of the water, watery; so
this is of the earth, earthy. Both have that
intenseness of feeling, which seems to resolve
itself into the element which it contemplates."

37   51   *crystal* : fairness.
38   53   This "Spousal Verse" was written in honour
of the Ladies Elizabeth and Katherine Somerset.
Although beautiful, it is inferior to the "Epi-
thalamion" on Spenser's own marriage—omitted
with great reluctance as not in harmony with
modern manners.

39   —   l. 9 *feateously* : elegantly.
41   —   l. 19 *shend* : put out. P. 421. l *a noble peer* : Robert
Devereux, second Lord Essex, then at the height
of his brief triumph after taking Cadiz : hence
the allusion following to the Pillars of Hercules,
placed near Gades by ancient legend.

—   —   l. 13 *Elisa* : Elizabeth. L. 29 *twins of Jove* : the
stars Castor and Pollux; *balderic*, belt : the
zodiac.

44   57   A fine example of a peculiar class of Poetry ;—
that written by thoughtful men who practised
this Art but little. Wotton's, 72, is another.
Jeremy Taylor, Bishop Berkeley, Dr. Johnson,
Lord Macaulay, have left similar specimens.

50   62   l. 28 *whist* : hushed.
51   —   l. 12 *Pan* : used here for the Lord of all.
53   —   l. 33 *Lars and Lemures* : household Gods and
spirits of relations dead. *Flamens* (l. 36) Roman
priests. *That twice-batter'd god* (l. 41) Dagon.
54   —   l. 13 *Osiris*, the Egyptian god of Agriculture
(here, perhaps by confusion with Apis, figured
as a Bull), was torn to pieces by Typhon and
embalmed after death in a sacred chest. This
myth, reproduced in Syria and Greece in the
legends of Thammuz, Adonis, and perhaps
Absyrtus, represents the annual death of the
Sun or the Year under the influences of the
winter darkness. Horus, the son of Osiris, as

the New Year, in his turn overcomes Typhon—

54 62 It suited the genius of Milton's time to regard this primeval poetry and philosophy of the season, which has a further reference to the contest of Good and Evil in Creation, as a malignant idolatry. Shelley's Chorus in *Hellas*, "Worlds on worlds," treats the subject in a larger and sweeter spirit. L. 15 *unshower'd* grass : as watered by the Nile only.

56 64 *The Late Massacre* : the Vaudois persecution, carried on in 1655 by the Duke of Savoy. This "collect in verse," as it has been justly named, is the most mighty Sonnet in any language known to the Editor. Readers should observe that, unlike our sonnets of the sixteenth century, it is constructed on the original Italian or Provençal model—unquestionably far superior to the imperfect form employed by Shakespeare and Drummond.

57 65 Cromwell returned from Ireland in 1650. Hence the prophecies, not strictly fulfilled, of his deference to the Parliament, in stanzas 21-24.
This Ode, beyond doubt one of the finest in our language, and more in Milton's style than has been reached by any other poet, is occasionally obscure from imitation of the condensed Latin syntax. The meaning of st. 5 is "rivalry or hostility are the same to a lofty spirit, and limitation more hateful than opposition." The allusion in st. 11 is to the old physical doctrines of the non-existence of a vacuum and the impenetrability of matter :—in st. 17 to the omen traditionally connected with the foundation of the Capitol at Rome. The ancient belief that certain years in life complete natural periods and are hence peculiarly exposed to death, is introduced in stanza 26 by the word *climacteric*.

60 66 *Lycidas*. The person lamented is Milton's college friend Edward King, drowned in 1637 whilst crossing from Chester to Ireland.
Strict Pastoral Poetry was first written or perfected by the Dorian Greeks settled in Sicily : but the conventional use of it, exhibited more magnificently in *Lycidas* than in any other pastoral, is

PAGE NO. apparently of Roman origin. Milton, employing the noble freedom of a great artist, has here united ancient mythology, with what may be called the modern mythology of Camus and Saint Peter—to direct Christian images.—The metrical structure of this glorious poem is partly derived from Italian models.

60 66 l. 15 *Sisters of the sacred well* : the Muses, said to frequent the fountain Helicon on Mount Parnassus.

61 — l. 32 *Mona* : Anglesea, called by the Welsh Inis Dowil or the Dark Island, from its dense forests. *Deva* (l. 33) the Dee : a river which probably derived its magical character from Celtic traditions : it was long the boundary of Briton and Saxon.—These places are introduced, as being near the scene of the shipwreck. *Orpheus* (l. 36) was torn to pieces by Thracian women. P. 62 *Amaryllis* and

— *Neaera* (l. 5, 6) names used here for the love idols of poets : as *Damoetas* previously for a shepherd. L. 12 *the blind Fury* : Atropos, fabled to cut the thread of life. *Arethuse* (p. 62 l. 22) and *Mincius* : Sicilian and Italian waters here alluded to as synonymous with the pastoral poetry of Theocritus and Virgil. L. 25 *oat* : pipe, used here like Collins' *oaten stop* l. 1, No. 146, for *Song*.

— — L. 33. *Hippotadès* : Aeolus, god of the Winds. *Panope* (l. 36) a Nereid. The names of local deities in the Hellenic mythology express generally some feature in the natural landscape, which the Greeks studied and analysed with their usual unequalled insight and feeling. *Panope* represents the boundlessness of the ocean-horizon when seen from a height, as compared with a limited horizon of the land in hilly countries such as Greece or Asia Minor. *Camus* (l. 40) the Cam ; put for King's University. *The sanguine flower* (l. 43) the Hyacinth of the ancients ; probably our Iris. *The pilot* (p. 63, l. 3) Saint Peter, figuratively introduced as the head of the Church on earth, to foretell " the ruin of our corrupted clergy, then in their heighth " under Laud's primacy. L. 22 *the wolf* : Popery. *Alpheus*

63 66 (l. 26) a stream in Southern Greece, supposed to flow underseas to meet the Arethuse. *Swart star* (l. 32) the Dogstar, called swarthy because its heliacal rising in ancient times occurred soon after mid-summer. P. 64 l. 10 *moist vows* : either tearful prayers, or prayers for one at sea. *Bellerus* (l. 11) a giant, apparently created here by Milton to personify Bellerium, the ancient title of the Land's End. *The great Vision* (l. 12) :—The story was that the Archangel Michael had appeared on the rock by Marazion in Mount's Bay which bears his name. Milton calls on him to turn his eyes from the south homeward, and to pity Lycidas, if his body has drifted into the troubled waters of the Land's End. Finisterre being the land due south of Marazion, two places in that district (then by our trade with Corunna probably less unfamiliar to English ears), are named——*Namancos* now Mujio in Galicia, *Bayona* north of the Minho, or perhaps a fortified rock (one of the *Cies* Islands) not unlike St. Michael's Mount, at the entrance of Vigo Bay.

64 — l. 21 *ore*: rays of golden light. *Doric lay* (l. 40) Sicilian, pastoral.

66 70 *The assault* was an attack on London expected in 1642, when the troops of Charles I. reached Brentford. "Written on his door" was in the original title of this sonnet. Milton was then living in Aldersgate Street.

67 — l. 2 *The Emathian Conqueror* : When Thebes was destroyed (B.C. 335) and the citizens massacred by thousands, Alexander ordered the house of Pindar to be spared. He was as incapable of appreciating the Poet as Lewis XIV. of appreciating Racine : but even the narrow and barbarian mind of Alexander could understand the advantage of a showy act of homage to Poetry. L. 5 *the repeated air Of sad Electra's poet*: Amongst Plutarch's vague stories, he says that when the Spartan confederacy in 404 B.C. took Athens, a proposal to demolish it was rejected through the effect produced on the commanders by hearing part of a chorus from the Electra of Euripides sung at a feast. There is however no apparent congruity

PAGE NO:

between the lines quoted (167, 8 Ed. Dindorf) and the result ascribed to them.

68 73 This high-toned and lovely Madrigal is quite in the style, and worthy of, the "pure Simonides."

69 75 Vaughan's beautiful though quaint verses should be compared with Wordsworth's great Ode, No. 287.

70 76 *Favonius*: the spring wind.

— 77 *Themis*: the goddess of justice. Skinner was grandson by his mother to Sir E. Coke ;—hence, as pointed out by Mr. Keightley, Milton's allusion to the *bench*. L. 8: Sweden was then at war with Poland, and France with the Spanish Netherlands.

72 79 l. 13 *Sydneian showers*: either in allusion to the conversations in the "Arcadia," or to Sidney himself as a model of "gentleness" in spirit and demeanour.

76 84 *Elizabeth of Bohemia*: Daughter to James I., and ancestor to Sophia of Hanover. These lines are a fine specimen of gallant and courtly compliment.

— 85 Lady M. Ley was daughter to Sir J. Ley, afterwards Earl of Marlborough, who died March, 1628-9, coincidently with the dissolution of the third Parliament of Charles's reign. Hence Milton poetically compares his death to that of the Orator Isocrates of Athens, after Philip's victory in 328 B.C.

80, 81 92, 93 These are quite a Painter's poems.

83 99 *From Prison*: to which his active support of Charles I. twice brought the high-spirited writer.

87 105 Inserted in Book II. as written in the character of a Soldier of Fortune in the Seventeenth Century.

88 106 *Waly waly*: an exclamation of sorrow, the root and the pronunciation of which are preserved in the word *caterwaul*. *Brae*, hillside : *burn*, brook : *busk*, adorn. *Saint Anton's Well*: at the foot of Arthur's Seat by Edinburgh. *Cramasie*, crimson.

89 107 *burd*, maiden.

90 108 *corbies*, crows : *fail*, turf : *hause*, neck : *theek*, thatch.—If not in their origin, in their present form this and the two preceding poems appear

due to the Seventeenth Century, and have therefore been placed in Book II.

92 III The remark quoted in the note to No. 47 applies equally to these truly wonderful verses, which, like "Lycidas," may be regarded as a test of any reader's insight into the most poetical aspects of Poetry. The general differences between them are vast : but in imaginative intensity Marvell and Shelley are closely related.—This poem is printed as a translation in Marvell's works : but the original Latin is obviously his own. The most striking verses in it, here quoted as the book is rare, answer more or less to stanzas 2 and 6 :—

Alma Quies, teneo te ! et te, germana Quietis,
  Simplicitas ! vos ergo diu per templa, per urbes
Quaesivi, regum perque alta palatia, frustra :
  Sed vos hortorum per opaca silentia, longe
Celarunt plantae virides, et concolor umbra.

94 112 *L'Allegro and Il Penseroso.* It is a striking proof
98 & of Milton's astonishing power, that these, the
 113 earliest pure Descriptive Lyrics in our language, should still remain the best in a style which so many great poets have since attempted. The Bright and the Thoughtful aspects of Nature are their subjects : but each is preceded by a mythological introduction in a mixed Classical and Italian manner. The meaning of the first is that Gaiety is the child of Nature ; of the second, that Pensiveness is the daughter of Sorrow and Genius.

94 112 l. 2 : Perverse ingenuity has conjectured that for *Cerbus* we should read *Erebus*, who in the Mythology is brother at once and husband of Night. But the issue of this union is not Sadness, but Day and Aether :—completing the circle of primary creation, as the parents are both children of Chaos, the first-begotten of all things. (Hesiod.)

95 — l. 14 *the mountain nymph* : compare Wordsworth's Sonnet, No. 210.

— — L. 40 is in *apposition* to the preceding, by a grammatical licence not uncommon with Milton. P. 96, l. 1 *tells his tale* : counts his flock. *Cynosure* (l. 14) the Pole Star. *Corydon, Thyrsis,* etc.

(l. 17) : Shepherd names from the old Idylls.
P. 97, l. 22 *Jonson's learned sock* : the gaiety of
our age would find little pleasure in his elaborate
comedies. L. 26 *Lydian airs* : a light and festive
style of ancient music.

98 113 l. 3 *bestead* : avail.

— — L. 19 *starr'd Ethiop queen* : Cassiopeia, the
legendary Queen of Ethiopia, and thence trans-
lated amongst the constellations.

99 — l. 17 *Cynthia* : the Moon : her chariot is drawn
by dragons in ancient representations.

100 — l. 2 *Hermes*, called Trismegistus, a mystical writer
of the Neo-Platonist school. L. 13 *Thebes*,
etc. : subjects of Athenian Tragedy. *Buskin'd*
(l. 16) tragic. L. 18 *Musaeus* : a poet in Mythology. L. 23 *him that left half told* : Chaucer, in
his incomplete " Squire's Tale." L. 30 *great
bards* : Ariosto, Tasso, and Spenser, are here
intended.

— — L. 37 *frounced* : curled. *The Attic Boy* (l. 38)
Cephalus.

102 114 Emigrants supposed to be driven towards America
by the government of Charles I.

— — l. 19, 20 *But apples*, etc. A fine example of
Marvell's imaginative hyperbole.

103 115 l. 6 *concent* : harmony.

114 123 *The Bard*. This Ode is founded on a fable that
Edward I., after conquering Wales, put the native
Poets to death.—After lamenting his comrades
(st. 2, 3) the Bard prophesies the fate of Edward II.
and the conquests of Edward III. (4) ; his death
and that of the Black Prince (5) ; of Richard II.,
with the wars of York and Lancaster, the murder
of Henry VI. (the *meek usurper*), and of Edward V.
and his brother (6). He turns to the glory and
prosperity following the accession of the Tudors
(7), through Elizabeth's reign (8) : and concludes
with a vision of the poetry of Shakespeare and
Milton.

— — l. 13 *Glo'ster* : Gilbert de Clare, son-in-law to
Edward. *Mortimer*, one of the Lord Marchers
of Wales.

115 — l. 13 *Arvon* : the shores of Carnarvonshire
opposite Anglesey.

115 123 L. 35 *She-wolf*: Isabel of France, adulterous Queen of Edward II. P. 116, l. 25 *Towers of Julius*: The Tower of London, built in part, according to tradition, by Julius Cæsar.

116 — L. 31 *bristled boar*: the badge of Richard III. L. 37 *Half of thy heart*: Queen Eleanor died soon after the conquest of Wales. P. 117 l. 5 *Arthur*: Henry VII. named his eldest son thus, in deference to British feeling and legend.

118 125 The Highlanders called the battle of Culloden, Drumossie.

— 126 *lilting*, singing blithely: *loaning*, broad lane: *bughts*, pens: *scorning*, rallying: *dowie*, dreary: *daffin'* and *gabbin'*, joking and chatting: *leglin*, milkpail: *shearing*, reaping: *bandsters*, sheaf-binders: *lyart*, grizzled: *runkled*, wrinkled: *fleeching*, coaxing: *gloaming*, twilight: *bogie*, ghost: dool, sorrow.

120 128 The Editor has found no authoritative text of this poem, in his judgment superior to any other of its class in melody and pathos. Part is probably not later than the seventeeth century: in other stanzas a more modern hand, much resembling Scott's, is traceable. Logan's poem (127) exhibits a knowledge rather of the old legend than of the old verses.—*Hecht*, promised: the obsolete *hight*: *mavis*, thrush: *ilka*, every: *lav'rock*, lark: *haughs*, valley-meadows: *twined* parted from: *marrow*, mate: *syne*, then.

122 129 The *Royal George*, of 108 guns, whilst under-going a partial careening in Portsmouth Harbour, was overset about 10 a.m., Aug. 29, 1782. The total loss was believed to be near 1000 souls.

124 131 A little masterpiece in a very difficult style: Catullus himself could hardly have bettered it. In grace, tenderness, simplicity, and humour it is worthy of the Ancients; and even more so, from the completeness and unity of the picture presented.

127 136 Perhaps no writer who has given such strong proofs of the poetic nature has left less satis-factory poetry than Thomson. Yet he touched little which he did not beautify: and this song, with "Rule Britannia" and a few others, must

PAGE NO. make us regret that he did not more seriously apply himself to lyrical writing.

129 140 l. 1 *Aeolian lyre* : the Greeks ascribed the origin of their Lyrical Poetry to the colonies of Aeolis in Asia Minor. *Thracia's hills* (p.130 l. 9) supposed a favourite resort of Mars. *Feather'd king* (l. 13) the Eagle of Jupiter, admirably described by Pindar in a passage here imitated by Gray.

—   —   *Idalia* (l. 19) in Cyprus, where *Cytherea* (Venus) was especially worshipped.

131 —   l. 4 *Hyperion* : the Sun. St. 6-8 allude to the Poets of the Islands and Mainland of Greece, to those of Rome and of England.

132 —   l. 25 *Theban Eagle* : Pindar.

134 141 l. 32 *chaste-eyed Queen* : Diana.

136 142 *Attic warbler* : the nightingale.

137 144 *sleekit*, sleek : *bickering brattle*, flittering flight : *laith*, loth : *pattle*, ploughstaff : *whyles*, at times : *a daimen icker*, a corn-ear now and then : *thrave*, shock : *lave*, rest : *foggage*, aftergrass : *snell*, biting : *but hald*, without dwelling-place : *thole*, bear : *cranreuch*, hoarfrost : *thy lane*, alone : *a-gley*, off the right line, awry.

141 147 Perhaps the noblest stanzas in our language.

144 148 *stoure*, dust-storm : *braw*, smart.

145 149 *scaith*, hurt : *tent*, guard : *steer*, molest.

146 151 *drumlie*, muddy : *birk*, birch.

147 152 *greet*, cry : *daurna*, dare not.—There can hardly exist a poem more truly tragic in the highest sense than this : nor, except Sappho, has any Poetess known to the Editor equalled it in excellence.

148 153 *fou*, merry with drink : *coost*, carried : *unco skeigh*, very proud : *gart*, forced : *abeigh*, aside : *Ailsa Craig*, a rock in the Firth of Clyde : *grat his een bleert*, cried till his eyes were bleared : *lowpin*, leaping : *linn*, waterfall : *sair*, sore : *smoor'd*, smothered : *crouse* and *canty*, blythe and gay.

149 154 Burns justly named this " one of the most beautiful songs in the Scots or any other language." One verse, interpolated by Beattie, is here omitted :—it contains two good lines, but is quite out of harmony with the original poem.

157 161 The Editor knows no Sonnet more remarkable
          than this, which, with 162, records Cowper's
          gratitude to the Lady whose affectionate care for
          many years gave what sweetness he could enjoy
          to a life radically wretched. Petrarch's sonnets
          have a more ethereal grace and a more perfect
          finish ; Shakespeare's more passion ; Milton's
          stand supreme in stateliness, Wordsworth in
          depth and delicacy. But Cowper's unites with an
          exquisiteness in the turn of thought which the
          ancients would have called Irony, an intensity of
          pathetic tenderness peculiar to his loving and
          ingenuous nature.—There is much mannerism,
          much that is unimportant or of now exhausted
          interest in his poems : but where he is great, it
          is with that elementary greatness which rests on
          the most universal human feelings. Cowper is
          our highest master in simple pathos.
160 163 *fancied green* : cherished garden.
—   164 Nothing except his surname appears recoverable
          with regard to the author of this truly noble
          poem. It should be noted as exhibiting a rare
          excellence—the climax of simple sublimity.
          It is a lesson of high instructiveness to examine
          the essential qualities which give first-rate
          poetical rank to lyrics such as " To-morrow " or
          " Sally in our Alley," when compared with poems
          written (if the phrase may be allowed) in keys so
          different as the subtle sweetness of Shelley, the
          grandeur of Gray and Milton, or the delightful
          Pastoralism of the Elizabethan verse. Intelligent
          readers will gain hence a clear understanding
          of the vast imaginative range of Poetry ;—
          through what wide oscillations the mind and
          the taste of a nation may pass ;—how many are the
          roads which Truth and Nature open to Excellence.
163 166 *stout Cortez* : History requires here *Balbôa* :

(A.T.) It may be noticed, that to find in Chapman's Homer the " pure serene " of the original, the reader must bring with him the imagination of the youthful poet ;—he must be " a Greek himself," as Shelley finely said of Keats.

167 169 The most tender and true of Byron's smaller poems.

168 170 This poem, with 236, exemplifies the peculiar skill with which Scott employs proper names : nor is there a surer sign of high poetical genius.

183 191 The Editor in this and in other instances has risked the addition (or the change) of a Title, that the aim of the verses following may be grasped more clearly and immediately.

189 198 *Nature's Eremite* : refers to the fable of the Wandering Jew.—This beautiful sonnet was the last word of a poet deserving the title " marvellous boy " in a much higher sense than Chatterton. If the fulfilment may ever safely be prophesied from the promise, England appears to have lost in Keats one whose gifts in Poetry have rarely been surpassed. Shakespeare, Milton, and Wordsworth, had their lives been closed at twenty-five, would (so far as we know) have left poems of less excellence and hope than the youth who, from the petty school and the London surgery, passed at once to a place with them of " high collateral glory."

191 201 It is impossible not to regret that Moore has written so little in this sweet and genuinely national style.

—   202 A masterly example of Byron's command of strong thought and close reasoning in verse :—as the next is equally characteristic of Shelley's wayward intensity, and 204 of the dramatic power, the vital identification of the poet with other times and characters, in which Scott is second only to Shakespeare.

200 209 Bonnivard, a Genevese, was imprisoned by the Duke of Savoy in Chillon on the lake of Geneva for his courageous defence of his country against the tyranny with which Piedmont threatened it during the first half of the seventeenth century.— This noble Sonnet is worthy to stand near Milton's on the Vaudois massacre.

PAGE NO.

243 252 *interlunar swoon*: interval of the Moon's invisibility.

248 256 *Calpe*: Gibraltar. *Lofoden*: the Maelstrom whirlpool off the N.-W. coast of Norway.

249 257 This lovely poem refers here and there to a ballad by Hamilton on the subject better treated in 127 and 128.

261 268 *Arcturi*: seemingly used for *northern stars*.— *And wild roses*, etc. Our language has no line modulated with more subtle sweetness. A good poet *might* have written *And roses wild*:—yet this slight change would disenchant the verse of its peculiar beauty.

264 270 *Ceres' daughter*: Proserpine. *God of Torment*: Pluto.

— 271 This impassioned address expresses Shelley's most rapt imaginations, and is the direct modern representative of the feeling which led the Greeks to the worship of Nature.

272 274 The leading idea of this beautiful description of a day's landscape in Italy is expressed with an obscurity not unfrequent with its author. It appears to be,—On the voyage of life are many moments of pleasure, given by the sight of Nature, who has power to heal even the worldliness and the uncharity of man.

274 274 l. 2 Amphitrite was daughter to Ocean.

— — l. 20 *Sun-girt* City: it is difficult not to believe that the correct reading is *Seagrit*. Many of Shelley's poems appear to have been printed in England during his residence abroad: others were printed from his manuscripts after his death. Hence probably the text of no English Poet after 1660 contains so many errors. See the Note on No. 9.

277 275 l. 21 *Maenad*: a frenzied Nymph, attendant on Dionysus in the Greek mythology.

— — l. 19 Plants under water sympathise with the seasons of the land, and hence with the winds which affect them.

279 276 Written soon after the death, by shipwreck, of Wordsworth's brother John. This Poem should be compared with Shelley's following it. Each is the most complete expression of the innermost

INDEX TO WRITERS

WITH DATES OF BIRTH AND DEATH

Reference to Number of Poem

INDEX OF FIRST LINES